Heroes, Plain Folks, and Skunks

The Life and Times of Happy Chandler

An Autobiography
with Vance H. Trimble

Foreword by Bob Hope

Bonus Books, Inc., Chicago

93 92 91 90 89   5 4 3 2

Library of Congress Catalog Card Number: 88-71521

International Standard Book Number: 0-933893-74-4

Bonus Books, Inc.
160 East Illinois Street
Chicago, Illinois 60611

Printed in the United States of America

My Old Kentucky Home
Stephen Foster

The sun shines bright on the old Kentucky home
'Tis summer, the darkies are gay.
The corn top's ripe and the meadow's in the bloom
While the birds make music all the day.
The young folks roll on the little cabin floor
All merry, all happy and bright:
By'n by Hard Times comes a'knocking at the door
Then my old Kentucky home good night!

Weep no more my lady.
Oh! Weep no more today!
We will sing one song for the old Kentucky home
For the old Kentucky home far away.

They hunt no more for the possum and the coon
On the meadow, the hill, and the shore.
They sing no more by the glimmer of the moon
On the bench by the old cabin door.
The day goes by like a shadow o're the heart,
With sorrow where all was delight.
The time has come when the darkies have to part
Then my old Kentucky home good night!

Weep no more my lady.
Oh! Weep no more today!
We will sing one song for the old Kentucky home
For the old Kentucky home far away.

The head must bow and the back will have to bend
Wherever the darkey may go.
A few more days and the trouble all will end
In the field where the sugar canes grow.
A few more days for to tote the weary load
No matter 'twill never be light.
A few more days till we totter on the road
Then my old Kentucky home good night!

Weep no more my lady.
Oh! Weep no more today!
We will sing one song for the old Kentucky home
For my old Kentucky home good night!

Written and composed by Stephen C. Foster, 1851,
and sung by Christy's Minstrels, 1853

Contents

Foreword

Happy Chandler slipped me into No. 10 Downing Street to meet Winston Churchill. That was World War II, and I was over there doing two a day for the USO. Happy came through London touring war fronts with a bunch of other senators. We ran into each other at the Dorchester, and Happy said since I had a day off to come along with his party. Sir Winston did a double take when he found me in his receiving line. While Happy and the other senators went out into the garden to talk secrets with the prime minister, I sat at Sir Winston's desk where all those confidential documents were piled around in boxes with ribbons on them. I felt like a spy.

I tried on his hat, and sniffed one of his cigars, and filched one of Churchill's little note pads. That was something—a shantytown mutt like me sitting in the prime minister's chair!

I've known Happy half my life, and we've always been pals. I've had so much fun with him, so many laughs. We've played many a round of golf; he could beat Bing, but not me. He can drive and he can putt, but I've spent more time on the golf course than he has. That's my sideline, the only way I make any real money. Dolores and I have had all the Chandlers out to the house for dinner, and we have been their guests at the Kentucky Derby and many other places, and always had a fun time.

One of my gag writers looked over my shoulder and said Happy Chandler couldn't miss with this book. "Why do you say that?" I asked. My guy snorted, and seemed a mite jealous. "Well, Bob, for crying out loud! Happy spent ninety years collecting material before writing his first line!"

That's not all bad, either. We have a different writing style, Happy and I. My books are supposed to brim with ad-libs, bon mots, humorous stuff in every paragraph. Happy doesn't have to be funny. He's just got to be himself. What he has done in this book is just haul off and fire away with some of the more interesting highlights of a truly fabulous life.

There's a lot in this book I never knew about him. He's had his triumphs and, like most of us, he's taken some tough licks, too. He got a raw deal from the owners as baseball commissioner, but he never let that change him. He's got this saying—a nifty he picked up as a kid running an oil field crew—that if you drill a dry hole, you don't fill it up with tears, you just move your digger and start over. That's not a bad philosophy.

I don't know anybody else just like him. He's about the strongest man I've ever known, and I mean that literally. I'm amazed at this man's stamina—I think he takes the same pills as George Burns. Happy is one of those churchgoers who knows the Bible; he doesn't drink, doesn't smoke—never did. No dirty stories, either. He doesn't even drive an automobile—quit nearly fifty years ago! That's not to say he hasn't always been a fierce scrapper, a never-say-die competitor. He's made himself something of a scholar, and a national expert in sports and politics, but he remains a man of the common people. He loves everybody, and neither race nor creed ever kept him from giving anyone that terrific handshake of his or that bone-crushing bear hug of friendship. Happy never let a friend down—maybe that's why he has so many. The newspapers down in Kentucky don't call him "the most beloved man in the Commonwealth" without high regard for the truth.

Couple of years ago Happy and I attended a big benefit for the race track people in Kentucky right across the river from Cincinnati. Happy closed the show by singing his personal signature song, "My Old Kentucky Home." I just marveled at the strength of his voice. His song just knocked me out. I wish Dolores had been there to hear that last note. Takes a lot of power from a guy his age.

Of course, Happy Chandler has always been legendary for his rare knack of remembering names and faces—even people he hasn't seen in a coon's age. If nothing else, this book proves that Happy still has that precious gift—and knows how to make splendid use of it.

For almost half a century Happy and I have had our own "theme" song—"You'll Never Know . . . ." Whenever I hear it a smile comes to my face because I think of him. He's a delight to be with, a great father, a great husband, and a great friend. And now, a great tale-spinner.

Bob Hope
January 1989

1

.38 Detective Special

Judge Bingham scowled at me and yanked out his pistol. In the garden of his Louisville mansion, we were strolling under the Kentucky night sky. We had been in friendly conversation about politics. This abrupt change of mood startled me. Instinctively, I recoiled from the weapon.

"Take this." He held out the revolver. "Your life may be in danger. You can never tell. You ought to have a pistol for protection. I always carry one."

I looked from the ugly gun to his strained face. We were good and close friends. He was the millionaire publisher of the powerful *Courier-Journal,* and an influential, active and determined citizen-politician. To challenge his judgment, to reject the proffered pistol, certainly would demean our relationship. The Judge had political savvy and strength not only in the state, but also nationally. Serving as county attorney, circuit judge and mayor in Louisville, he had acquired his practical political skills firsthand.

I felt something of a father-son relationship with him; actually Judge Bingham was almost exactly the age of my own dad. Certainly he considered me one of his political protégés.

I took the pistol. It was a Colts .38 calibre Detective Special.

His concern gave me a momentary flutter of unease. I well knew that in pioneer days Kentucky politics was marred by factional fighting. Gunfire and other violence erupted. Governorelect William Goebel was assassinated in 1900 on the steps of the Capitol. Rough stuff was so common that every elected official is still required to affirm he has never fought a duel before he can be sworn into office.

That night on the quiet garden path on the bluff high above the Ohio River, I could not imagine that I would ever need this Colts revolver Robert Worth Bingham had just pressed on me.

It is staggering now to realize that incident took place more than sixty years ago. In the intervening years I have encountered some danger. There have been startling and surprising close calls with tragedy. But not too many. My life has unreeled largely in the public eye. It has been full to the brim. Much of the time hectic. Rarely has it lacked for action and excitement. Not only has it been tremendously interesting, but also rewarding for me and the Kentuckians I call my people.

Judge Bingham was one of my most beloved friends. He believed in me—bragged that I had extreme leadership potential. I could not have fallen under the influence of a more astute political mentor. His reward for supporting F.D.R. in 1933 was appointment as Ambassador to Great Britain. Even in the great royal halls of London, Judge Bingham's heart was still in Kentucky. Every now and then the transatlantic operator would ring my phone and it would be Judge Bingham eager to talk fifteen or twenty minutes about political affairs back home.

In the fall of 1937 Ambassador Bingham fell ill. British doctors were stumped. He was rushed back to Johns Hopkins in Baltimore, where exploratory surgery disclosed a rare and obscure disease, abdominal Hodgkins. He died in a matter of days, at sixty-eight.

Had he lived he would have played a powerful—and perhaps astonishing—role in pushing my political aspirations. I aimed high. About as high, I guess, as anyone can go in America. I thought I had a fairly good shot at becoming President of the United States.

Of course, I never made it to the Oval Office. I haven't cried about that. In other ways I didn't do so badly. First I jumped from high school coach and country lawyer to governor of Kentucky. I was thirty-seven, the nation's youngest governor. I next went to serve in the United States Senate—three times.

The major league club owners drafted me to succeed the late Judge Landis as the high commissioner of baseball. World War II was on and I refused to leave the Senate until we'd vanquished the enemy on both fronts. The baseball moguls agreed to wait and keep the job open for me. If I'd known the snakepit I was stepping into, I'd have passed.

Many of the owners were greedy. They were cruel to the players and umpires. They abused the fans. They tried to dominate me—but I fought 'em. I took charge. I handled the Mexican league raids, the threat of a player strike and other tough disputes. I banished "Leo The Lip" Durocher for a full year for besmirching the game. I just didn't sit around. For the first time players got pensions and a fair shake on rights, pay and contracts. And I helped integrate baseball. The avaricious owners began to boil. After seven years they finally greased the skids—and railroaded me out.

I came back home, hurting, of course. But I couldn't cry about being fired. I just went out again and won the best job I ever had—governor of Kentucky—for the second time.

Among the baseball moguls I had several good friends, but not enough. These friendly owners thought I was doing a good job. Most of the others felt so personally thwarted that they tried to demean the really notable accomplishments of my short and busy years as baseball commissioner. Experts like Bowie Kuhn, one of my successors, wouldn't buy that. He said bluntly I was one of the best commissioners baseball ever had.

My enemies in baseball could never take away credit for my unprecedented—and bold—action in permitting Brooklyn Dodger owner Branch Rickey to break the baseball color line by bringing the first black—Jackie Robinson—into the major leagues. Except for me, that would have not happened. The other fifteen major league club owners had turned thumbs down on Rickey putting a Negro in a major league uniform, out-voting him fifteen to one. But I had the power—absolute power—and I told Rickey to go ahead.

I was known as a "players' commissioner." The club owners who were skunks held a grudge against me. They took their re-

venge by turning me into baseball's "forgotten man." For years
I languished in near oblivion, snidely deprived of my World Series box and given other slights. Finally baseball veterans had
a change of heart; belatedly came the recognition that I deeply
had yearned for. In 1982 I finally was inducted into the Baseball Hall of Fame. That was a great moment!

Lately I have been running over in my mind the significant
events of my life, collecting notes for this autobiography. It
seems to me that measured by the quotidian affairs of mankind
my years from 1917 through the 1930s were nothing short of
remarkable—as bush league player, umpire and manager, as
college quarterback and pitcher, as coach and scout in high
school and college, as amateur thespian and ambitious tenor
who sang the "Miserere" from *Il Trovatore* in the 1918 Cincinnati May Festival . . .

For years people have urged me to recount my life. I always
begged off. Some people may have thought I had secrets to
guard. I don't. I tell the truth, and admire candor. Some folks
ask me what changes I would make in my life. I say, none. I was
sober and I meant to do everything I did. I wouldn't change
any of it. I still wear the world like a loose jacket. I live every
day like it's going to be my last, and sleep every night like I'm
going to live forever.

I haven't yet felt Old Father Time trying to hobble me, but
nobody can argue with the calendar. On July 14, 1988, I
reached my 90th birthday. I realize, of course, nobody lives forever.

That Colts Detective Special Judge Bingham gave me—I
still have it. I keep it in my bedside night stand. It's getting a
little rusty, but it is always loaded!

I wish I could say that I never had to fire that revolver. But
I can't.

I didn't use it when some skunks poisoned my drinking water and nearly killed me. That occurred in my 1938 Senate race
against Alben Barkley, a bitter battle that took the national
spotlight as a test of F.D.R.'s political power.

Nor did I have it in my pocket when goons in the mine
fields boasted I would be assassinated if I made a campaign appearance in 1955 in Breathitt County. Once we got wind of that,
one of my own men—a big, strong, angry-looking fellow—took

bold and direct action to diffuse that threat. He simply stomped into the hall and took the seat beside the known leader of the goon squad. My man leaned over and hissed in his ear.

"You got rifles in here. I know that. Anyone makes the slightest move, your ass is cold! My pistol is out, and under my coat. It's already cocked and aimed right at your heart!"

Don't let me leave the impression that I have constantly lived on the brink of a precipice. Or that my friends are badly outnumbered by enemies. I certainly have people who hate me; and plenty others who love me. I, too, harbor some pretty tall grudges. Those people who have done me wrong—well, I try to outlive them. In that, partner, I have succeeded remarkably well.

In the worlds of politics and sports I have developed hundreds, nay thousands, of singular associations and friendships. That should not be surprising. I've spent ninety years at it— close to thirty-three thousand days.

Fate threw me into some pretty tall cotton. Imagine me being able to smuggle Bob Hope into Number Ten Downing so he could shake hands with Winston Churchill. But the most rewarding and exciting days of my life involve the everyday Kentuckians—country folks, city sophisticates, black and white, male and female, rich and poor, young squirts and old codgers, people you've probably never heard of.

My panoramic mind's eye flashes back to visions of Franklin D. Roosevelt trying to charm me, and failing, reaching for his club...Churchill sending a personal cable applauding my Senate speeches...Ike and MacArthur sharing secrets with me in the warfronts...Harry Byrd of Virginia (The Great One) tutoring me how to be a good senator...Harry Truman (The Bad One) drinking too much whiskey and hurling poison-tipped daggers....

I think of the years of being a pal with Bing Crosby, Bob Hope, Greer Garson, Jimmy Stewart and a host of luminaries in Hollywood, where I struck up my warm and lasting friendship with Ronald Reagan...Ty Cobb, who was not too busy to give my hometown kids tips on batting...Babe Ruth, when he was crying and dying, and I could help rescue him—briefly... Jack Dempsey startling me with a hot-foot and laughing his head off...Connie Mack making my daddy's day...Walter

Hagen whipping me at golf... A mere handful of the hundreds of solid friends who have enriched my venerable years....

Then right here in my beloved bluegrass... My political strategists Dan Talbott and Joe Leary... All-American Frenchy De Moisey who drove me a million miles and volunteered—not the least joking—to kill one of my obnoxious enemies... Quixotic "Walking" Munn who couldn't rest until he danced in a pair of the governor's shoes... Dick Gallagher who claims he threw a football pass that actually turned me into a governor... Ella V and Porter, the black couple who came off murderer's row—by my executive clemency—to serve Mama and me faithfully for forty years....

Yes, the characters in my life story are heroes, plain folks, and skunks... quite a cast, quite an interesting and unusual cast....

But getting back to that .38 Detective Special, the only time I fired it was at a night prowler at the back fence of my home in Versailles, Kentucky. I love dogs, really love 'em, let 'em sleep in my bed, even today. But this prowler was a mean black alley cat and it came around howling every night. Finally I grabbed the revolver and rushed out to the back gate. I saw the old tomcat and fired off a couple of quick rounds.

I only meant to give him a lasting scare. But unfortunately for the cat, my shooting eye was too accurate—and deadly.

2

Boyhood Without a Mother

Angry voices came from the bedroom. My mother and father were quarrelling. She was packing her suitcase. Out at the front gate someone waited in a buggy. My mother was leaving home, abandoning us. I was just four years old. This is my earliest memory.

"Do you want to take the children?" my father asked.

"I'll take Robert," she said. He was two, my brother. Her tone turned harsh. "I don't want Albert—he looks too much like you."

My father shook his head. "No. If you don't want both—just leave them with me."

I followed mother out to the buggy, crying. Dusk was beginning to settle over our little Kentucky hamlet. She gave us two boys a quick kiss, and Robert a long, long hug. The buggy wheels crunched off toward the depot. I sat down at the gate and tears rolled down my cheeks. Robert whimpered, looking bewildered. Likewise I was too young and innocent to comprehend this awful tragedy that was inaugurating my life. Under ordinary circumstances, it might have turned me into an introvert. It didn't. Mainly, I think, that was because of my father's innate goodness.

He was a son of the soil, strong and industrious, content and not goaded by ambition. He was a carefree optimist, usually flashing a warm Will Rogers grin. Life on a fifty-acre homestead on the edge of Corydon suited him just fine. It was by no means enough for my vivacious, energetic and pretty mother, not yet twenty years old. "She wanted city lights," he used to explain, hugging both his sons. His voice was gentle and sympathetic. Not a single harsh or critical word about her passed his lips.

There was no denying Corydon was a *small* small town. The population was eight hundred, as Daddy said, "four hundred whites and four hundred blacks." It was just a wide place in the road, really, with a post office, railroad depot, bank, general store, drug store, picture show, livery stable, a couple of cafes and a handful of other businesses and offices—all either on Main Street or just off it.

It was the turn of the century and roads were deplorable. When we would load our tobacco harvest for market in Henderson, ten miles away, the wagon wheels sank half-way to the hubs in near-freezing mud. The mules strained for ten hours to reach Henderson. In summer the trip was different, but somehow worse—with the mules kicking up gritty clouds of red dust that stung our faces. Henderson was a nice county seat town. But the nearest "metropolis" with bright lights was Evansville, Indiana, another eight miles or so further north across a great horseshoe bend in the Ohio River. That's where my mother went—and vanished from my life, I thought, forever.

Strangely, I have never lost the memory of my mother's young pretty face and her luminous blue eyes, too crystal and deep to fathom. Her name was Callie Sanders, born into the foremost family in Garrard County, in east central Kentucky, sixty miles below Lexington. But she grew up outside Corydon on Diamond Island Road on the farm just opposite my father's. Propinquity most likely helped inspire their marriage. But it was a sad mismatch. Callie wanted to escape her "hired girl" drudgery. Unfortunately my father was ten years her senior, serious and already set in his ways. When I was born on Bastille Day, July 14, 1898, my mother was only sixteen or seventeen.

Two years later she was again thrashing around in painful labor in the rustic upstairs bedroom of our tiny unpainted clapboard farmhouse. She cooed over fair-faced Robert. But she cringed at the thought of what fate offered: more babies, unending slave work in house and field until, washed-out and sickly, she would wearily sink into an early grave like many near-poor women of her time. All she could think of then was escape from a meager home devoid of running water, inside plumbing or electric lights—before the wine of laughter in her frisky veins soured into the stale vinegar of lost youth.

Kentucky was largely settled, of course, by hardy pioneers who followed Daniel Boone and other adventurers through the "Gap," fighting Indians and other wilderness perils. The Chandlers migrated from Virginia about the 1830s and my grandfather, Daniel Madison Chandler, was born in Trimble County, Kentucky. On the fertile plains along the banks of the Ohio River he became a fruit farmer. His knack of producing choice strawberries, grapes, peaches and apples made him well-to-do. Then came the Civil War, which split Kentucky families, sometimes pitting brother against brother, turning the Commonwealth into a bloody no-man's land.

Reckless and daring, Dan Chandler served as second sergeant for General John Hunt Morgan's Confederate cavalry raiders. At Shiloh, he was shot in the heel. "Grand-daddy," I said when he recounted his war experiences, "it looks like you-all were running."

"Son," he said, "everybody was running!"

Grand-daddy liked to talk about the war. "Son, we could have whipped the Yankees with corn stalks!" His booming laugh would rattle the windows. "Only trouble was, the damn Yankees wouldn't fight with corn stalks!"

From the surrender at Appomattox, my grandfather came back to bitter unrest at home. He pulled up stakes and took his wife, Mary Terrell, into the Ozark hills in Camden County, Missouri. My father, Joseph Sephus Chandler, was born there in 1870. His unusual name is my Grand-dad's own spelling of that famous historian of Biblical times, Josephus. Dad had three sisters and four brothers.

When my daddy was ten, the old second sergeant again loaded up his wagons and came back across the Mississippi and the Ohio and settled on a fruit farm on the outskirts of Corydon.

Long before I was even a gleam in his eye, my father set my work-clock. He grew up a happy workaholic, flourishing on hard labor—and that is the foremost and most satisfying characteristic I inherited from him. Also, perhaps, the most beneficial. Despite long hours on the farm, daddy grew up an excellent student. He became an avid reader, especially of history. His penmanship was beautiful. He was intelligent, friendly and helpful to everyone. He was graduated from Corydon High School in 1886, valedictorian at sixteen of his small class. The principal praised his graduating address and said he wouldn't be surprised but what Joseph Sephus Chandler would become president of the United States.

There was no high ambition niggling my dad's brain. He was an easygoing man, content to own his fifty-acre farm and become to a certain extent the town handyman for Corydon. For several years he was the night operator in the telephone exchange. He pushed a wheelbarrow to the depot and hauled the incoming mail to the post office. When I was seven or eight he began the first rural mail delivery route—twenty-five miles long—in Henderson County. At another time we occupied a tiny apartment in the rear of the bank, so he could serve as night watchman. One night burglars smashed a window and started crawling in. My father drew his two six-guns and blazed away in the dark. The surprised intruders returned fire before turning tail. Bullets whistled all over the place but nobody was hit. Unfortunately I was not on hand to witness my father's heroism, having at that time been sent to spend a year with family friends in Evansville.

The night my mother decamped Uncle Ed came and carried Robert and me over to his house. Loving, patient Aunt Julie became our temporary mother. Mother's sister came from Missouri and looked after us a week or two. She was not at all sympathetic with Callie; but she decided my mother planned never to return, so she went back to Missouri. The task of mothering Robert and me largely fell to Aunt Julie and neighbor women, chiefly Mrs. Albert Wetzel. I was named for her husband, a blacksmith. He was a strong-willed German, a good man. They were the folks I lived with for a year in Evansville. My middle name came from a local physician, Dr. Benjamin Compton.

I cannot imagine what my life would have been like without the vigorous mothership of my father. He was not mean or stern but he was dedicated to work—by man or boy. As soon as I was big enough to carry a stick of kindling, I was assigned chores. Robert, clinging to me like a shadow, began to help, too. I felt it was my job to look out for my little brother.

As I grew older the more physical became my farm work. It is unbelievable how punishing is a twelve-hour day spent pitchforking pea hay into a barn loft. It's heavy, there's a little kernel that tangles it, and the strain of lifting makes the butt of the pitchfork handle kick a deep dent in your belly. I got twenty-five cents a day for carrying my pail into the neighbors' fields and dropping tobacco plants ahead of the setters. My hours were sunup to sundown. Worse was worming and suckering when the burley plants began growing. I'll never forget when I first lifted a green leaf and found a big fuzzy-faced worm barking at me. They were vicious, too, I discovered when one nipped my finger before I perfected the knack of grabbing its neck and pinching off the head. Often at the end of the day I helped milk fifteen or twenty cows for a neighbor.

I guess I actually enjoyed hard work. I watched my biceps grow large and tawny; I was becoming something of a young bull. Subconsciously I must have been trying to emulate my father, noticing with pride how the muscles flexed and rippled across his back. I wanted to grow as tall and as strong as my dad.

Barely an hour into the morning sweat began streaking his denim shirt; and working next to him I would tingle when I sniffed his vigorous, manly odor. Conversely there was something inspiring, too, in our pungent soapy smell when we emerged from the Saturday night washtub ritual in the kitchen before heading into town for a drink at the soda fountain.

In the last summer before I finished high school I worked alongside a husky six-foot Negro named Bill Blunder on the railroad loading dock at the Anchor Milling Company. My job was to put an empty burlap bag under the spout of the corn sheller, fill it, hoist it on the scales to make sure it weighed one hundred pounds, and then carry it on my shoulder to the freight car and dump it in. Bill did the same thing. Occasionally the two of us would leap into the car with big shovels and spread out the corn.

Once Bill Blunder leaned a moment on his shovel and gave

me keen appraisal. "They's one thing to say about you, Irish,"
he said. I had somehow picked up that nickname around Corydon; everyone seemed to think our Chandler ancestors sprang
from Ireland. "You's the only white boy I knows that's shonuff
got the willie."

That was a sincere testament to his regard for my "willingness" to do hard work. Ours was no easy job. Every day we
filled and dumped into the railroad car 880 sacks—440 each.
Our pay was not bad, a dollar and a quarter a day.

For four or five years I had a regular afternoon chore that I
literally despised. That was currying the horse when my dad's
box-like rural mail buggy rolled in from his day-long route.
Only someone who has done it can imagine how dried country
mud can snarl a horse's mane and tail. To this day, I have never
been very fond of horses—not even Kentucky thoroughbreds.

Naturally I spent free time at my grandfather's fruit farm.
My memories are still bright and vivid of lying on my back in
the warm sun between the strawberry rows, picking that deli-
cious fruit and avidly munching it.

But old Dan Chandler became, as I grew into boyhood, not
so much a beau ideal or godling, but an object of some scorn
and pity. And an awesome object lesson—pointed out by my
father—of the evils of drink and profligacy. Ever so often,
Grand-dad, a widower since 1892, would be struck by an overpowering thirst for liquor and companionship. He would limp
out to the stable and hitch up his buggy. When he climbed in,
he usually laid a wad of one hundred dollar bills on the seat.
Then he drove off to cavort.

To my father or other of his sons fell the mission of going
out to bring him back home. Always the old soldier was tanked
up and usually his C-notes were scattered across the country-
side. These debauches turned my father firmly against
whiskey—and smoking as well.

"Your grandfather," he lamented to me, "has wasted a fortune in riotous living. It's a shame. Promise me, son, that until
you are at least twenty-one you will never touch alcohol or tobacco."

My response was wide-eyed and fervent. "I won't, Dad!"

I didn't know then that was a promise I would keep all my
life. Never have I had even one drink, or smoked tobacco.

From my earliest childhood religion played an important role in my life. My father regularly attended the little Christian church in Corydon, whose members were known as the "Campbellites." It was only natural that both his sons sat in the pew with him. We attended every Sunday morning, sometimes evening services as well, plus frequent "protracted" or revival meetings.

Instead of being reluctant, I was eager to attend church. In one of the revival meetings as a young teenager I joined the church. In the usual custom, I was "dunked." Soon I was teaching a Bible class, and finally, as a high schooler, became superintendent of the Sunday school. My father not only was a church pillar, he was the voluntary custodian, making a lifetime chore of cutting the grass in the churchyard and in the little cemetery. In the beginning he used a hand scythe; in his eighties he was still at it, but with a power mower—and tragic consequences.

The discovery I made in that little church that most remarkably affected my life was not so much that my imagination was dazzled by the canticles of the Scriptures, but that I had a splendid singing voice. I was booming out the hymns so magnificently that soon I was leading the choir. Singing became my passion. Robert, too, had a good voice, and often we were unabashedly giving duet performances at school, for our neighbors, even down on Main Street on request, as well as just for ourselves.

Except for the plasticity of healthy childhood, I do not see how I could have crowded such varied activity into my days of growing up. Fortunately I was as healthy as an ox, not even a trifle lazy. Baseball began to rival singing as my main passion. My father had always been a fan, following the big leagues from afar, and usually through the pages of *The Sporting News,* published in St. Louis by the family of J. Taylor Spink, who later became my close friend. Dad even arranged for me to deliver *The Sporting News* in Corydon. And then I took on delivery of the daily newspapers that came in by train from Henderson, Evansville and Louisville, serving thirty or forty subscribers.

Somewhere Dad rustled up a couple of gloves, a scuffed-up ball or two and some old bats. He set about teaching me all he knew about baseball. Fortunately, I was an adept pupil. I could run, and catch, and throw—pretty hard. With my strong arms and country swing, once my bat connected, the ball just took off. Usually I kept a ball in my hip pocket and my glove, oiled and supple, stuck under my belt. I always had some time to kill at the depot mornings waiting for the train to bring the newspapers. Like my father, who made friends easily, I got on well with the ticket agent, Bob Bransford. If he wasn't busy, he'd come outside and hit me a few fly balls.

Mr. Bransford—my father was ultra strict about his boys showing proper courtesy to their elders and that made a lasting impression—was the means of Dad and me having the next best thing to a box seat at the 1909 World Series. The ticket agent could read the telegraph ticker and we stood beside his chair and heard him "broadcast" for us a play-by-play account. It was big excitement, with both Ty Cobb and Honus Wagner starring. Pittsburgh finally took the championship for the National League, besting Detroit four games to three.

My best and favorite morning newspaper customer was Mrs. Pentecost, the mother of the postmaster. She'd greet me with a smile at the kitchen door, through which wafted an aroma that would make a growing boy's mouth water. She invited me in and set before me a generous plate of bacon and eggs and hot biscuits. I must have done a lot of blabbing about baseball for she started calling me Ty Cobb. The new nickname stuck and seemed to spread all around town. For some reason my father objected to me playing football, but let me go out for baseball in high school. I made the team, a pretty fair hitter, and developing into an effective pitcher. One of my school mates, Owen Stapp, a couple of years back reminisced about my high school pitching, asserting I would literally jump at the batter, wave my arms furiously, and then beat him with a roundhouse curve. Maybe I was something of a maniac on the mound; all I remember is that Corydon High won a lot of games.

It was not uncommon for Robert to tag along after me, but I never minded that at all. Somehow—perhaps because we were both motherless—I felt it was up to me to watch out for him. He was a hard worker, too, and hired himself out for farm chores.

The summer he was fourteen he was out in the country helping pick a cherry crop. He was scrambling around on a limb about ten feet off the ground. Suddenly it snapped, plunging him head-first to the ground. Word of the accident was relayed to me at home and I hopped on my bicycle and furiously pedaled out there; it was five or six miles. I rushed into the house where they had lain Robert on a pallet. The poor little fellow was as pale as a ghost, slack and motionless, except for a strange flutter of his eyelids. There was a big bruise and a little gash on his forehead; one of the women crowding around kept wiping away a trickle of blood. Everyone kept remarking that the fall had badly stunned him. Robert's fluttering eyes turned to me; he just stared and didn't speak. I was fearful, and terribly upset.

My father came and took Robert to my grandfather's nearby farmhouse. He was tucked in between clean sheets. Somehow the family verdict seemed to be that he needed "to rest." In those medically-impoverished days there was no thought of rushing him to a hospital. I'm not even sure there was much discussion of getting a doctor. Generally, people said with sad resignation that the one or two physicians around Corydon "don't know much."

I sat beside the bed and watched over him. The next day he still seemed stunned, but managed to talk to me a little. Every now and then he would go back into a speechless daze. I took it for granted the family adults knew best, but I grew more and more fearful as my uncomplaining little brother lay quietly in that big four-poster—day after day. Every now and then his face flushed like he had fever. No one seemed to realize that his neck was broken; I was too uninformed to even guess that.

On the seventh day Robert mumbled to me that he wanted a cold drink, "orange pop, if you can find any."

In the icebox I found an Orange Crush and took it in to his bed. He lifted up a little and took a few sips. He handed me the bottle, lay back and closed his eyes.

Vaguely I heard a gentle gasp and noticed his mouth go slack.

Never before—or since—have I seen the black angel come. It took me a few minutes to realize that Robert, only fourteen, had just died.

Later I went out and sat beside the front gate. I cried just like I did when mother left, perhaps even harder. But I was older now and I tried to avert my tear-streaked face when neighbors came to offer condolences. Perhaps it was not considered manly to cry, but the sense of ineffable grief was crushing and overpowering—and the tragedy seemed so mysterious. It was something my sixteen-year-old mind could not comprehend. Why? I asked myself. Why? And I didn't have any answer. Surely God had made a mistake. What reason was there to punish Robert, or me, or Dad? I would see suffering etch deep marks on my father's face; it was a loss he never got over.

For me it was the blackest moment of life. I have never felt more hurt or depressed than that Sunday afternoon I grieved at the gate over the shocking and unexpected death of my little brother.

Some evenings I used to follow Dad up to the small cemetery when he went to cut the grass. At his little headstone I knelt and talked to my brother. I kept trying to tell him how sorry I was; with the perfume of fresh-cut grass in my nostrils, the golden rays from the western horizon flickering in my eyes and the sweet song of the night birds gently in my ears, I somehow felt that Robert knew how much I loved him and missed him.

In high school I was a diligent student. Classes were small, only seventeen in my senior year. Our schools were of course segregated; the Negroes had their own school on the other side of town. That was the southern way of life, and accepted by both races. I can't recall any trouble or conflict in my boyhood with Negroes. I had many friends among the blacks; I'm certain I was taught they were inferior, but I respected all I knew well.

My ardor for sports, fortunately, was not a stumbling block in the classroom. I fell under the influence of some excellent country school teachers with old-fashioned dedication. My English teacher, Mrs. Rexie Raymond, stuck my nose in a book of poems and figuratively pounded on me until I developed a liking for the classics. Once I had a taste I became a glutton. I stayed after school so Mrs. Raymond could guide my studies of the great poets.

In the process I discovered that I possess a remarkable memory. Even today I recite with ease perhaps the first of the poems my English teacher introduced me to, Oliver Wendell Holmes's "The Last Leaf":

> *The mossy marbles rest*
> *On the lips that he has prest*
> *In their bloom—*
> *And the names he loved to hear*
> *Have been carved for many a year*
> *On the tomb.*
>
> *I know it is a sin*
> *For me to sit and grin*
> *At him here;*
> *But the old three-cornered hat,*
> *And the breeches, and all that,*
> *Are so queer!*
>
> *And if I should live to be*
> *The last leaf upon the tree*
> *In the spring,*
> *Let them smile, as I do now,*
> *At the old forsaken bough*
> *Where I cling.*

Perhaps that is my favorite of all the poems I know.

During our study period, I had permission to dash off to the depot on my bike to catch the bundle of afternoon papers off the train and deliver them. Most of them went right along Main Street and I was never late getting back for the next class. The principal, L. H. Gehman, observed me and detected something I didn't yet recognize, a hidden or latent ambition. I was aping my father's easygoing dogma. If Corydon was good enough for him, it was good enough for me. Strangely, I had more or less willed myself a mental block on the future.

Being motherless threw me totally into my daddy's realm of values. I was not a mischievous lad, but that is not to say I never had a trip to the woodshed for misbehaving. I had no fights in school. I noticed the pretty girls—one in particular, the banker's little daughter everyone called "Hon"—but I had no genuine crushes. I was not deluded; even young girls looked for what prospects a boy had. Mine were but two—slim and none. My dad gave me a good code of values, especially the necessity to be thrifty and avoid going into debt. "Never spend more than you take in, Albert," he said, "and you'll never go broke. If you do, you will." It was a lesson that has stood me well all the days of my life.

From his indirect hints, my father seemed to be urging me to take up the ministry. I wanted to be a dutiful son, but somehow I could not see myself a preacher. I didn't have any goal at all in mind, so I just left his preacher suggestion fluttering around in limbo.

The summer of 1916 I was sent, as superintendent of our Sunday school, to attend a religious methods seminar in Lexington. For a week or ten days I studied with other Kentuckians at the School of the Bible at Transylvania University. I heard lectures by some of their most dynamic men—President Richard Crossfield, Drs. Alonzo Fortune, William C. Bower, and rough-hewn Elmer E. Snoddy, who became widely known for his unorthodox teaching style and Socratic mind.

That trip seemed to open my eyes to the future. These teachers and their bright ideas and the studious atmosphere of the Transylvania campus—old but small—vaguely stirred my ambition. Principal Gehman was the first person to ever talk seriously to me about going to college. I told him we were not impoverished but I doubted we could afford it. He put his hand on my shoulder and said he'd help me try to get a scholarship. Or I could work my way through; a lot of lads were doing that. When I broached this idea, my father's grin quickly vanished. He drew back and folded his arms. The principal tried to talk to him, too, but got the same rebuff.

"Son, you ought to get yourself a job in Corydon."

"But, daddy—" Something inside was triggering rebellion. "I could do that any time—if I can't make it any place else!"

"Ask down at the drug store," he suggested. "Maybe they could use you behind the soda fountain."

I set my face defiantly, an unaccustomed pose. "I hate, I really hate...not being able to go to college." I was naturally downcast, but I was not about to actually go up against my father's will. I never had.

There were seventeen graduates in my senior class. One of the local ladies who liked me and appreciated my singing in church, Mrs. Anna King, widow of the owner of the general store, gave me my best graduation present. It was a Bible, which I still treasure. She marked a passage, Romans 12:11. That Scripture has always been a source of inspiration. Just the other night I got out of bed, turned on the lamp and re-read it:

Not slothful in business, fervent in spirit, serving the Lord.

I have to smile now at the little prophecy printed under my photograph in the High School annual of 1917:

Work hard and study while you wait,
And you'll be governor of your state.

The rhyme was meant to be humorous. No one had the least notion it would come true, least of all me.

Just at that juncture to Corydon came the man who first changed the course of my life, Dr. Homer W. Carpenter, the chancellor of Transylvania University. Because this college was closely associated with our Christian Church, I'd heard as long as I could remember about its great contribution to education in the West.

On a trip, Dr. Carpenter paused in Corydon to deliver a sermon to our little congregation. He took special notice of me. Perhaps Principal Gehman had put a bug in his ear. Dr. Carpenter invited me to come to Transylvania. "I will see that you get a scholarship for your tuition," he promised. "Moreover, we will assist you in finding work so you can pay your way through."

It seemed to me that Transylvania must be one of the most important colleges in the whole country. It was chartered when the West was just barely being opened, in 1780. "Transylvania," said Dr. Carpenter, "has had among its trustees some of the greatest leaders in Kentucky's political, military and judicial life." He mentioned three: Isaac Shelby, the first governor of Kentucky; George Rogers Clark, the Revolutionary War hero who won the Northwest from the British; and Henry Clay. He talked of graduates who had come up in the world, men like Stephen F. Austin, who opened Texas for settlement; Albert Sidney Johnston, who lost his life as a Confederate general at

Shiloh, where Grand-dad was wounded in the heel; Cassius M. Clay, the fighting abolitionist; and Jefferson Davis, the president of the Confederacy.

I looked Dr. Carpenter squarely in the eye. He was dead level serious. He wanted me to enroll at Transylvania. He would give me all possible help. Dare I refuse such an offer? Sort of in a flash, my suppressed ambition exploded. Even if Dad still held back, I suddenly knew where my future lay.

With vigor and an iron clasp, I seized Dr. Carpenter's hand. "I'll come! Thank you, sir! I'll come!"

3

Transylvania's Singing "Terror"

The ring of the alarm clock rolled me out at 5 A.M. and sent me hurrying down to the ink-misted pressroom of the *Herald*. I scanned the page one headlines. America had been at war with Germany just over three months. Our first doughboys were arriving in France. Stuffing my bag, I threw the strap over my shoulder and scurried out on the quiet, dim-lit downtown streets, to leave the morning newspaper at the closed doors of a hundred or so stores and offices. By 6:30 I was at Ma Hager's boarding house waiting table.

I had come to Lexington in July, 1917. From the railroad station I walked out Broadway to the Transylvania campus. Dr. Carpenter made me welcome. In fact, he took me home with him that first night. Next day he got me assigned to a dormitory and lined up my first two jobs.

Legend has it I arrived at Transylvania with no resources other than a red sweater, a five dollar bill, and a smile. That's about right.

I didn't expect help from my dad. He never got enthusiastic about my hunger for a college education. I did have affluent kinsmen in Lexington—Dan Terrell, dean of engineering at the University of Kentucky, and Claude Terrell, who had been speaker of the Kentucky House of Representatives during the second term of Governor James Bennett McCreary, 1911–1915.

They were my older cousins, but neither took the least notice; certainly offered no assistance. Their family may have felt some vague resentment over my grandfather's escapades after Mary Terrell died. I don't know. At any rate the Terrells were pretty slow to ever get concerned about the Chandlers.

Later in my embryonic political days, my wife encountered one of the Terrell matriarchs at a family gathering, and tried to initiate a friendly conversation about family ties. The Terrell lady fixed her with a stare of disdain.

"I ain't interested," she observed, "in looking up any new kin."

Indeed, the Albert B. Chandlers were of no concern at all to the Terrell clan until I became governor. I never harbored any resentment; but I never fell all over myself either about those "new" kinfolk.

As a Transylvania freshman, keeping busy twelve or more hours a day was nothing new to me. I got along fine. Getting to work for Ma Hager was a lucky break. In the kitchen I could eat my fill of meat, beans and vegetables. It was plain grub, just the menu to nourish an athletic nineteen year old from the country.

In Dr. Carpenter, bright and young, I found an empathetic ally, and I tried to repay his interest. Whenever the chancellor and his wife had an opportunity for a night out, I gladly volunteered as babysitter for their only child, a girl about two years old.

Somehow the Transylvania atmosphere kept me optimistic, chipper, even bouncy. I threw myself into every activity I could find—baseball, basketball, football, the glee club, the theatre, even trying out for Shakespearean roles. I was not shy, and I had the knack of making friends quickly and easily.

One morning I was plunging along the sidewalk in front of Old Morrison, with my usual vigorous, quick stride, smiling and whistling. A senior from Lawrenceburg, "Happy" Hawkins, shot me a pleasant look and turned back to his companions. He said: "Fellows, there goes Happy Chandler." The nickname stuck—for my whole lifetime. Thank God he didn't dub me "Stinky." That probably would have haunted me just as tightly all my days.

Though I was strong and quick, the coaches at Transylvania had to knock off the rough edges that clung to me from Corydon's cow-pasture sports. The baseball coach, Jim Park, who later played professionally for the St. Louis Browns and the Cleveland Indians, took me under his wing. Soon he had put some polish on my game, showing me how to throw a better curve as well as a fastball, and what Satchel Paige always called a "hesitation" pitch.

Soon I had a chance to show my new "stuff." We took on two small colleges, Kentucky Wesleyan and Georgetown of Kentucky. I was invincible on the mound. We won both games. Then I went up against a stronger school down at Danville, Kentucky. That was Centre College, which already was getting a national reputation for its "Praying Colonels" under Coach Charley Moran.

As against the other opponents, I was—I thought— overpowering and faultless. It turned out to be a long and tiring game. But I was strong even when we went into the eleventh inning. I could already smell the roses of victory.

Then I wound up and unleashed my "hesitation" ball. The Centre batter managed to get a little piece of it. It was a dribbler, floating down the third base line—a cinch out. Our third baseman grinned and stuck out his glove. But, horrors! The ball skittered past him, letting in the winning run. We lost 3 to 2. However, the game paid one unexpected dividend—it caused me to catch the approbative eye of Coach Moran. He was one of the heroes of my college years. He was intelligent and long on character. I called him "Uncle Charley," and he was a benefactor and a strong influence on my life.

My most memorable collegiate baseball encounter took place in Lexington when Transylvania played the awesome University of Tennessee. Their student body was maybe ten or fifteen times the size of ours, giving them a bigger pool of good players.

Their pitcher and captain was Frank Calloway. He was good enough to later make it to the major leagues. I was pitching for Transylvania. I came up with the bases loaded and Frank Calloway struck me out. It was a terrible feeling, but it turned out to be not a momentous calamity. Despite the David-

Goliath overtones, I pitched the entire game and we walloped mighty Tennessee 10 to 4.

My tenor voice impressed the Transylvania music professor, Ernest Woodruff Delcamp. He was, incidentally, a remarkable man, who also taught Latin and would remain on campus for fifty years. He promptly put me in the glee club as soloist. I began to feel the glow of acceptance and success, but experienced a good deal of trouble learning to parcel out my hours in the hectic and constant rush from my newspaper delivery, to table waiting, to classes, to music and sports.

In the spring of 1918 I was dazzled with the idea that I might have a chance for a career in opera. Our glee club was invited that year to sing in the Cincinnati May Festival. Mrs. Delcamp had a lovely voice and the professor decided that the two of us would offer a duet. He chose the beautiful but difficult "Miserere" from Verdi's *Il Trovatore*. The star of the festival was Evan Williams, who rose from Ohio steelworker to become a famous tenor, veteran of a thousand concerts. Evan Williams—and the audience—enthusiastically applauded the Transylvania glee club, and especially our "Miserere."

I was flattered when Evan Williams asked me to sing for him. I sang "Friend of Mine." He returned the compliment by singing for us "Oh Dry Them Tears." I was stunned barely two weeks later to pick up the newspaper and read that he had suddenly died, at only fifty-one.

My success in Cincinnati triggered a sudden effort by all my musical friends in Lexington to convert me exclusively and single-mindedly to music. Miss Catherine Cochran, the city's leading voice teacher, began giving me lessons, at no charge.

"You might go on the circuit," she assured me, "or have a career in opera. But, of course, you must study hard and train your voice."

Oh, what a far cry from pinching the fuzzy, barking heads off tobacco worms. Or bruising my belly button all day with the handle of the pea hay pitchfork.

Another friend undertook to teach me to play the piano. I thought I might like that. But it only took a few lessons at the keyboard to dash any dreams I had of becoming a pianist. My hands just were not made for the piano; my fingers were too stubby and too inflexible. I struggled for a few weeks. There was no joy for me in this pursuit. My forlorn gaze kept straying to the window; I yearned to be out on the field with the players. Baseball, basketball, football—even track—seemed more attractive and enjoyable. While I fingered the keys, my mind's eye was watching me throw a crushing body block or a sizzling strike.

So I made a compromise, of sorts. I decided I would continue to sing and I would study voice as much as time allowed. But first and foremost I would go out regularly and heave and sweat and exercise at baseball, football, basketball and occasionally track and field.

One truth was clear to me: I was more of a jock than I was a musician.

Now the shadow of the war in Europe was falling darkly across the Transylvania campus. In a patriotic fever more than a hundred boys had rushed to recruiting centers. Some went to Texas to learn to fly. Others were quickly in France. With most regulars in khaki, the football team collapsed. Coach Willis T. Stewart did his best with untried raw material, but took lop-sided pastings from larger schools, losing 41–0 to Vanderbilt and 72–0 to Sewanee. The coach then quit and joined the army engineers.

During the 1918 summer vacation I went back to Corydon and worked in nearby Henderson in the circulation office of the *Gleaner.*

When I got back to Lexington in the fall, the war was bringing Transylvania to an unequivocal halt. Scores of students were stricken in the terrible flu pandemic. Those who remained were needed as doughboys. Eighty-five Transylvanians promptly volunteered for the Student Army Training Corps. I was one of them. That October the school shut down and became our military camp, with Ewing Hall converted into a barracks. Some young lieutenants took charge, filling rigorous days with drills, inspections, signalling, athletics, bayonet work and fatigue duty. One of the lieutenants was Dutch Meyer, who became a famous coach at Texas Christian University.

I felt patriotic, fit and ready. I remember my dog tag number was 5311754. They made me corporal of the fourth squad. I considered myself a good soldier.

But the Transylvania SATC was short-lived. In November

came the armistice. By year's end Transylvania's campus soldiers were demobilized. Quickly, the university returned to normal and I made up all my sophomore credits.

As a student, my level of sophistication was undergoing
sharp change. I was learning so much from the wonderful professors, lessons that would enhance my career in the years to
come. But I had no desire to abandon my heritage as a true
country boy. I loved the land and I felt I appreciated and understood the manners and mores of the plain rural people. At that
time, when I was nineteen or twenty, I had not the least glimmer of suspicion that this knowledge and *feel* for the everyday
hopes and dreams of the plain folks of my state, the people who
in the main were so much like my father, my grandfather, the
friends and neighbors I had in Corydon, was perhaps my most
powerful future asset.

I was making it a practice to look every new man or woman
in the eye, listen carefully to our introduction, and silently repeat the name to myself. I shook hands firmly, and I was not
too shy to give warm and sturdy hugs to the motherly women.

That knack of sincere greeting and avid listening to what
the other fellow had to say—not just with a polite head-shake
and a deaf ear—probably got me a million votes in politics.

Even in Lexington—a so-called metropolis of twenty
thousand—it was possible to reinforce my rustic intuitions.
Once a month "country" came to town—for what was called
"court day." In Lexington it was held the second Monday of the
month, drawing country folk from miles around to transact
business with the justices of peace in the courthouse, and create a sort of shopping festival in the public square. Frequently
I visited these raucous bazaars, savoring the antics and patois
of back home.

It was a festival the like of which apparently is common
only to our commonwealth. My friend Squire J. Winston Cole-
man, Jr., a noted Kentucky historian, succinctly captured the
flavor of Lexington's "court day"—just as I saw it—in one of
his books:

> Here, on Cheapside, the public square, were assembled a
> motley collection of livestock—lean cows with bawling
> calves, shaggy mules with tails full of cockleburs, braying

jacks, sway-back broodmares with colts, old plug horses and, occasionally, a blooded animal—all to be traded or offered for sale to the highest bidder. Along the courthouse yard were lined up various articles for sale or trade—farming implements, worn-out stoves, broken beds, old furniture and clothing, ax and plow handles, tools, plow gear and buggy harness, jars of pickles and preserves, home-made baskets and chairs, sugarcane "sweetening" and molasses by the gallon.

Here also were gathered itinerant vendors, junk dealers, petty fakers, cheap-jewelry salesmen, patent menders of glass and tinware, "painless" tooth extractors, long-haired "doctors" in long-tailed coats selling their all-curing medicines, hucksters with their watermelon carts, and traders of every kind and shade of reputation. Over on the sidewalk a blind mendicant with a tin cup around his neck sang mountain ballads and songs to the halting accompaniment of his squeaky fiddle. The public square on court day was the trading center and gossiping place for all rural Kentuckians; the talk was free and easy and every man had his say . . . .

The summer of 1919 I made my debut as a semi-pro baseballer, joining the Lexington Reo's. Generally I played in the infield, and occasionally pitched. Another rookie joining the Reo's was Earle Combs, who later went on to real greatness in the majors and wound up in the Baseball Hall of Fame. I had just turned twenty-one, and Earle was a little younger. I'll never forget our first game together. I was playing shortstop and he was in left field.

My God, he had more energy than anybody I ever saw. He wanted to run over everything and everybody. Our opponents would hit a line drive. And Earle would run in and grab every one, just jump at the ball.

I yelled over and tried to give him a little advice. "Son, those line drives will get to you. You don't need to board-fence 'em or run in on them. . . . Relax a little, let them come to you."

In the fourth inning I hit a single and he followed me with a home run over right field fence. He could hit and he was fast. Before I reached third he ran up behind me. I turned around, and cracked wise: "You didn't see that one very good, did you? The dust must have got in your eye when he threw that one."

To show you how Fate works, the Reo's sold his contract at the end of the season to Louisville for a mere hundred dollars. But he went right on up in the majors and hit .325 for twelve years with the New York Yankees. He was as good as Joe Di-Maggio. Unfortunately he was knocked unconscious when he crashed into centerfield fence in St. Louis chasing a fly, and was never very good after that as a player. We remained friends and I was able to be of some help to him later in baseball; and then during my second term as governor I named him banking commissioner in Kentucky.

Another rookie with the Reo's that year was a cute little Georgia boy named Joe Burman. He was something! And we became the closest of lifetime friends. Joe Burman would join me in my first gubernatorial administration as a jack-of-all-trades assistant with a variety of duties, not the least of which was to serve as my bodyguard.

That fall, beginning my junior year at Transylvania, I encountered good luck—and bad. I was still a poor boy from the country, but I yearned to join a fraternity. I hoped for a bid from Kappa Alpha, which in 1900 established the first Greek letter chapter on campus. Those fellows didn't seem to know that I existed. But Pi Kappa Alpha did. I was overjoyed to move into the PKA house with fifteen brothers. It was a rather modest set up, actually just sleeping rooms; we had to eat at the boarding house. But at last I was a fraternity man.

Bad luck came in football practice. I was playing quarterback, but on defense I was blocking back. During one afternoon drill I lunged at the tackling dummy. My shoulder pads slipped up just before the moment of impact. I felt the crunch of shoulder contact—and immediate searing pain. I doubled up on my knees and marveled that the strangled nerves in my neck and shoulder could torture every fiber of my body.

I limped off to the doctor's office. My collarbone was broken.

"You'll be out four weeks," the doctor said. "Maybe five."

That meant I was sidelined for the best part of the football season. On the gridiron I had already picked up a reputation as a sort of "Transylvania terror." My senior yearbook would put it this way:

...when the Lord made "Hap" He used up the end piece so that there can never be another like him, and then sent him off to the Class of 1921, for the singing athlete to make good...His "rep" on every team is best explained by a young Wesleyan rooter: "Kill 'Hap' Chandler; the rest of them won't hurt you; kill 'Hap.'"

My skill and verve in sports had attracted considerable notice among the Lexington high school athletic directors. Henry Clay High School suddenly needed a girls basketball coach. I was offered the position. Naturally I needed the money. It was a part-time job so I could manage to work it into my hectic schedule.

The girls were suited up in the Henry Clay gym when I arrived for our first practice. They were lively and interested, a group of all size and shapes, ranging from about fourteen to eighteen years old.

One of the tallest on the squad was a slender brunet, strikingly beautiful.

"What's your name?" I asked, holding my roster.

She studied me with a long look. Her eyes seemed to twinkle.

"Shelby Northcutt." She whirled and arced the basketball toward the hoop. It plopped through cleanly. "I play center, Coach."

Our eyes met again. Hers were smiling, quizzical, daring. It was an electric moment.

Not only was Shelby Northcutt the star, she indisputably was the strongest, quickest, sharpest-eyed player, vivacious and good-humored. Academically she was also a top gun, and in addition she played the piano—a skill I still envied.

My debut as a coach might have proved awkward if for no other reason than that I had a hard time masking my natural youthful ebullience with an authoritarian sheen. Hardly could I appear a father figure to these girls, being not much over twenty-one.

But I hit it off with them from the first.

Especially with Shelby. Naturally her role as the sparkplug of the team required my close attention. When I gave her pointers, she eyed me narrowly. For an instant she would seem distant, then a stunning smile would explode across her pretty face.

I began to feel my blood rise when she would give me a long quizzical stare, taunting and daring. I felt myself blushing. The situation did not seem to bother her. Her emotions did not interfere with her playing, which was superb. And I kept my mind strictly on coaching—most of the time.

Never before had I been seriously in love. It seemed pointless; I couldn't think of marriage.

But the beautiful vision of tall, slender Shelby Northcutt began to haunt me. Any coach who becomes enamoured of a high school girl runs several risks. First, his sweetheart's teammates may become jealous and think he's showing favoritism. From the academic ranks may come jibes, taunting him for trying to rob the cradle.

Nothing like that happened. All the girls looked up to Shelby. Besides, there wasn't that much of a gap in our ages— she was close to eighteen. Finally I asked for a date and called at Shelby's home to take her to a movie. Her mother came to the door. She was smiling. I could tell right away that she approved. With her father it was a different matter. He put down the evening newspaper, came across the room and warily shook hands. His eyes drilled into mine, not at all friendly.

Shelby explained. Father favored her other boyfriend, a young Lexington man who was waiting for an appointment to the United States Naval Academy.

"Dad hopes I'll marry him." She gave a gentle little laugh. "Daddy says he's sure to be an admiral!"

I courted her steadily. We swam together and played tennis. Took boat trips down the river. Attended a summer camp together. I have reason to believe she loved me and would have married me, but I could not ask her. At this point I could barely support myself.

Her father proved something of a soothsayer—Shelby finally married the midshipman as soon as he graduated from Annapolis. And he did become an admiral in the United States Navy. They had one child, and then got a divorce. She later married again. She is gone now, but I'll never forget her. Ours was a wonderful romance—my very first.

My Lexington memories are not all innocent, warm and

beautiful. During my Transylvania days I was jolted by a darker encounter with real life—eye-witness to the fury of a lynch mob, and unexpected retaliation by the law.

The episode began with the brutal murder of a ten-year-old girl. A man named Will Lockett was arrested and held for trial in the Lexington courthouse. This was in the first part of February, 1920. Tension quickly rose to a dangerous pitch. Agitators got ropes and muttered that the prisoner ought to be lynched.

People began milling around the courthouse with their ropes, shouting wildly, angrily demanding Will Lockett be brought out.

The Lexington sheriff, frightened that he could not control the mob, appealed for state troops. A National Guard company arrived from Louisville. With loaded rifles, they ringed the courthouse.

The commotion drew curious spectators, including me. I rushed from the Transylvania campus down to the Cheapside square. Just then the angry crowd turned into a mob, and surged forward. At a command, the Guardsmen began firing their rifles. I was close enough to hear the rattle of gunfire and see men in the mob stagger and fall, gushing blood. I was safely out of the range of the bullets, and certainly had no notion at all of joining them in storming the jail.

The mob fell back at once. Men rushed around retrieving casualties. More than fifty in the mob suffered rifle wounds. Some victims, cursing, screaming and bleeding, were carried past me. A few went by on stretchers, with closed eyes, pale, quiet, lifeless. The death toll was six.

My young mind was stunned by this bloody eruption. I hated the thought of overwrought citizens, however badly intentioned, being brutally shot down by their own state troops. Of course, the law had to be upheld, and every prisoner—no matter what—is entitled to trial. Finally the vivid vision faded in my mind, but it would come back with great force when I sat at the governor's desk examining a sheaf of death warrants for convicted murderers awaiting my signature. . . .

Most of my summers in the Transylvania years were devoted to playing baseball for money. I was getting a pretty good reputation as a pitcher. Over at the University of Kentucky, the much bigger college on the south side of town, varsity baseball coach Andy Gill had been watching me. He liked my arm.

Andy Gill looked me up and said he was taking a team from Kentucky up to the wheat country on the Canadian border. "Those Swedes and Norwegians up there are crazy about baseball," he said. "You never saw such rabid fans!"

His semi-pro team would play under the aegis of Grafton, North Dakota. He offered me one hundred dollars a month.

"Lordy, yes, partner. I'll go!" To me it sounded like a gold strike and jamboree combined. And that's how it more or less turned out.

Andy Gill wanted me to pitch. He was taking along some of his University of Kentucky players including a Casey County native named Floyd Wright. Wright was a baseball hotshot and everyone called him "Rasty." In every way he was a remarkable and extraordinary man, and we enjoyed a lifelong friendship. He eventually had a stint in the major leagues as a Cleveland Indians outfielder, but made his success as a tobacco warehouse manager in Lexington. He became wealthy enough to leave six million dollars to the Albert B. Chandler Medical Center at the University of Kentucky.

In World War One he was an aviator. When the Armistice came, Rasty just couldn't contain himself. He whooped and hollered, and then rushed out to the air strip. He hopped into his little Jenny biplane and took off for Paris. He didn't have in mind landing—just showing off.

He flew low over the Champs Elysees, heading straight for the Arc de Triomphe. Happily he waggled his wings in a salute to victory and dived down, just above the roofs of the taxicabs, and burst beneath the center and highest of the monument's arches.

It was perhaps a foolhardy gesture, but it was brave and daring. If Rasty said he did it, I know he did. That's the kind of fellow he was.

In Grafton we lived in a boarding house run by a sturdy Swedish woman. Every time I saw her she was scrubbing, cleaning, cooking, busy inside the house and out—I had never before seen a woman work that hard.

She asked me what I was doing for a living.

"I play baseball."

She threw up her hands and a grimace ran across her face. "Ah, baseball! Is one hard yob!"

Of course I thought it was real fun, almost child's play. Just turned twenty-two, my pitching game was sharp. I had a good fastball and an improving curve. And my Satchel Paige "hesitation" number seemed to consistently confuse the batters.

I started thirteen games, and won twelve of them. In neighboring Minnesota, I was on the mound against the Mahnomen Indians. This was one time I thought I might have the Indian sign on the Indians. For three or four innings every one of their batters who came up to the plate sat down mighty quick. If I didn't throw three strikes, I managed to feed 'em something soft that ended in a miserable pop-up.

By the seventh inning, Rasty and my other teammates were beginning to buzz, and shoot me warm glances. Andy Gill stopped me when I picked up my glove and started out to the mound. "Tell me, Happy, have you ever pitched a no-hitter?"

I gulped. "No, Coach, I never have!"

He gave me a look and his eyes seemed to be dancing. "Well son, you might today!"

Up to that point, I hadn't really thought about that. For a split second I felt flustered and insecure. But I was too cocky to get a case of nerves. My arm actually was getting a little tired; I didn't have my old throwing strength since breaking my collarbone on that football dummy. I walked out, toed the rubber, got the sign. . . .

Then I hurled the last two innings with no more worry than if I was still getting two bits a day for dropping tobacco plants in Corydon.

The Mahnomen Indians sent up their final batter. He looked mean and desperate. I ran the count to one ball and two strikes and then sailed him my country curve. He took such a lunge, missing by a foot, that he nearly fell over.

I had my no-hitter—my first ever!

It was perhaps the biggest thrill of my sports life. But a little later in the season I just about equalled that achievement, as far as our Grafton fans were concerned.

This was a game where we seemed to be somewhat outclassed, or at least off our feed or out of synch. The opponents had the lead. I had done a pretty good job pitching, but it looked like we were going to lose.

Suddenly, in the last inning, our team came alive. Three of our men rapped out little hits, and all at once we had the bases loaded! That was the good news; the bad was that we had two outs, and I was walking to the plate as the last hitter.

I wasn't worried at first, but I took a called strike and then hit a foul. I stepped out of the box and glanced out across the diamond. Our three baserunners were tense as jackrabbits. All they wanted was for me to connect, and give them a chance to run. It was ironic; if I took another strike I'd lose my own game. I tightened up on the bat.

I saw a good one coming and whacked it—for a double. Our three runners came in. We had chalked up another win.

Something akin to pandemonium erupted in the grandstand. These Scandinavians take their baseball seriously. They were whooping and hollering. All at once pellets began flying out of the stands. Several thudded against my flannels, falling harmlessly into the dirt.

Andy Gill, beaming, rushed out to me.

"Hey, kid!" he exclaimed. "You're their hero!"

"But, Andy—they're throwing at me! What are they throwing?"

"Silver dollars, you idiot! Pick 'em up!"

That was a North Dakota custom I could easily get used to. Silver dollars seemed to be flying out from every seat. Rasty Wright and several other players rushed out to help me scoop up the cartwheels. In a few minutes they had filled up every pocket of my uniform, and dumped big handfuls into the bat bag. Later I counted them—one hundred and fifty!

That wasn't the end of the victory celebration. There were no saloons up in that wheat country, but the fans all clustered into the corner drugstore to relive the excitement of the game and congratulate the victorious players. The locals began passing out cigars.

"Thanks, sir," I said, shaking my head when someone offered me one. "I don't smoke."

A little later I was walking down the street when I felt the thud of a swift kick. I turned, startled, ready to fight. It was Andy Gill.

"Listen, Sonny Boy," he snapped. "You don't smoke—but old Pop does. Take them cigars!"

Afterwards I did.

It is interesting that they have named the Grafton ball park Chandler Field. It wasn't so much that I was a 1920 "star" there, but actually because when I became baseball commissioner I showed so much interest in the minor leagues.

Of course my daddy always hoped I'd get into professional baseball and be a big leaguer. At one time I may have even thought I could achieve the impossible dream.

At the end of the summer up on the Canadian border I came face to face with the truth about the big leagues. Rasty Wright hooked on with the Saskatoon club in the West Canadian League. He built me up to the Saskatoon manager, Sammy Beer. Finally, Beer agreed to take me on for a tryout.

I had high hopes. I got in the Saskatoon lineup for a few games, playing second base and shortstop. Then Beer called me aside. He put his hand on my shoulder. "I'm sorry, Happy. I don't think you're good enough for us." End of dream.

I wasn't big league material, not even good enough for the minors. I had one consolation—I still could play baseball and loved the game. That broken collarbone was really bad luck; except for that I might have made the Saskatoon club. And from there, might have had an entirely different career.

In the back of my mind were some vague and latent urgings to follow my father's injunction to take up the ministry. I had close friends among the student preachers in the College of the Bible. One of them, Kenneth Bowen, grabbed me the moment I returned from North Dakota.

Kenneth had been hired to lead a "protracted meeting" or revival at the Christian Church at Taylorsville in Spencer County. He wanted me to accompany him and lead the choir and sing solos. For those two weeks, I would get about sixty dollars. I still needed money for my final year at Transylvania, so I accepted. I knew all the old church songs—"Beautiful Isle of Somewhere," "In the Garden," "Abide with Me" and dozens of other favorites.

I couldn't escape that vague but strong religious tug. I continued to be drawn toward preaching. Maybe Dad knew best, after all.

I frequently attended Sunday services at what was called "Everybody's Church," conducted in a Lexington picture show by Dr. J. Archer Gray, who got to be a good friend of mine. One day he said something that caused me to believe there was something special within me, vague and mysterious, a secret inner element that would channel my thoughts and shape my destiny.

Dr. Gray sat me down and spoke very earnestly.

"A lot of people," he said, "look at you and say, How does this fellow get along? I'm as smart as he is—and they are. I'm as good looking as he is—and they are. And they'd try to explain how it is that you get along and they don't get along. I'll tell you why it is, Happy."

"Why is it, Dr. Gray?"

He looked deeply into my eyes before he spoke.

"You have the divine spark."

Of course, there is no way I would know if I had the divine spark. I can't say. I don't know whether I do or not. But he said I had it. And if I have, it has been good luck for me. I know that some people do have some inner fire that could be called the divine spark. I have felt *something* all my life.

Without being critical of anyone, my close observation of some of the "preacher boys" finally cooled me off on going into the ministry. I just decided it was not the life for me. This decision forced me to rack my brain about the kind of career I ought to pursue. Certainly, whatever it was to be, I wanted to live in Kentucky.

It is not clear just when the idea jelled that I would become a lawyer. But I remember precisely the moment in the Transylvania library when it struck me that I should go to the most prestigious law school in the United States.

That was a truly frightening decision, and a monumental hurdle to leap. My grades were good enough, I felt, to get in. But going far away from home and financing myself through an Ivy League university might be impractical and perhaps impossible. But once I had fixed the goal in my mind, I started scratching to try to do it—and scratching hard.

4

Harvard Nothing, Centre Six

"Colonel Moore, do you know if anyone around here needs a coach?"

The athletic director of Harvard University stared across his desk, considering my question with a quizzical but not unkind expression.

"I've just enrolled in your law school," I added hastily. "I need part-time work to get by."

"As a matter of fact, I do. Tell me about yourself, son."

This was August 1921 and I had come with my A. B. from Transylvania to Cambridge, Massachussetts as a freshman in Harvard Law. Emerging from the South Street station, I was dazzled by my first view of the famous campus, sharply taken aback by the obvious age of everything. Most impressive of all was the walled-in Harvard Yard. I was staggered by the size of my law class, numbering 400 or 500. Lord, that was about twice the size of the whole Transylvania enrollment.

In every way this was a far cry from Kentucky. I had never before seen ivy climbing old buildings. The climate was different. So were the people. I guess they considered me a unique character. "Where," asked several young men, mocking my southern drawl, "are *you-all* from?"

At 19 Irving Street, I found inexpensive lodging. It had to be cheap. I was wearing my only suit, bought for nineteen dollars in Cincinnati, and carried everything else in one small suitcase. I came to Harvard with only two hundred dollars, borrowed from a fraternity brother, Lexington automobile dealer John Field. I explained my urgent situation to Colonel Moore.

In recounting my experience in sports, I observed that Uncle Charley Moran had often had me scout for Centre College.

"You can't beat us!" Colonel Moore snapped. He seemed to take for granted that my collegiate loyalty still remained with my home state.

The "Praying Colonels" had created such a stir in collegiate football that Harvard had scheduled the Kentucky team for a three game series. In the 1920 opener Harvard had soundly whipped the Danville eleven, 31 to 14. Mighty Harvard expected to thrash Uncle Charley's team again this fall—and then kick Centre off their schedule.

My response was cautious.

"Well, sir," I said, timidly in view of the fact he hadn't yet disclosed the potential job, "I guess we won't know that until after the final whistle."

Colonel Moore, his eyes narrowing slightly, looked pensive. Doubtless he was rolling his impressions of me over in his mind. Then he spoke. "Listen . . . Take the train and go out to Wellesley Hills High School. They're looking for a football coach."

I got the job.

My law school classes were mornings. I got on well with my professors. Woodrow Wilson's son-in-law, Francis Bowers Sayre, taught criminal law. He was nice to me. But my most interesting and valuable course at Harvard was six hours on contracts. That helped me immensely in my legal career.

Weekdays at about 12:30 P.M. I hopped the train for the twenty-five mile ride to Wellesley Hills. My pay was bare-bones, twenty-five dollars a month, but I couldn't have survived without it. Luckily, I had a lively squad. Some of the players were super. The quarterback was a bright kid named Herby Gibelein, who was easy to coach.

I got on famously with one of the ends, Sherman Glendenning. Every now and then he would invite me to come home to supper with his family. That helped a lot; Lordy, I was always hungry!

My Wellesley High team had a very good year. It was a real coup for me when we managed to defeat arch rival Needham.

The winter weather in New England was the most severe I had ever encountered. I really didn't have clothes heavy enough for it. But I just gritted my teeth. I told my friends that Mark Twain had said it for me on climate: "When the Lord sorts out the weather and sends rain, rain is my choice." Same for snow and sleet. Brr!

Every Sunday I attended church in the Harvard Yard. Visiting preachers delivered the sermons and I heard some impressive speakers. That remains to this day one of my most memorable Harvard recollections.

At nearby Wellesley College I looked up a girl from back home. She was Mary Pringle Barrett, from a well-to-do Henderson County family. In Corydon High School I had a crush on her. It was not totally unreciprocated, but Mary Pringle was a practical lass. She knew all about my meager financial prospects. Besides, now in college she was romantically involved with a young medical student named Fitzgerald. I must say that years later she confided that she might have made a mistake not waiting for me.

At Wellesley College, Mary Pringle showed me around and took me to several afternoon dances where I met other girls. One stands vividly in my memory. She was the youngest of the three celebrated Soong sisters, Mei-ling. A petite intellectual beauty, Mei-ling later became the wife of the Chinese generalissimo Chiang Kai-shek. Over twenty years later, when I toured the war fronts to report to the United States Senate, I visited the generalissimo's headquarters where I saw her again. She had the reputation of being brilliant and haughty. Still beautiful at forty-nine, her eyes twinkled as she recalled our carefree Harvard-Wellesley days. Generously she tried to load me down with gifts to carry back to my wife and children.

A letter came in the fall of 1921 from Centre. Uncle Charley Moran was inquiring whether I'd have time to scout the Harvard football team. I told Colonel Moore that I was going to squeeze in that assignment. Scouting by rivals was a common and open practice. Harvard, too, obviously had someone go to Danville and study the Centre players and tactics.

I took careful notes and diagrammed critical Harvard formations. There is no doubt in my mind that my scouting made significant contributions to the outcome of the Harvard-Centre contest that year.

When the Centre team reached Boston, I was waiting at the railway station. Setting off for headquarters at the Lennox Hotel, I strode along with Uncle Charley, pouring into his ear my last-minute intelligence and ideas on the Harvard game plan.

Of all the people I've known in sports, Charley Moran is one of the most memorable. He was only about five-ten, but very powerful in the legs and shoulders. Usually he kept a wad of chewing tobacco in his cheek. When things didn't go to suit him, he could explode in a rage with more cussing than a sailor in a Calcutta hell-hole. Our paths kept crossing for years because he was a summertime umpire in the National League.

Not many years ago I said—fondly, of course—in a newspaper interview that Uncle Charley was as tough as a Mississippi boarding house steak. You never heard such an uproar from down south! I made haste to apologize to the state—and every boarding house in Mississippi.

I had three special friends on the Centre team—Alfred "Bo" McMillin, Red Weaver and Red Roberts. That was the year all three would make All-American, helped in a great measure by what was about to happen on the Harvard gridiron.

In my last year at Transylvania, I had tangled with all three of them in one of the most lopsided contests I ever played. Centre massacred us, something like 49 to 0. I was quarterback and had to stay in on defense as blocking back. We had only seventeen players on the Transylvania squad.

By the end of the third quarter, I thought I was going to die, and then I was afraid I wouldn't, and then it didn't make any difference. I still think playing a full game against that Centre powerhouse was a sheer problem of survival. Nobody else much did that; I was one of the few Transylvania fellows who lasted the whole game.

Black and blue and groggy, I was about to collapse when

the final whistle blew. Red Roberts, who had spent the afternoon banging me around, rushed over and grabbed me. He lifted me up in his arms. He was a powerful big brute but he held me as tenderly as a baby. Red Roberts carried me all the way in to our dressing room. I felt that was a pretty damn good display of real sportsmanship.

When the Centre team suited up on Saturday to take on Harvard, Uncle Charley called everyone together in the Lennox Hotel dining room. Once again he had me diagram the Harvard plays.

Emotion was already running high with the Kentucky invaders. They were still smarting from the previous year's defeat, and were embarrassed that the Cambridge athletes held them in light regard, as upstarts from a little country college.

"That play you keep talking about," Uncle Charley said to me. "Diagram that again."

"This fellow," I said, pointing, "will be two and a half yards back for the snap. He will offer to pass to the halfback, but he won't. He will turn and come right back through the middle of the line."

The Centre blocking back, Ed Kubale, spoke up.

"Happy, will he do that?"

I said, "Yes, sir. And when he does that what are you going to do?"

"I'm going to gore him like a bull!"

The "Praying Colonels" had come to fight.

Uncle Charley was a past master at the psychologic twists of getting his players up on an emotional high. He wanted them to be thinking of pride and home when they charged out to meet Harvard.

"Happy," he said, "sing us a song."

I stood before the team and began singing a very nostalgic, moody melody, "Down the Road to Home Sweet Home."

It created a spell. Glancing around the room, I could see tears glistening in practically everyone's eyes—mine included.

That was a charged-up Centre team that took the field. I sat on the bench beside Uncle Charley.

The first half ended nothing to nothing.

Centre kicked off to Harvard to start the second half and

held the home team on downs. Harvard punted and Tom
Bartlett from Owensboro caught the ball on the Centre 35 and
ran it to midfield.

I jumped up screaming an angry protest. It looked like the
whole Harvard team piled on Tom. The referee blew his
whistle—he thought the same thing. He picked up the ball and
started walking off the penalty.

The referee was Tiny Maxwell, who had been an All-
American guard at Swarthmore. His nickname was perversely
apt—he weighed something like 380 pounds.

Tiny Maxwell walked off the fifteen-yard piling-on penalty,
putting the ball on the Harvard 35.

On the first play from scrimmage, Bo McMillin followed
Red Roberts over their right tackle and immediately cut for the
sideline and raced furiously downfield. He ran 35 yards for a
touchdown.

Harvard was emotionally worked up, too; they had a national image to protect. They blocked the Centre try for extra
point. The score, of course, stood Centre 6, Harvard zero.

After that it was a furious and desperate struggle. The defense tightened up on both sides of the line. The players surged
back and forth, sweating, panting, cursing, getting brutal.

Both offenses were getting ground up.

Finally the clock ran down. Tiny Maxwell blew his whistle.
He picked up the football. "B-b-boys," he said with his stutter,
"t-t-this g-g-game is o-o-ver."

Bo McMillin stood there with tears streaming down his
cheeks. He was a little Irishman from Fort Worth, a dirty little
fellow, and one of the greatest football players I ever saw.

Tiny Maxwell threw the football to Bo.

Everybody rushed out and picked Bo up on their shoulders. Bo McMillin tossed the football to me.

In the melee that ensued I missed my ride back to the Lennox Hotel. Clutching the football, I walked up to Harvard
Square and took the subway over to Boston. At the Lennox Hotel I waded through the jubilant crowd and found Bo.

"Here." I handed him the football. "You won the game with
this. Take it. Keep it!"

For me it was enough to know that from the sidelines I had played a role in a sports shot heard round the world.

That game became known as the football upset of the century.

5

Hanging Out My Shingle

I fell in love at first sight with the little Kentucky town of Versailles. That occurred on the first day of July, 1922. It has been my hometown ever since. In fact I've lived on the same corner of Elm street since 1934. At heart I've always been a country town fellow. But I got to Versailles in a roundabout way.

I was on a summer job up in the mountains when Stanley A. "Daddy" Boles tracked me down by phone. He was athletic director at the University of Kentucky.

"Just got a call from Versailles High School," he said. "They're looking for a new football coach. I recommended you. Go see 'em."

It was a Saturday afternoon, the first, when I got over there and looked up Principal Beaman. He took me down to Fisher's Drug Store on Main Street to see two members of the school board, Bob Berryman and "Doc" Fisher. We sat around and talked. I sipped a coke. They sized me up.

I was struck at once that the town seemed friendly, with a comfortable look and feel. The population was about eleven hundred, maybe only a third bigger than Corydon. But Versailles was the county seat of Woodford county, with a two-story courthouse right on Main Street. It had an old fashioned clock on a bell tower. In the drugstore we could clearly hear the hours striking. Somehow that was sweet music to my ears.

Versailles is ten or twelve miles west of Lexington and, on the bottom corner of a somewhat flat triangle, about the same distance southeast of Frankfort, the state capital. Over the years our town has grown to about 8,000, but it has managed to retain its rustic charm. On my first afternoon there plenty of farm wagons were rolling along Main Street.

Beaman was apologetic. His school had sorry equipment. But he'd buy what was needed. They planned to build a new high school. And a better football field. The football coach, he explained, had to also teach two history classes.

"I'm qualified to do that," I said. "But I would have to have my mornings free." They looked at me. "I've enrolled in law school over at the University of Kentucky. I'll be taking morning classes."

My year at Harvard Law School hadn't worked out. My grades were good. But trying to scrape by in Cambridge on odd jobs was just too rugged. I decided not to remain in New England. Kentucky was home. I transferred to U.K. to finish law.

The principal and the school board members retired behind the drug counter to confer. They came back smiling.

"Okay," said Beaman. "Eighty dollars a month. Next year, if you work out, a hundred and a quarter. Can you start August first?"

This job wouldn't make me rich. But I could live on it, and fortunately it would be easy for me to jump back and forth between Versailles High and my law classes in Lexington. An interurban ran about every half hour.

With my coaching job nailed down, I returned to Lee County where I was working for the Swiss Oil Corporation when "Daddy" Boles phoned me. Head of the firm, which later became the Ashland Oil Corporation, was J. Fred Miles, who had followed my college athletic career. He hired me for the summer to drill oil wells, build shack lines—and manage the Swiss Oil semi-pro baseball team.

All of us—oilfield roughnecks and ballplayers alike—worked hard during the week and perhaps even harder on the weekends when we took on surrounding towns on the diamond.

One lesson I learned that summer up in the eastern Kentucky hills has stuck with me always: If you drill a dry hole, you don't stand there and fill it up with tears, you move your digger! Jumping right in and starting anew after any defeat seemed then to make a lot of sense to me, and still does.

I saw to it that my Swiss Oilers got good food and equipment. That paid off. We won every game. I had brought in four or five crackerjack players from the outside. One youngster was a heavy-hitter. The locals couldn't remember his name. They called him "That long-legged son-of-a-bitch from Winchester."

Working so much as a scout and player, I have over the years been able to spot promising youngsters and got some a chance to go to the big leagues. Not all my finds made it, though. I remember sending a hotshot pitcher from Kentucky to the New York Giants. Manager John McGraw kept him a couple of months and turned him loose. I asked why. "Happy," McGraw told me, "that fellow has a million dollar arm and a ten-cent head."

In August I showed up in Versailles. I met the mayor, Dr. W. C. McCauley. His daughter had just gone away to college. Mrs. McCauley agreed to rent me the girl's room. I went around Main Street and the courthouse telling everyone I could find, "I'm Happy Chandler, your new football coach." In those early years I learned to call every store owner in town by name, and knew most of their families. Today not a single original store owner remains.

It took a lot of sixteen-hour days but I managed to successfully meld my two careers—law student and football coach. I got up early in the morning and rode the interurban to Lexington. It took more than thirty minutes. I got off at the top of the hill over there at the Southern Railway station and walked across the dump to the law school. I stayed until about noon and caught the interurban back to Versailles. I had my first class at the high school at one o'clock and the next at two. Then I went to coaching. And sometimes when the moon came up I was still coaching.

I worked hard. I worked like a dog. Coaching football is hard work, and coaching high school football is double hard. It's one of the hardest jobs you ever saw. Not harder than pea hay; pea hay's got the prize. But standing out there on the sidelines for hours and watching a bunch of youngsters continually do what you expressly ask them not to do—that'll run you crazy!

Most of my boys were light, but they had heart. I remember playing Frankfort. My boys probably averaged 140 pounds. From end to end the Frankfort team ran about 175 pounds. Generally people thought if they outweighed you in high school they'd run over you. I thought I was a pretty good coach, especially on defense. If they don't score on you, they aren't going to beat you.

We played those big fellows for what seemed like all day and at the half it was nothing to nothing. Before we went back out, the little Gaines boy rushed up to me. "Coach," he said, "I mean to win this game or I intend to die on the field!" He was serious. "Stanley," I replied, "we'll win it, and you'll live."

I don't know where I got it but I had a certain power of persuasion—the power of getting a team emotionally up for a game. You can't get 'em emotionally up for every game. If you do that you make a mistake. Sometimes you have to let 'em off. So I didn't try to get my boys up for every game. And I had an unusual experience on that.

I used to tell the boys: "This is a special day tomorrow. This is one we got to win. So go down to the butcher shop and get you some raw meat and eat some raw meat and be ready when you come up here tomorrow to take those fellows apart!"

Well, I had a big country boy who played center. Rasty Brandenburg sidled up to me after practice. "Happy, do I have to eat that raw meat?"

"What's the matter?"

Rasty made a face. "The last time you said to eat it, I ate some. It sort of made me sick at my stomach."

I looked at him and kept a straight face. "No, not this time. You've already done it. You pass it by."

I didn't want him to know that I thought anything of the fact that he took literally all I said. If I had said go and kick the goal post over, he'd have done it. He did what I said.

During the time I coached football, Versailles High School had a record to be pretty proud of: thirty-six wins, fifteen losses, and five ties. That covers seven years. In 1924 we didn't lose a game.

That first year it was difficult to get everything done in Lexington and Versailles. But I was never late for class. My daddy told me that I had a right to waste my time but I didn't have a right to waste yours. So I'm the most on-time fellow you ever saw in your life. I've been doing business with a fellow for thirty-five years and he's been on time five times, in those thirty-five years. I said to him, "You bastard, I wish you'd have been late those other five times, then you'd have a clear record." He always has a plausible excuse. There is no excuse for not being on time except occasionally. Time is important to me—it's important to you.

Daddy's warning about going in debt haunted me when I started in Versailles. I wanted to heed his advice. But I was struggling, counting my pennies. I walked into the clothing store on Main Street looking for a suit. The owner showed me one for nineteen dollars. I fingered the gray fabric, hesitating. "Can I get it on credit?" I asked.

"No." He gave me a fishy eye. He knew who I was, the football coach. He set his jaw. "Cash."

I left and crossed the street to the bank. I sat down at the bank president's desk. He, of course, knew who I was but we were still more or less strangers. I said I needed to borrow fifty dollars and had no collateral.

That old man—he certainly seemed old to me then, but he really wasn't—talked very kindly to me. I didn't realize it but he was drawing me out, analyzing my character. He launched into a long story about a loan he had made to his son-in-law. The day the note was due the son-in-law disappeared. My mind fidgeted, wondering if that would sour the banker on every young fellow who came along.

Finally he made up his mind. He reached in his drawer for a blank note, scribbled in fifty dollars, and shoved it across the desk. He handed me his pen. "Just make sure," he grunted, "you show up when it's due."

I did, of course. I paid it off on time. We became good friends. And later in my first term as governor I had the pleasure of appointing him (Hiram Wilhoit) banking commissioner of Kentucky.

With that fifty dollars in my pocket, I walked right past

the clothier where I'd been turned down and took the interurban to Lexington. I bought a suit over there. It cost twenty dollars, but it certainly seemed of much better quality. To this day I have never set foot inside that store in Versailles.

Perhaps I don't easily forgive people who treat me mean, but that incident on the suit of clothes was certainly not typical. Most everybody else in Versailles trusted and liked me. I made it my business to look everyone in the eye, listen to their names, and give them a hearty and sincere handshake. That— and a friendly hug for the mothers and grandmas—became my trademark. As I said, I could call by name a heck of a lot of the people in Versailles.

The most influential lawyer in town, Field McLeod, became an early friend of mine. Talk about somebody born with a silver spoon in his mouth, that was Judge McLeod. His father started the newspaper here, the *Woodford Sun,* and they lived in the big house on the hill that once was the residence of Marquis de Calmes. General Lafayette came here in 1825 to visit his countryman the marquis. That is the reason our town has a French name, though its pronunciation is Americanized, sounding not like ver "sigh" but like ver "sales."

Judge McLeod became a big fan of my football and basketball teams. I took my Versailles High girls basketball team to the state tournament and they knocked off favorite Lexington in the first round. I invited Judge McLeod to make the speech at our basketball banquet. When I first met him he was about sixty, very distinguished, and I suppose the richest man in town.

In May 1924 I was graduated from the University of Kentucky law school and passed the state bar with a score of eighty-seven and eleven-sixteenths.

Naturally I could not afford to abruptly quit my job as coach—my only source of income—to hang out my shingle and plunge exclusively into the practice of law. But I had my mornings free, now that I didn't have to shuttle over to Lexington for classes.

My friendship with Judge McLeod proved a great boon. He offered me rent-free desk space in the law office he shared with Judge Edelen. And he even loaned me a desk! Of course, I was not a member of the law firm, just strictly on my own.

When I got ready to hang out my shingle, Judge McLeod and Judge Edelen were all frowns.

"I believe I'd get rid of that nickname," Judge Edelen said.

Everyone in town called me "Happy."

"Why?" I asked.

"It's not dignified."

"How would you go about getting rid of it?"

The two lawyers pondered my question.

"Give me some time," said Judge Edelen, "and I'll let you know."

A couple of weeks went by. Finally Judge Edelen called me over and shrugged elaborately.

"I've thought about it," he said, "and I don't believe you can do it. . . . I'd just keep it."

I didn't try to bury or disown "Happy"—but my shingle went up: Albert B. Chandler, Lawyer.

"Gentlemen," I announced to the two lawyers, "what I want is a client who is scared—and rich!"

That was quite a while in coming. My first client was a man who wanted a mortgage drawn. I charged him three dollars. I was so proud of my first fee that I framed the check and stuck it on the office wall for years. I may still have it around somewhere.

I used to say in those days that I was a lawyer by profession and made my living coaching football. I got more money generally for coaching football than I did for my law practice.

A colored fellow came in and told me: "Mr. Happy, I bought me a little country place."

"Fine." I said. "I'll make you a deed."

He gave me a sharp look. "Mr. Happy, I wants a mortgage!"

"What the hell do you want a mortgage for?"

"Well," he said, "Ah had de deed de last time and de other fellow he had de mortgage, and he got de farm!"

You weren't going to fool him any more. Finally I explained the law and wrote him a deed. He went out muttering and shaking his head, still not too certain I knew what I was doing.

My first appearance in court was to represent a couple of local men accused of taking an automobile from some Louisville folks. I don't remember why they hired me. I tried to be on good terms with the sheriff and other people around the court-house. Maybe the jailer suggested my name.

Anyhow the prisoners told me they weren't guilty. There were circumstances. Some lawyers will take a case for anybody, but I would never defend a person who admitted to me his guilt.

I demanded a jury trial. Somehow, luckily, I got them off. I seemed to have a way of persuading jurors, too, just like I could inspire little football players to eat raw meat.

Little by little my law practice grew. I hung onto my job as high school coach, though. Judge McLeod and his partner Edelen quietly—and generously—steered a few clients my way. One was the Episcopal girls school, Margaret Hall, located on Elm Street just a block or two from where I now live. One after-noon in October 1924 I was summoned by the headmistress to discuss some legal matter.

While we were talking the door burst open and a tall girl in a rumpled gym suit started in. "Oh...Pardon me, Miss Gaither. I didn't know you were busy."

The girl in the doorway had honey blonde hair hanging to her shoulders and dazzling blue eyes. Her eyes fascinated me; they seemed full of wit, of shrewdness, of humor, of spunk and courage. She must have just come from a workout, for beads of sweat stood out on her face. Her hair, fine-spun as silk, was matted up from perspiration, but even so it twinkled with all kinds of wonderful lights. I caught my breath. Though hot and unkempt, she was about the prettiest girl I had ever seen.

"That's all right, dear," said Miss Gaither. "Come in and meet our attorney, Mr. Chandler. And I'll talk to you later." The headmistress turned to me. "May I present Miss Mildred Watkins, our instructor in athletics and drama."

Later, when we finished our legal conference, I smiled at the headmistress. "That girl from the gym is most attractive. Tell me about her."

Miss Gaither gave me a sharp look. "Mildred is engaged, Mr. Chandler. A very nice boy up at Kenyon College in Ohio, where we were last year. He's a football player."

I asked a few questions, though, and found out about Mildred Watkins. She was a Virginian, and her father was a railroad engineer. She left college after a couple of years to join a friend at Harcourt Place, a girls school at Gambier, Ohio, which shares a campus with Kenyon College. There she developed an outstanding athletic and drama program. When Miss Gaither was asked to become headmistress at Margaret Hall, Mildred had come with her. My guess was Mildred was about twenty-four (which was correct), about a year younger than I was.

For days I kept thinking about her and toyed with the idea of making some pretext to go out to Margaret Hall so I could get a better look.

Those were the days when we were barely out of the horse-and-buggy age. Henry Ford's flivvers were chugging along Main Street, their propensity to "kick" while being cranked leaving an unwonted roster of broken arms. There was, of course, no television and very little radio. In the mid-twenties there were Victrolas with scratchy seventy-eights. The young people of Versailles, or in other cities and towns, largely had to create their own entertainment. So we put on lots of plays and musicals. Sometimes we even brought in a professional director.

In these productions I usually had some part, often as leading man.

One evening I came into a rehearsal and heard a beautiful soprano voice emerging from the far end of the stage.

"Who's that?" I asked.

"Mildred Watkins."

I was tickled that we were going to be singing together in this musical. It was a chance to get better acquainted with her. It didn't matter to me that she was supposed to be engaged to some football player at Kenyon College. I knew at once that this was the girl for me. I wanted to marry her.

But Mildred Watkins didn't seem much impressed by my personality. In fact, she gave me the cold shoulder. But I kept trying to get a smile from her.

Finally I asked her for a date.

She looked at me for a long moment, and shook her head.

"Why not?" I asked.

She looked away and seemed quite hesitant.

"Tell me," I insisted.

Mildred sighed and measured her words. "I don't like the

way you sing. You can't see it but when you sing all the veins and cords stand out on your neck—terribly. I don't care whether you hit those high notes or not...but hit 'em softly. Please. Don't try to blow a door down. Remember, mister, you are singing in somebody's ear!"

She started to walk away.

"Your big problem," she said, snappishly, "is you sing too loud!"

6

Courting the Confederate "Flapper"

In the little Versailles hospital, Mildred, red-faced, puffy-eyed and in anguish, lay propped up in bed. I stood around, useless, awkward and uncomfortable, wishing I could do something. She was almost crying, it hurt so bad. A young surgeon had come down from Shelbyville for a clinic at Margaret Hall and he took out a lot of bad tonsils. Mildred was his last victim.

"I'll come back this evening," I said, leaning over her bed. Sudden inspiration had hit me. I hadn't given up on getting a date with her. We were together a good deal in the musical. And we sang a duet at a funeral. She was going to be my girl—and my wife! I was desperately in love now. She wasn't going to get away.

About an hour later the florist's little van pulled up at the hospital. The driver carried in a big basket of flowers and set them next to Mildred's bed. He went out and came back with another huge bouquet. Then he made a third trip. That was my big idea—to practically cover Mildred's sickroom with flowers. The ploy worked. It softened her up. She confessed to one of her friends that she thought I was "sweet." Even the surgeon was startled by all my flowers. He had been trying to sweet-talk Mildred himself.

When I visited her hospital room that evening, Mildred gave me a wan smile. "My doctor," she said hoarsely, "saw all my flowers with your cards and said, 'Looks like I'm out of it. You've got somebody who really loves you.'"

Of course she finally agreed to a date. I had a friend, a colored man, who owned a taxi. I gave him five dollars and he drove us to Lexington so we could have dinner and see a movie. He waited and drove us back to Versailles.

I started working on Mildred to break her engagement. I told her I heard from friends over at U.K. that her fiancé, Al Wade, had two left feet. She just gave me an enigmatic smile. She said Al's sister had invited her to come back up to Kenyon for a Christmas visit and Miss Gaither might take her up there.

That bothered me. But my brand new courtship was just one of the many balls I was trying to juggle at once. It was not enough to be starting a law practice and coaching football and teaching those two history classes, I had taken on other assignments.

For one thing, I was basketball coach for girls at the University of Kentucky. My team in 1924 was pretty good. Not long ago I looked at an old picture of those five girls, in their middy blouses and dark scarfs, with me standing in the back row, dark-haired, serious-meined, and with rather visibly large ears. The young lady in the middle, captain, and holding the basketball, was Sarah G. Blanding, who went on to become president of Vassar College.

My perhaps more important, and certainly more appealing, sideline was to take scouting assignments for Centre College. Since the Harvard game Uncle Charley had concluded I was some sort of a whiz at that. Often he would give me a hundred dollars to go study their opponents in some upcoming game.

Perhaps my most outstanding contribution to the "Praying Colonels" in 1924 was to scout the Georgia team that was coming to Danville on December 1 to meet Centre. It was a game for the Southern Championship. It turned into a hard-fought battle, and Centre won, 14 to 7. When they took the photo of the championship team, Uncle Charley stuck me right close to him in the back row. I have always been proud of being in that picture. But it saddened me to look at it hanging on the

wall of my bedroom the other day and realize that every one in
that photograph—except me—is gone.

The reason I welcomed the chance to scout for Centre was
that it put me on close terms with Uncle Charley. I had a secret
dream. My heart was set on succeeding Moran as the head football coach at Centre. Of course, not before he was ready to re-
tire, but you could tell he wouldn't be staying too many more
years. He gave me some broad hints that he thought I was
pretty well qualified for the job. I certainly thought so. And
Fate almost put it right in my hands—until I hit an unexpected
mean streak of the damndest kind of rotten luck.

By January 1925 I was spending a lot of time vigorously
courting Mildred. I gnashed my teeth when Miss Gaither took
her back to Kenyon College for that Christmas visit. I could
gladly have wrung the neck of Al Wade.

I was a typical silly suitor. Nearly every afternoon I'd leave
my law office and walk out Main Street to Elm and turn and
stroll past Margaret Hall. Just beyond the courthouse I'd start
whistling *our* love song, "Honest and Truly, I'm in Love with
You." Mildred thought I could whistle beautifully. The girls
would all hear me come whistling up the hill. I would see a lot
of them hanging out the dormitory windows, smiling and waving. Instead of embarrassing Mildred, my serenading seemed
to please her.

Rarely had I encountered a more confident and self-assured
young lady. She was outgoing, full of vim, good spirits and excellent moral judgment. They were just inventing the term
"flapper"—but she had already developed that kind of brisk
and lively personality as a teenager. Not wild and not bad in
that sense. She was a talented and brilliant student. But she
confessed that back in her small hometown—Keysville had a
population of only 500—she was a sort of tomboy hellion in
school.

"I was always in trouble at school," she confided, laughing,
in one of our intimate chats. "If the boys had itch powder, you
know, and the principal sent somebody to the room to check out
everybody to see who had that itch powder, they gave it to me
to get rid of. So I raced to the bathroom just as hard as I could
go."

She apparently didn't let convention hold her back.

"I guess I was about the first girl," she told me, "to ride bareback through town—you know, Happy, astride. When I was growing up proper ladies rode sidesaddle. I'd just jump on a horse, wearing jeans, or with an English saddle—I loved those flat English saddles. And I'd go sailing down Main Street lickety-split, legs a-flying."

Was that girl ever proud of her family and her Dixieland heritage! She was—even when I met her in the twenties—no less a Confederate than Robert E. Lee. She still thought damn Yankees was one word. Hatred for those Union troops had been planted deep inside her by her Virginia grandmother.

"General Lee surrendered at Appomattox," she recalled, turning somber, "which was just fifteen miles from our family home. Our farm was just run over by those Yankees time after time, and all our silver taken. That part of Virginia was a real battleground . . . it was captured, lost, and recaptured seventy-two times."

Her father, the railroad engineer, was the youngest in a family of ten, born in the last year of the War Between the States.

"He had grown sisters who had beautiful clothes, but . . ." She fell silent and a shadow came across her face. "Those Yankee soldiers came in looking for contraband, and they drew their sabers and just slashed through those dresses hanging in the closet—just like that!" Mildred ground her teeth. "If there had been a nigger in there hiding he would have been cut in two."

The source for most of this intelligence was her grandmother, who lived with them and died when Mildred was fourteen.

"You can see my background. My grandmother would tell me story after story. My grandfather was a big slave holder. And my grandmother had a slave for every child and one for every brood of turkeys." Mildred grinned at me. "If you wonder why in the world she had that, turkeys are the damndest fools that ever were—they'll drown if it starts to rain. They'll hold their mouths open, and just drown."

Mildred chuckled, recalling another incident. "I used to love to have my head scratched, and grandma told me, 'I'm telling you right now you were born too late, honey. 'Cause if you had come along when your father was coming along, you would have had a slave just to scratch your head.'"

I was an ardent suitor, but Mildred played hard to get. She kept me dangling. Worse, she had a date or two with Bob Massie. He was nice enough, but I didn't want him to beat my time. She kept me fidgety.

One evening she stuck her hand in front of my face. "Look," she said.

"What?... I don't get it."

She sighed and smiled. "No ring. I sent Al back his jewelry. I'm not going to marry him."

My heart leaped, my blood surged frightfully, and I felt like trying to handspring. Now there was no obstacle to my asking her to marry me. Except—well, there was one big drawback on my side.

I was still working myself to death but just scraping by financially. I didn't own a house, a car, any land—not even a horse and buggy. Actually I possessed little more than the clothes on my back. Every now and then I still had to borrow from my friendly banker. Mildred came from a substantial family. Al Wade, I had to confess to myself, was actually a high calibre fellow; he was getting an advanced degree in geology and was soon to leave for Antarctica with the Byrd expedition. I was afraid the object of my affections might develop misgivings about a husband whose prospects were barely out of the slim and none category.

We kept dating. I escorted her nearly everywhere. We appeared together in a few more plays and musicals. I toned down my singing style, and she liked that. We were in love but we only skirted talk of marriage. I wanted to be fair and honest with her. But it began to get close to the end of the school year and I knew that she would be going back home to Virginia. That was risky. I might lose her. She might meet a better man, and not come back.

So one Sunday afternoon while we were walking down by the clearing on the banks of the Kentucky River at Clifton, several miles from Versailles, my fear and my courage finally combined to bring me to direct action. I teetered dizzily, goaded by the desire that rankled the secret places of my spirit, a tremendous backwater of emotion about to burst through its walls in an inundating flood.

But I could barely utter, in a voice that cracked, a prosaic cliché. "I want you to marry me, honey."

Mildred abruptly stopped, and turned to me with a stricken look on her face. She reached out and put her hand on my arm, her eyes intently searching my face. She seemed to choke up a little, on the verge of tears.

"I've been dreading this," she said.

"What?" I stammered. "What?"

She looked down at the ground. "You may not want to marry me, Happy. I didn't tell you—I've been married before."

For a moment I was staggered. It was just the surprise. It had never crossed my mind that she had been seriously in love, much less married.

"But...but..." I reached out and drew her roughly into my arms. "I love you, sweetheart, oh! how I love you. That doesn't matter."

Mildred stiffened and her face turned even more grim. "That's just part of the story," she whispered. Something started trembling inside me, and I stared fearfully at her. Once more she spoke hesitantly, quietly. "I have a child, a little girl."

That was a shock—a big one, a really big one. Something that would have been the last thing in the world I expected. I caught my breath, and after a long moment hugged her tenderly in my arms.

"Oh, Happy," she said, "I'm already a mother!"

I squeezed her tighter. "Sweetheart, sweetheart...That's just a break for us—a head start on our family!"

Her story was not tragic. It was really not extraordinary. It was just commonplace and sad.

Small town girl. Lively and frisky. Modern and daring. Chafing under her dull confines. Wanting adventure and excitement. Looking for any excuse to get away from home. Along comes a young soldier from a nearby camp. He has just inherited ten thousand dollars. She thinks she has fallen in love with him. Unwittingly, it may have been the money, not the man. They marry. And they leave town. They blow the ten thousand. They quarrel. He is selfish and fickle. He begins chasing other women. She leaves him and returns to her parents. Then the discovery—she is pregnant. Her husband has abandoned her and gone off with a new girl. He would eventually marry and divorce three or four wives.

Poor Mildred knew her marriage was a total failure. She filed suit and was granted a divorce. Three months later her daughter was born. Then came the chance to go out to Ohio and start a new life as gym and drama teacher. She takes the job, leaving her little girl in her mother's care at Keysville.

Listening to my sweetheart's bleak recitation, I felt dismal and melancholy vibrations begin to throb along my own heart strings. Oh! how similar to my own mother's rebellion and escape from the desolate and uncultivable restraints of backwater existence.

I knew if I could somehow make it up to Mildred for her own sorrow and disappointment, I would perhaps somehow expiate the idiosyncratic guilt pangs my mother had welded to my heart. I felt vaguely responsible for some of her unhappiness. She could not have loved me very much, saying in effect she hated my face. Even so I was her flesh and blood, and at times I was very, very lonely for the sight of her. But in my heart I realized that I would never see her again.

"What is your little girl's name?"

"Marcella."

I turned on my most handsome smile. "When am I going to get to see my new daughter?"

Mildred sprang up, threw her arms around my neck, and kissed me vigorously.

Our wedding would be, of course, back in Keysville. Congratulatory letters came from her parents. Mildred said they knew all about me—and approved. My own father sent his good wishes—and a rather big surprise. He, too, was thinking of going to the altar. After being unattached for twenty-two years, Dad was courting a woman in Corydon. I knew her, a handsome lady of the very finest character. I hoped that he married again and found happiness.

An unexpected obstacle to our marriage sprang up. Miss Gaither was pleased by our betrothal, but found a flaw. She was a stickler in following the canons of the Episcopal Church.

It was doubtful, she asserted, that the church would recognize the validity of Mildred's divorce, which had been obtained on an abandonment statute.

"You must go back into court," she advised, "and get your divorce on grounds of adultery. The church will accept that."

As a lawyer I could certainly initiate that procedure, and did. My own disappointment was that the new litigation meant a delay of about six months. Finally we were able to set the date—Thursday, November 12, 1925.

I could put the interlude to good use. I had to find us a place to live, and collect some furniture. And think about increasing my income so I could support a wife and daughter. It surprised Mildred, but I was truly pleased that I would start off with a ready-made family. I buckled down. I figured it wouldn't be a bad idea to learn a little more law. In my spare time I hung around the courthouse, picking up pointers from the established lawyers, and making more friends.

Naturally I was getting a post-graduate education in the art of practicing law. It was exciting, and I was brash enough— and I guess clever enough—to hold my own with the old-timers, to earn their respect, and not develop any unnecessary enemies.

Perhaps the most imposing, or at least most bombastic, lawyer in town was old Colonel Bob Franklin. He used to stomp into Judge Ben Williams court and parade up and down in front of the bench, glowering at everyone in the chamber.

"Get these little feists out of here," he bellowed, waving his arms, "and let the big dog bark!" He was not jesting.

But he couldn't intimidate or bamboozle the other veteran attorneys. Some were too clever and subtle for him—especially Edward C. O'Rear, who had offices in Frankfort but spent about half his time in the Versailles courthouse. He was not predisposing, but was a rather studious fellow, medium height, with gray hair, long eyebrows, and a beard and mustache. He was a distinguished old-fashioned Kentuckian; his father was in the Civil War. On one occasion O'Rear was making an argument before Judge Williams when Colonel Franklin stood up and objected.

"Judge Williams," said the big dog, "that's not the law."

O'Rear turned and looked at Franklin for a moment. He was as smooth as lace. He didn't get flustered, didn't say a word to defend his statement. He let his quiet gaze wander around the courtroom and come to rest on Judge Talbott, who was Bob Franklin's partner, and was sitting beside him.

O'Rear took half a step toward Talbott, and addressed him.

"Judge Talbott, isn't that a correct expression of the law I just cited?"

Talbott sat up. "Yes sir, Judge O'Rear," he said, "that is a correct expression."

O'Rear turned back to the bench. "Judge Williams, I've always insisted 'twas well for some member of every law firm to know some law."

Cut old Colonel Bob down slick as a hog knife.

Over the years maybe I felt a little sympathy for Franklin on account of tragic consequences. He had taken in as a law partner his son-in-law Virgil Chapman, who turned out to be an astute politician. Chapman got himself elected United States Senator from Kentucky. Unfortunately, he developed a bad drinking problem. One dark night in Washington, D. C. he turned into a one-way street and was killed in a collision.

I developed a real fondness for Judge O'Rear. He once got bit by the political bug. He was nominated for Governor on the Republican ticket, and got pretty badly beat. But he was a rather clever fellow. He never attended law school, but he passed the bar easily and was very knowledgeable about the Kentucky statutes.

Once he was in a conference with ten or fifteen so-called influential lawyers. They were all telling where they came from and where they went to school. He knew his turn was coming. Finally someone asked, "Judge O'Rear, where did you go to school?"

The old gentleman didn't bat an eye. "The University of Camargo," he said. He was born in Camargo, up in Montgomery county.

He knew they didn't know where Camargo was. No one asked. My God, that was just a crossroads up there. He was quite a lawyer.

I think I was a good jury trial lawyer. I was always on defense; I never prosecuted anybody in my life. My professor said the dice are loaded for the defense. And that's right. You have more challenges, and more opportunities . . . .

But I never took a case for somebody if I knew they were
guilty. I'd ask 'em first. They had to tell their lawyer. If they
were guilty, and wanted to plead guilty, I'd argue the extenuating circumstances, if any existed. You have an obligation to the
court, but you don't have to tell the judge, and you don't have to
represent a guilty client either and try to thwart the will of the
law.

Funny thing about juries and will contests. Oftentimes a
jury will try to rewrite the will. They shouldn't. But usually it's
hard for a lawyer to keep them from doing it. I faced that challenge in a will I wrote for a fellow named Mountjoy. I remember
it well. Not much of an estate. Fighting over a pittance. One of
his sisters challenged. She was not given the part she thought
she ought to have been—because the other sister looked out for
him.

He preferred one over the other and that was natural. I
thought it was. It went to a jury trial. How did I win it? Well,
the jury just said this fellow was of sound mind and he made
the will and he knew what he was doing, and indeed he did.

Somebody may wonder if this was because of my skill in
seating the proper jury. That had something to do with it. I
knew them all. I knew everybody in the county nearly. About
ten or twelve thousand.

Tell you what happens in a case like that. You see, in order
to make a valid will you have to know the objects of your
bounty. You have to know the extent of your estate. And then,
according to the law, you make disposition of it *according to a
fixed intention of your own.*

You've got a right to give. You got a right to leave people
out. You got a right to put people in. You distribute what you've
got according to a fixed intention of your own. And the jury is
not supposed to interfere with that, but more times than not,
the jury will look at it and say this one is entitled to this and
this one is entitled to this . . . he left this fellow out and he ought
not to have done it. The jury thinks they can make a better will
than the fellow who made it. It's a rare occasion when they attack a will they don't break it.

My pleas to jury, they were listened to, and generally, I
think, were reasonably persuasive. The results were good. I enjoyed myself. Very much. Did I make the right choice in going
into law? I wouldn't second-guess myself about it. It seems sort

of natural. As to whether I had any special skills or abilities, I'm not sure there weren't plenty of people just as good or better. But I did have this power to have the jury listen to me. They listened to what I had to say, and believed it most of the time.

During the early years I never had a better friend than Field McLeod. I asked him to go to Virginia and stand up as my best man when I married Mildred. He accepted enthusiastically.

Practically anything I undertook won his instant approval—except card playing. Judge McLeod was a brilliant poker and bridge expert. One night, after several rounds of play in which I didn't do too well, he wagged his head solemnly.

"Happy," he observed. "I'm so glad you've got some other way of making a living than playing cards."

Our wedding in Keysville was beautiful. I was so happy and proud to slip the wedding band on Mildred's finger. It was studded with some little diamonds—actually they were tiny. I bought the ring in Louisville, and—violating my deep-seated credo—had to buy it on credit. I could not afford an engagement ring. But those little diamonds from the wedding band— we've hung on to every one of them and managed to incorporate them in some of the diamond rings I bought years later when we got better off.

At first sight I was absolutely taken with Marcella. I was truly happy to be getting a bride and a two-year-old daughter at one and the same time. I had already filed the petitions and legally adopted Marcella just as quickly as possible. Mrs. Watkins, my wife's mother, a fine Southern lady, brought our daughter out to Versailles in time for Christmas.

The best I could manage was a tiny upstairs apartment on the scruffy side of town. Fortunately I had a matronly client who had quite a bit of unused furniture in storage. She let me borrow a bed, chest of drawers, a breakfast table and a couple of chairs, perhaps a small sofa. I received a five hundred dollar fee and went to Louisville and made one important purchase, a beautiful gas stove with a gleaming oven, for $104. We didn't start off with much but we were in love and gloriously happy!

Mildred just couldn't wait to have another baby. Actually I guess she tried too hard

She felt something was wrong. She went to her doctor.

"Well, Mildred," he said, giving her a curious look, "you-all were married the middle of November and here it is barely the first week in January. There's no reason in the wide world why you shouldn't get pregnant. You just gotta give yourself time."

The physician tilted back his chair. "Lord have mercy! I get plenty of requests to help somebody stop. But this is the first one I've had like this."

By sometime in February Mildred was pregnant—and happy.

That girl really was a good wife. She wanted to help me get ahead. She thought she ought to entertain my lawyer friends, the ones who had been so good to me.

Now she was quite a cook. But we didn't have enough room to entertain. Not even enough furniture for everyone to sit down. She fixed that by going around to a couple of grocery stores and finding some empty apple boxes.

Seven or eight lawyers crowded into our little breakfast room for lunch, sitting on those upended apple boxes. Of course Judge McLeod had the seat of honor—Mildred's piano bench. She laughs now looking back on that enchanted and innocent event. We didn't even have enough china to set the table. Mildred served our guests on pie plates she had received in a shower back in Keysville. And in ridiculously ironic contrast laid out the sterling silver flatware that her parents had given as our wedding present. Everyone ate hearty and had a good time. I'd say that Mrs. Chandler's very first party was a great success.

On October 15, 1926, my wife was in the hospital in labor. She had a kindly old doctor and she wasn't worried. Except about one thing. She thought all football coaches wanted only sons, husky youngsters to carry the family name to glory on the gridiron.

While she threshed about on the hospital bed, I knew what was going through her mind. She held onto my hand, but she was a brave girl. I didn't know how to keep her from worrying about it. All I wanted was a safe delivery and a healthy baby.

Finally the old doctor straightened up with a squalling red infant in his hands.

"Lookie here," he said. "You've got a beautiful girl!"

Mildred let out a little gasp. She covered her face with trembling hands. But just for a moment.

"Don't you worry, sonny," she chirped, brightly. "I'll get you a boy!"

7

The Last-Gasp Pass
That Elected Me
Governor

From the stands college football may look heroic and inspired. But standing on the sidelines at Danville I mainly felt gut-wrenching apprehension. Don't let anybody ever tell you there isn't a lot of hair-trigger micro-second luck—sheer bloody luck—in snatching victory off any football gridiron. I was just about to rediscover that truism the hard way.

It was December 1927. Winter had come to Kentucky, covering us this afternoon with a dirty canopy that hinted sleet or snow, stabbing viciously at our thin padding with brisk icy wind gusts. I was now coaching freshman football at Centre College. This was the last game of the season. My frosh eleven was spirited. We'd had a good season, beating Sewanee, Maryville and Georgetown, all small colleges.

Now we were playing the freshman squad from Kentucky Wesleyan, and we were ahead, 6 to 0. There were twenty seconds to go. Our opponents had the ball, but they were back at midfield. What could they do? Everyone thought the game was over. Except me. I had my enchanted dream riding on the outcome. I paced up and down, just about holding my breath.

Everybody, I guess, knew what I dreamed of. That was to follow Uncle Charley Moran as head coach of Centre College's "Praying Colonels." He liked me, and I believe talked me up pretty good. After taking his little backwater school to national prominence in football, he left the coaching post in 1923. But he stayed in sports. His other love was umpiring in the National League, where he officiated from 1917 to 1939.

I didn't get his job. Centre picked Robert Meyers. Knowing he was plopping down in Uncle Charley's old squeaky chair was a blow to my ego. But I remembered the lesson I'd learned up in Lee County. If you get a duster, you don't fill the dry hole with tears, you just move your digger.

Meyers stayed just a couple of years. They had to find another Centre head coach. I perked up and figured maybe I had another shot at it. But they picked an All-American end from Wisconsin, Harold "Hod" Ofstie. During his second year with the "Praying Colonels," in 1927, Hod called me down to Danville and offered me a spot on his staff, coaching the freshmen. That looked good to me. I resigned my old position at Versailles High School and started shuttling back and forth to Danville.

There was nothing easy about wearing two or three hats. But I was used to it. I kept plugging away at my law practice, gaining ground all the time. Danville was close to sixty miles away, over some poor, crooked roads. But, like always, I managed.

Hod Ofstie turned out to be a real friend and admirer. He watched me in action and decided I had a lot of ability as a coach.

About the middle of the 1927 season, Hod called me into his little office.

"Sit down, Happy. I want to talk to you."

Ofstie got right to the point.

"I'm not going to stay after this season. I'd like to see you take my place. Give me the word, and I'll recommend you to Dr. Turk."

"Why . . . why . . ." Surprised and pleased, I found it hard to get the words out. "Oh, great, partner! Sure. Please do."

Hod did. It was up to Centre's president, Dr. Charles J. Turk, to hire the football coach.

So now in this last game of the season with long-time rival Kentucky Wesleyan I felt a lot of pressure on me, and on my chances of at long last making come true my enchanted dream.

Twenty seconds to go!

Kentucky Wesleyan had the ball right on the fifty yard line. Their quarterback, a boy named Dick Gallagher, faded back and looked for a receiver downfield. He finally spotted one, and scrambling out of the grasp of our running backs, let the ball fly.

I watched it sailing, sailing, sailing—a long ways down field. That ball flew like it was shot out of a cannon. One tall and skinny Wesleyan back went like a blue streak, watching the ball's arc, trying to get under it. The ball kept going, and going. It went across our line—but so did the enemy speedster. He snagged it for a clean touchdown.

They say they caught that ball behind my goal line. But I'd have sworn it went all the way across the river into Garrard county. What a throw!

Now we were tied 6 to 6. What a lousy piece of luck. But in about a minute it got even worse. Kentucky Wesleyan kicked the extra point as the game ended in my 7 to 6 defeat.

Some days later Dr. Turk called me to his office. I knew he had reached a decision. I felt it was between me and another fellow on Hod's staff, Frederick Potthoff.

"Will you come back next year," said Dr. Turk, "and help Mr. Potthoff? I've decided to give him the job."

I swallowed hard, and felt something inside me crumbling and my nerves shrieking. I had come so close—so damned close—to my enchanted dream—and missed again. It hurt like hell.

"No, sir," I said. "This is my year. I'm either going to be the head coach of Centre College, or I'm going home."

I went home.

Incidentally, the next year Potthoff won only two of ten games, and Dr. Turk bounced him.

What cost me the head coach's job was that last-gasp pass. At least that's the way it looks to that Kentucky Wesleyan quarterback Dick Gallagher. It's pretty true that I went almost straightway from the humiliation of my rejection at Centre into the equally enchanting arena of Kentucky politics—and did right well, if the records don't lie. And they don't. But politics didn't beckon overnight; it was a couple of years happening. That game really triggered it.

On my birthday I always get a letter from Dick Gallagher. Year after year it always starts out the same way:

> Dear Happy:
>   Remember me? I'm the fellow that threw that pass that made a governor out of you . . . .

Dick Gallagher did all right for himself, too. He became head of the Football Hall of Fame.

In those early years I still made frequent trips to the bank to borrow money. I had responsibility as husband and father of two little girls—and yet we just barely skinned by. We were not desperate, but God knows we were poor. Still, I'll tell you, partner, we lived a happy life. Mildred still loved to sing. She had the most beautiful soprano voice you ever heard. We were constantly called on to sing together. And we would always go if we could.

Being a friendly type, I was frequently consulted on small legal questions by friends who considered I was just doing them a favor. That was par for the course. Most of my fees were still little five and ten dollar things, anyhow. Every now and then a good fee would come along.

Judge O'Rear and I took a case together, suing for damages for a woman whose horse and buggy was struck by an automobile. The buggy was destroyed, and she was hurt. We won the trial and collected a fair sized amount that entitled us to a nice fee. It came time to settle up.

"Partner," said Judge O'Rear, "we did pretty good, didn't we?"

"Yes, sir," I answered. "I'm going to divide the fee now, and I'm going to give you two-thirds and I'm going to take one-third, because your superior knowledge and your time here is worth more than mine."

The old gentleman gave me a sharp look. I'll never forget it.

"We're partners, aren't we?"

"Yes, sir."

"Well," he said, "partners split fifty-fifty."

That was generous of him. But I felt that under the circumstances I was not entitled to half the fee. But he insisted. And Mildred was right glad to see that kind of money for a change.

Years later, when O'Rear was up in his eighties, I remembered that incident and got a chance to repay him.

The Southern Pacific Railway had pulled out of Woodford County and I was employed, along with my partner Judge Rouse, to sue the railroad for damages. The county also made a contract with Judge O'Rear to pay him $3,000. We won the case and got a fee of twelve or fifteen thousand dollars. Judge O'Rear went back and tried to get the county to give him more money, and they wouldn't. I just made a better deal than he did.

When we got ready to settle, I called him in.

"We're gonna lump these fees all together," I told him, "and split it three ways."

He looked at me just as funny. "Are you going to do that?"

"Yes sir," I said. "You remember what you said to me a long time ago when we had that suit with the woman who got hurt in the buggy? You said we were partners. You gave me half the money. There are three of us lawyers in this case—and we're still partners. I'm gonna give you a third of this one."

That old man was just as pleased as he could be. He lived to be ninety-six. And he was one of the best friends I had on earth.

For some reason I had a notion that I ought to keep some distance between my law office and my home. Mildred wanted to come down to the courthouse and see her husband in action. I told her not to do it. I thought that settled it. But nothing stops my wife when she gets a notion in her head.

She was bound and determined to come to the courtroom whether I approved or not. She worked out some conspiracy with the sheriff. They slipped her up the outside stairs on the back of the courthouse. I turned around from questioning a witness, getting ready to sit down. I looked and jumped. There she was perched in the second row and grinning with pleasure at my startled look. Well, that didn't seem to jinx my case. As I remember I won that one.

Along about then I got a three thousand dollar fee out of a damage case involving an explosion. There was a little house on High Street we had been thinking about. They wanted $3,050 for it. With that fee and the extra fifty, I bought our first house. It was a great feeling for both of us to have *our own house,* and better yet to have it free of any debt.

That I recall as one of my proudest moments. That was the first piece of ground I had ever owned. I used to walk out there on it and say, "Boy, this is mine!"

That house wasn't very big. There were two bedrooms and a bath upstairs. We were pretty crowded, especially when our family grew.

We bought our first car, too. It was a second-hand Dodge that cost $250. That played out, and I bought a Wyllis-Knight. I got rooked on that; the valve sleeves slipped in it. It was a bad car. I don't know why I bought it; somebody talked me into it. Then we got a Dodge coupe. You could get one for five or six hundred dollars. Paid cash every time. I never wanted to buy anything I couldn't pay for on the spot.

With Mildred it was a different story. I've always called her a financial disaster. She doesn't understand the first thing about banks. She couldn't balance a checkbook if her life depended on it. She throws all that financial stuff in my lap. She always has an overdraft, even to this day.

When I came home during the Depression and told her the bank was closed, she shouted, "Oh, goody! That means I won't have to pay my overdraft!"

But she has always been a worker. That little house on High Street had a garden plot, not a very large one, out in back. Every spring she would put in a garden, and get out there and hoe the weeds herself. That was something she picked up from her folks back in Keysville; they always planted vegetables. Mildred kept her hand hooked around a hoe handle until just a few years ago when the doctor advised her she couldn't do those chores any more.

She liked her High Street garden, but not the vacant lot next door. It was a convenient place for the country folks coming to town to tie up their buggies and wagons. There were times when the horses and mules kicked up a veritable cloud of dust and clatter, and left behind odious mounds of manure. But we lived through it. And those farm families—they were the kind of people we liked real well.

Mildred kept saying she was going to give me a son. But it didn't seem all that easy to have another child. We had named our newest baby after her mother, Mildred Watkins Chandler, and we called her "Mimi." When she was in diapers I called her "Little Stink"—but that was just a private nickname.

In Mimi's honor, I went to Louisville and bought her mother her first diamond solitaire. It was maybe a three-quarter carat. Mildred simply loved it. That was another of the things I had to buy on credit, and I didn't like that at all, but Mrs. Chandler certainly deserved it. Sadly, it later vanished, we think a case of sticky fingers by a housemaid.

The kick in the teeth from Dr. Turk at Centre was followed in 1928 by a little flurry of good luck for the Chandler family. Judge Ben Williams of Frankfort, who presided over Woodford County, really threw me a prize plum. I guess he had been impressed in the many times I appeared in his court, by my knowledge of the law, my ethics, and my willingness to do the hard work that is sometimes required of lawyers willingly and without complaint. And cheerfully. Frankly, I was still living up to my name "Happy."

Judge Williams called me into his chambers. "I propose to appoint you Master Commissioner. Is that agreeable?"

It was all I could do to restrain myself from jumping up and shouting. Agreeable! Good Lord, it was an appointment some lawyers might give their right arm for. The Master Commissioner is the conscience of the court. He makes deeds for the court, handles many, many duties. It was a very important thing at the time and very important to me because I was paid legal fees that I would not have made otherwise. Judge Williams knew that. He meant to do a big favor for the Chandlers, and he sure as hell did.

At first I was giving hardly five minutes' attention or thought to a political career. It was all I could do to stay up with my business and family obligations. The extra work as Master Commissioner cut down some on the time I had for keeping tabs on sports. I did, however, follow the World Series in 1928 when the New York Yankees swept the St. Louis Cardinals in four games.

But the whole country seemed to be in some kind of unusual and fresh ferment—in business as well as politics. We were crossing new frontiers. There seemed another surprise every day. I remember strides in aviation—Amelia Earhart, just thirty, the first woman to fly the Atlantic, and the Graf Zeppelin floating through the sky 6,000 miles from Germany to Lakehurst, New Jersey.

Prohibition was the law of the land, but it was openly flouted. New cars were being advertised heavily in newspapers and magazines—not just the Ford, but Plymouth, Chevrolet, and Packard, with powerful six and eight cylinder engines. Naturally Mildred and I were following music. There seemed to be a great outpouring of wonderful new tunes: "Digga Digga Do," "I Can't Give You Anything but Love, Baby," "Lover Come Back to Me," "Let's Fall in Love," "Love Me or Leave Me," "I'll Get By," "Carolina Moon," "She's Funny That Way," and Eddie Cantor's "Making Whoopee."

Thinking back on it, that was the year that began the careers of Rudy Vallee, Lawrence Welk and the Mills Brothers. Amos 'n Andy were breaking into radio, which was trying to climb out of the crystal-set stage. In Lexington, Mildred and I saw two movies that struck us forcefully, Janet Gaynor in "Street Angel" and Douglas Fairbanks in "The Gaucho."

But the event of 1928 that intrigued me about politics and whetted my appetite to see what I could achieve in this new kind of a game—for it seemed almost like a sports contest to me—was the thundering campaign for president between Herbert Hoover and New York's Catholic governor Al Smith.

I was staggered at times by the eruption of charges and counter-charges, the blatant demagoguery and religious partisanship. I remember Hoover's speech asserting the slogan of progress was changing from the full dinner pail to the full garage. He left himself wide open; that statement was twisted into the infamous misquote that he was calling for "A chicken in every pot, and two cars in every garage."

Even so, of course, Hoover ran away with the election. Smith lost five states in the "solid South" and got only forty-one percent of the popular vote to Hoover's fifty-eight percent. The Republican nominee hogged the electoral votes, getting something over four hundred.

But far from the national scene, people in my neck of the woods were talking about the upcoming race for state senate. Our district—the 22nd—was comprised of Scott, Woodford and Jessamine counties, which form a sort of crescent around Lexington. There was a quid pro quo and the three counties took turns—as is customary in Kentucky and other states—of sending a senator to the legislature. Woodford County's turn would come in 1929.

"Why don't you run, Happy?" I kept hearing that question from my friends around Versailles. In the beginning I thought it was just pleasant flattery. Then it became so persistent I began to weigh the possibilities and the problems.

I started thinking about making the race—of course, as a Democrat. The Democrats in Kentucky, a deep Southern state, outnumbered Republicans by three or four to one, maybe in some areas as much as ten to one. Eastern Kentucky, at least part of it in the mountains, was Republican territory, but the state usually went heavily Democratic. That certainly was true of the little 22nd State Senate district.

So, of course, I succumbed—"to the call of my people," as we used to say. I jumped in, filing as a candidate for the Democratic nomination in the summer primary election. Another fellow, who had served in the House of Representatives in Frankfort, also filed. I'd have the senate seat if I could whip him in the primary, where getting the Democratic nomination normally is tantamount to election in November.

Well, I encountered a startling surprise, something that I had not really expected. I liked politics; in fact, I *loved* it! I took to campaigning like a June bug to a duck's back. This was work I enjoyed, and an endeavor that I was good at! I was amazed by the way people responded to me.

I didn't have the slightest idea that when I was attending classes in Transylvania and the University of Kentucky Law school that I was also getting schooled in the art of successful campaigning for political office.

Dr. Edward Saxon, the Transylvania speech teacher, was a Shakespearean actor, and his mannerisms, tonal hijinks, and secrets of eye contact—all the magic of the Old Bard—sprang adroitly from my memory and helped me create a stage presence.

There's an old law professor to whom I am deeply indebted. He would get up and begin a lecture to my class in a quiet voice, almost a whisper. His students would strain to try to catch his words. He might quietly begin with something like: "Gentlemen, in the case of Jones versus Simpkins in the Third Appellate Court of the State of New York...." His voice, already low, would drop even more, and his poor students would concentrate even harder, strain all the harder to hear him.

The professor would pause—almost as though he had lost his concentration. Everyone would lean forward.

Suddenly the professor would open his throat and literally boom out the last part of his sentence. It was a trick, pure and simple. He wanted to get the attention of his audience, their ears tuned totally to what he was saying. And, believe me, he did!

I used that "pause" technique—to my very good advantage. I guess the pause, maybe, was one of the best aces I had up my sleeve as a campaigner. There were other important ones, such as quoting the Bible and reciting poetry. But the pause was very effective. One of my political associates, Joe Leary, the Frankfort lawyer who has been close to me practically since he was a little boy, once described this to a university researcher:

> When a speaker gets up to speak and hesitates, this immediately attracts attention and everybody in the audience thinks that he may have forgotten. Whether this is the reason or not, I do not know—but he [Chandler] is the master of the pause. Almost every speech begins haltingly, low key, and builds to a crescendo, and then cuts off.

That certainly was true, about cutting off. Practically the first thing I learned about the stump was to make it short. Talk thirty to forty minutes, and then stop! Don't wear out their ears. Then hop off the platform and get out and mingle with the folks, the voters.

I didn't make long speeches. There was a story I told about that. A fellow went to church and the preacher spoke twenty minutes and the fellow said, "I'm going to give him a hundred dollars." He spoke ten more, and the fellow said, "Fifty will do." The preacher went on another ten minutes. "Well, twenty-five will do." The preacher spoke ten minutes more and the fellow stole ten dollars from the collection plate.

I had a strong feeling that nobody is saved after twenty minutes. After twenty minutes, time is running. I made short speeches and I never told a dirty joke. My daddy would have whipped me.

I had personality, I didn't have to work at that. It came natural. Somebody wrote: "There are juices in him that appeal strongly to those who watch him and hear him."

Would you guess that I took advantage of my ability to sing? You're doggone right, partner. I was proud of my voice. I didn't need an orchestra for accompaniment, not even a piano. I could just haul off and sing. Audiences loved it.

In my first race, for the state senate, I sang every time I made a speech. They were the songs I loved, and knew the people loved, too: "There's a Gold Mine in the Sky," "Sonny Boy," "My Old Kentucky Home" and "Happy Days Are Here Again." That was a Broadway tune from a new show called "Chasing Rainbows." I grabbed it first in politics, on account of my nickname, but damned if F.D.R. didn't later capitalize on it in a much bigger way as the theme song for his 1936 presidential campaign.

For some reason I was smart enough to not agitate the audience by getting in front of the microphone and using a lot of arm gestures. I just took a solid stance and, as the *New York Times* once observed, relied "for emphasis on a rasping, high-pitched voice that is capable nevertheless of a wide range of dramatic shading." Another reporter commented that I "attempted no fine oratorical flourishes but stood with his hands in the side pockets of his coat, his gaze fixed straight on the audience, his feet planted squarely on the platform."

It may be immodest to say, but I wasn't a run of the mill old-time politician. I guess I was refreshing and natural, talking to people on their level—not down to them. And what I was saying, partner, was honest, and from the heart. Not any bombast. No bull crap. No flowery flights and no garbled promises.

If I said it, I'd do it. And if I couldn't do it, I wouldn't say it. People believed me. They liked that.

The reporters were surprised that I didn't use prepared speeches, you know, read 'em from a typewritten sheet. I think my most effective speeches were ones that I didn't prepare except for outlines. I rarely used notes. And if I did I never referred to them. Knowing so many people and remembering their names . . . who their daddies were . . . what they did for a living . . . maybe how they got rooked selling their last tobacco crop . . . when the heifer died—those little details stuck in my memory. Well, I wasn't going to let all that inside information go to waste.

So I started directly addressing specific individuals in the audience from the platform and getting them to talk back to me as I spoke. The *New York Times* said: "He peppers his speeches with homely asides to members of the audience: 'You know that's the truth, don't you Billy-Boy Morgan? You too, Johnny Jones—doggone you, I love every bone in your body, Johnny-Boy!'"

The reason I kept my speeches short was to give me more time to get out in the crowd and mix with people. *Time* magazine picked up on that, reporting that "[Chandler] calls first names and nicknames of people in the crowd, calls oldsters 'Dad and Mom,' old Negroes 'Uncle.'" That's true, and further, I talked to them about other days and places down the road and members of their families that I had known, and some of whom were gone. Not every politician could do that, of course. But I could, because I knew these people and who they were.

Joe Leary used to say that I could go to a town of five hundred to seven hundred people and draw a crowd of several thousand. Of course that was long before television, when there was very little radio—and people, the citizens, were hungry for honest talk. *Time* also whooped it up that I had a fervent handclasp, a quick embrace, a big smile and a cheery hello for everyone. What's wrong with that?

Newsweek reported that I kissed babies with the gusto of a man who really likes babies, and that when I asked a voter, "How's the wife?" it sounded like I really cared. I did—guilty on both counts.

In my race for the senate, my first time out, I brought Mrs. Chandler into my speeches. Just in name only. I was very, very proud of her, and I knew everyone was conscious of that. So I cracked jokes—making her the butt of them. Even she got a kick out of them. I didn't call her Mildred—I called her "Mama."

I would go up to the microphone with a phony pained expression and say: "Mama's complaining I never take her any place interesting. So tonight I'm going to take her someplace where she's never been—the kitchen!"

There was a reason "Mama" popped into my mind. Marcella was now five and Mimi was a pretty and precocious three. And, Lordy Mercy, Mama finally was again pregnant.

So here I was in the dog days of late summer 1929 awaiting two big blessed events in my life—the outcome of my first election campaign, and the arrival of our new child, which the doctor expected to come any hour.

Some people probably thought I was pretty calm about it all. I had contributed just about everything I could to both events. And I was certain everything—in both cases—would turn out just fine.

So what did I do? Well, I went down to George Stipp's barbershop in Versailles on election eve and got a haircut—I called it a *good luck* haircut.

That's what it turned out to be, partner. And I made it into a tradition. I never went through a political campaign without on the last night climbing into that same barber chair for a fresh trim. Of course, you got to understand that over these mighty long years I've outlasted quite a passel of different barbers.

8

On the Front Line in Politics

Mama has a country expression for my political style. The way I campaigned was as simple as a goose going barefoot. I guess she's right. Whatever philosophy has dominated my public life has pretty much been with me since boyhood. Somebody suggested that I have been driven by a sense of fair play and being honest and doing something that somebody else couldn't do.

"Have you ever rationalized it?" I was asked. "What is your philosophy of life and public service, what are you trying to do, what do you want to do, and where are you going?"

I want for the other fellow the same thing I want for myself. I want reasonable security. And what's that? Well, freedom from want as much as possible. So many people are not free from want. And I don't want to make the burden of the average fellow more difficult. I don't want people to impose on him so that you limit his opportunity to life, liberty, and the pursuit of happiness.

All my life I have been a strong advocate of self-sufficiency. I don't reward people for not working. I don't reward people for sitting around on their backsides and complaining. And I don't reward people who want to take care of 'em and pay their bills. I'm not much for that.

To be a politician you have to have a great deal of self-confidence. Some people call that vanity. I enjoyed being in the limelight. I enjoyed the respect.

When I started out I said all I wanted to do was win the respect of the respectable people of my commonwealth, and the love of some of them. Now everybody ain't going to love you. I learned that long ago. Some of them are going to hate you and some of them are going to wish you well. And some of them will rejoice if you fail. I have no idea of failing. It never occurred to me that I was going to fail.

Political reporters have always commented on my emotional nature and my ability to personalize. It was true that I never looked on a crowd as a mass of people, but as a group of individuals. I always smiled and laughed a lot. I used to walk in front of them, you know, just like you would talk to a jury. One of my campaign managers put his finger on one effective trait; he said I could read a crowd well and decide what they liked to hear and bear down on that.

I grew up with the folks. I thought I knew what they had in mind, and I did, too. What the average fellow had on his mind was the health and welfare and education of his children. And he didn't want anybody to make it more difficult. He had enough trouble, enough difficulty, enough hard times, you know.

And my job, I thought, was to see to it that the pursuit of happiness was not made more difficult on the average fellow. I fought the sales tax in Kentucky for the reason that it levied on things people must have in order to live, necessities. Some things they don't have to have and I don't mind putting taxes on things you don't have to have, but you must have bread and meat and shoes and shirts . . . Well, my God, to add a bump on the head for that! You know, I thought that won't do. And I was right. I never relented on that.

Political observers also thought that my being in sports or identified with sports helped. It gives you recognition that otherwise you wouldn't have. I started out as a country baseball player. Other teams occasionally borrowed me and gave me ten or fifteen dollars to play with them. I played pretty well and played around four or five counties down there in Western Kentucky. Everybody knew me down there.

Then I went to college and played on the college teams and

the college players knew me and the sports writers knew me. I was captain of all the teams at Transylvania and I was once mentioned for all-Kentucky guard on the basketball team.

I've been comfortable with people. I've not been high-hat or high-handed, not demanding anything more of them than they can give. They were not awestruck by me. They were not overwhelmed by anything I said or did. You understand I took 'em on even terms.

My skill at recalling names has helped immensely. I've been asked the secret of that. It's simple. You don't need any complicated memory code. I learned a long time ago. When you meet a fellow you'll look him in the eye and shake his hand and hear his name. Now the average fellow doesn't hear his name and really doesn't give a damn. If you never heard his name, you've got no way to call it again. And a lot of folks don't pay any attention. They just say hello and how do you do and think well I'm never going to see this peckerwood again.

I always tried to concentrate on the name. I have been able to astound fellows. I would say I saw you at a certain place at a certain time, and they'll say, "My God—unbelievable!" In 1918 I met a fellow in a churchyard at Ewing, Kentucky. I never laid eyes on him again until twenty-five or thirty years later. I called him by name and mentioned where we met. He like to have fell over.

Something similar happened on one of my many trips to New York. A cabbie picked me up at the railroad station. He muttered something about being from Brooklyn. I said, "Yes, I know you are." And I called him by name. He almost stopped his cab.

"You're a bum," he said, shaking his head, "like all the rest of 'em. But you're a good bum."

Will Grimsley, the Associated Press sports editor, never got over telling how I was introduced twice at a cocktail party to his assistant, Harold "Spike" Classen, once as "Spike" while standing and another time as Harold while sitting. "Every time after that," Classen told Grimsley, "Happy called me Spike if I was standing and Harold if I was sitting."

Mama tells everybody about the time I met a farmer down in Kentucky and picked up a discussion we were having about milk cows the last time we met—four or five years before.

Not everybody can do that. Senator Alben Barkley sure as hell couldn't. He didn't know anybody. They tell about the time he was down in Hazard campaigning for re-election. Barkley was walking down Main Street and passed some fellows sitting on a wall next to the courthouse.

"Hello," said Barkley to one farmer, "How are you? How's your father?"

"I'm sorry, Senator," the fellow responded, "Dad died last year."

"Well, I'm sorry to hear that," Senator Barkley said. He walked on down the street, and came up the other side.

Meantime, the fellow had got off the wall and crossed the street where he was standing in front of a store.

Barkley came down the line with his "hello, hello, hello." He greeted the farmer, and said "Hello. How's your father?"

"Senator, he's still dead."

Barkley was never one of my favorite people. His stump speeches were long and windy. He never really said anything. Two bushels of chaff and two kernels of wheat.

It was practically a tradition in Kentucky that a politician inaugurated his stump speech by uncorking a bottle and downing a big slug of red-eye. Usually, I think, Barkley gulped quite a few—even when he was a paid lecturer for the temperance people.

Anyhow, from my first days in politics the folks knew I didn't drink. In a whiskey state like Kentucky it was not necessarily a plus to be known as a teetotaller. That struck some people as incredulous.

One evening after a rigorous day of campaigning, I lay on my belly in the YMCA gym down in Harlan while my bodyguard-friend Joe Burman, who had learned the massage knack as boxer, baseball player and golfer, gave me a rubdown.

Not wanting to waste any time from the campaign, I had invited a delegation of local men into the gym to talk about Harlan County's problems.

One of the visitors watched curiously as Joe, massaging me, occasionally picked up a bottle and splashed the fluid on my back.

"What's that?" the man asked Joe.

"Why," said Joe, "rubbing alcohol."

"Oh, oh!" The fellow turned and gave his companions a triumphant look. "So that's how they get it into him!"

I was thirty-one when I won my first campaign—the state senate race. I had an opponent, a fellow from Woodford County who had been in the House of Representatives. I beat him badly, carrying Scott County by around 3,500 votes and Woodford by eleven or twelve hundred. I think my opponent carried only two precincts in the whole 22nd district.

Just eight days after my primary election victory—August 8, 1929—there was another cause for the Chandlers to celebrate. Mama went to the hospital and gave birth again. I remember old Doctor Stedman, a fine old country doctor, turning the infant over and saying, "Let's see what we got here. . . Lordy, lordy, we got us a fine boy. Just look at that little thing sticking out there."

We named him Albert Benjamin Chandler Junior—and I don't think any man could have had a finer son.

Of course I wasn't at all well known in the state capital when I took my seat in January 1930 in the State Senate. I wanted on the Rules Committee, because that's where you can help run the thing. It was unprecedented, but I made it. I immediately got into trouble with my first political friend, Johnson N. Camden. He had come out from West by God Virginia and was a banker and horseman in Versailles, with a beautiful estate just about a mile and a half out of town. Also he was a former United States Senator from Kentucky, serving around 1915 under appointment by Governor James B. McCreary.

Our rift came over appointment of the chief clerk for the State Senate. I had pledged my vote to Bill Perry. Senator Camden wanted me to support somebody else, but he hadn't told me.

Camden was considerably irritated. "How long do you expect to be in politics?" he asked me.

"Maybe I'm already in there longer than I'm supposed to be," I responded. "But I expect to keep my word."

He still looked sour. "Now you didn't tell me," I continued, "and I can't agree to do what you want to do if you don't tell me. Now you tell me and it's too late. I've already promised somebody else."

So I kept my word. I've always made a practice of that.

And it wasn't long before Senator Camden got over his grouch. He continued to be a staunch friend and political advisor.

Two big controversies erupted in my first Senate session, an attempt to repeal the parimutuel betting law and an effort to turn beautiful Cumberland Falls into a hydroelectric dam site. I was drawn into both, on the front lines. Those battles catapulted my name into statewide notice.

Some of the church leaders and other do-gooders wanted to do away with racetrack betting in Kentucky, chiefly on religious grounds. They contended it was gambling and the state was taking part in the gambling business, and indeed it was. Ironically, the anti-parimutuel forces were led by Dr. Charles J. Turk, the Centre College president who had turned me down for Charley Moran's old coaching job. Somehow Dr. Turk had it in the back of his mind that if he could outlaw racetrack betting it would be a springboard for his election as governor.

Oddly enough, the *Louisville Courier-Journal* and publisher Robert Worth Bingham were crazy about Dr. Turk and supported his fight on the parimutuels. At that time I was not yet a protégé of Bingham, so I was vigorously and openly fighting him and his newspaper. It was not so much that Bingham was against horse racing; he was opposed to the bipartisan combine that was then largely calling the political shots in Kentucky.

As chairman of the Senate committee on criminal law, I was right in the middle of the fight. I felt obligated to the horse people. Senator Camden, of course, was opposed to repeal. He thought if they abolished parimutuel betting it would put all the hoss people out of business.

We had to figure a slick way to handle the bill. My committee could have killed it, just thrown it out the window. That naturally would have triggered a violent cry of outrage. So we had a strategy meeting and decided that we'd report the bill with no expression of opinion. When that is done, the proponents are required to get twenty votes to read it into the calendar.

So a knock-down drag-out fight took place on the Senate floor. Senator Bartlett of Ohio County led the repeal forces with me defending the parimutuels. I made a two-point argument. The hoss industry was vital and without parimutuel betting it would be destroyed. That would throw hundreds of workers out of jobs. Secondly, Kentucky farmers would be hurt, deprived of the breeders' market for their hay and corn. My argument was effective. The anti-parimutuel forces couldn't muster the required twenty votes. They could only get ten. And that was the last time a frontal attack was made to bar parimutuels in Kentucky.

About Cumberland Falls I felt deeply. I can't be too harsh on the Governor, Flem Sampson. He wanted to get electric lights for his people out in the country. He had no way of knowing that in a couple of years the Insull people would be bankrupt.

But I led this fight, too.

"If we give them this," I told my Senate colleagues, "they'll have a dam site and we won't have a damn thing. And that will be a tragedy."

There is nothing else like Cumberland Falls, I told them, except one other place in the world. In North Africa they had one comparable to that. Cumberland Falls was a natural treasure, and I said we ought to keep it.

The battle was furious, and close. We won that by a vote of 20 to 18. It pleases me that Cumberland Falls is still intact, unspoiled—and there is a hydroelectric dam *downstream* and *below* the falls.

Except for these highly-publicized encounters in the Capitol my name would never have become so well-known in Kentucky so quickly.

I was being noticed by the political kingpins. Senator Camden stopped me at church one Sunday morning. We attended the same little Episcopal church in Versailles, where his family had a chapel bearing their name.

"Happy," said Senator Camden, "how would you like to be lieutenant governor?"

That question startled me a little bit. I had been in the Senate only half a term—two years. I could envision myself as the proud leader in politics. But I really hadn't thought of going the lieutenant governor route.

I beamed at Senator Camden. "Why, I'd like that fine!"

"Well," he snapped, "you won't be elected if you don't run."

"I'll run, Senator."

"I'll see if I can make arrangements for you then."

And he did.

Senator Camden was influential and he was very rich. He got hold of the various political leaders—from rival factions—and told them he wanted me to be lieutenant governor. They agreed to give me their support, and just like that I was elected.

All Camden wanted was to become chairman of the state racing commission. Of course I couldn't do anything about that unless I was governor. But eventually I was able to hand him that one job he so badly wanted.

9

Finding My Mother

"You're Mr. Chandler?" I turned around and looked at the young woman. I smiled and nodded affirmatively. "I think," she said, "I know your mother."

Her words stunned me. "Surely not!" I stammered. My mother? Not my mother—some mistake. For all I knew my mother was dead. I had never seen her since that terrible evening when I listened with tears to the clatter of the buggy wheels carrying her away, and presumably forever out of my life. In all the years we had heard from her but once—a belated sympathy card that came some weeks after Robert's tragic death.

Now I stood in a room full of people at a cocktail party in Jacksonville, Florida, hearing a young stranger say she knew my mother. Even this encounter was something out of the blue. It was merely happenstance that I was killing time at the cocktail party. Dinwiddie Lampton, a Louisville insurance executive, had taken me along with him. I was in Jacksonville acting as his attorney in a business deal.

This was 1931, late summer. I had last seen my mother in 1902. Almost thirty years had gone by. Sometimes I thought of her and wondered about her. But, truthfully, not often. I had a reason. She had abandoned us, and she made it clear she didn't love me, her first son. That was a bitter memory, so I didn't like to prod an old mystifying sore. All that did was to stir up fresh pain.

I stared at the woman; a strange flutter of emotions rippled my skin, difficult to sort out. Surprise hit me hard. I kept blinking at the woman, no doubt looking as dumb as an ox.

"She's talked about you," the woman explained. "That's how I know. She told me she's your mother."

This was a purely accidental meeting, but I could see what might have happened. My election as lieutenant governor had recently made the wires, and the Jacksonville papers probably carried a little item.

About two hours later there was a knock at my door in the George Washington Hotel.

I opened it, and she stood there, still a pretty woman, not yet fifty, with the deep blue eyes I remembered, long lashes, and long blonde hair.

"Albert," she said.

I knew her instantly. This was my mother. We stood for an awkward moment in the doorway before, trembling, I led her into the room. In a Hollywood movie this might have been a stunning scene of long-lost mother and son throwing their arms around each other, sobbing, and kissing. Our reunion didn't come even close to that. We were stiff, formal, very reserved and careful, but at least we were smiling at each other.

My mother seemed well—though I found out later she really wasn't—and well-dressed, about five feet six or seven inches tall, weighing maybe one hundred thirty or forty.

We sat and talked for quite a while, long enough for me to hear the story of her search for bright lights. She didn't really find them. She was married twice, first to a man named Fortune and then to a Mr. Chamberlain. They both died, leaving her with a second family, several children.

Oddly enough, my mother had also gotten into politics in Jacksonville. She had a patronage job for a while as warden at the jail.

Our visit was pleasant, and I asked her if she would like to come back with me to Kentucky and meet my family. That suggestion suited her. She rode back to Versailles with me in the Lampton automobile, and stayed for a week or two.

Our lives were now separate. It was clear from the outset

that she would be returning to Jacksonville. I was struck by her ruggedness and her courage. She was forthright, and independent. I can see where some of my own traits come from.

It was amusing when our son Ben came into the living room and saw her for the first time. We had always tried to teach our children that good manners pay great dividends. But little Ben was not yet three years old and hadn't yet got courtesy down pat.

Ben took one look at her and put his hands on his hips.

"Well, who are you?" he demanded.

"Sonny," my mother said, "I'm your grandmother on your father's side."

Ben wrinkled up his nose and gave her a look.

"Huh. You'll not be here very long until you find out you're on the wrong side!"

He was a little smart ass. But there was a great gulf between my mother and our lives that couldn't be fully bridged. Mama was not very enthusiastic about Callie; and my mother didn't make any real moves to establish filial ties. She never went back to Corydon, and of course never again met my father who had remarried and had his own family.

On my part I was not enthusiastic about her children, even though they were my half-brothers and half-sisters. The little contact we had over the years was unsatisfactory. I didn't think they measured up well. But that doesn't matter.

A story surfaced that my mother fell on hard times and begged me for money, threatening to go back to Jacksonville and complain to the press that her own son—at that time I was governor—was treating her shabbily unless I forked over fifteen hundred dollars. That is wholly false. She never did that. I did give her some money from time to time, out of respect and love for her.

She eventually died of cancer, too young, much too young. I went to Jacksonville and helped carry her to the grave.

As far as a normal mother and son relationship goes, we just never had it.

I came into politics in hard times. The nation was just starting Act I of a cruel scenario. The stock market had crashed in 1929. Now banks failed by the hundreds. Businesses by the thousands closed their doors. Millions were unemployed.

The poor in big cities queued up in breadlines. Franklin Delano Roosevelt came along. His fireside chats with their familiar "My friends . . ." raised hopes and things began stirring under his New Deal programs. But, as it turned out, the country had a long, long way to go to recovery.

The Depression obviously posed a problem for a neophyte just plunging into Kentucky politics. Conversely, it offered me an unusual opportunity. I knew that the commonwealth was being sloppily run, with great waste and inefficiency. We didn't live on a pay as you go basis, like my Daddy taught me. We had a huge disorderly debt. The whole bureaucracy was out of hand, needed shaking up and reorganizing.

That was the goal I set for myself: To get elected governor and make those needed changes. I was already thinking of how to do it.

My race for lieutenant governor was an eye-opener into just how vicious and treacherous was the Kentucky political battleground. I didn't intend to indicate that Senator Camden pushed me into office with a snap of his fingers. I had to fight for the nomination at the state Democratic convention. In doing so I got a close look at long-knife tactics of the feuding political overlords. I had to campaign, too, and win the race. But endorsement and support by the strongest of the divergent factions was necessary.

I saw that in running for lieutenant governor. Louisville's powerful Fourth Street Organization of regular Democrats seemed ready to go with my rival. Somebody talked to them, warned they were about to back a loser. Of course they didn't want that. At the last minute they threw me their support. That might have been the difference in the outcome of the election.

That time it worked in my favor. But it had another side, too. A friend and ally today, I discovered to my dismay, may tomorrow be a rival and an enemy. Loyalty in this political world is a scarce commodity.

But I found loyalty and true friendship, too, early in two men—Judge Bingham and Dan Talbott. I owe them a lot of credit for my success in politics.

My relationship with Judge Bingham was very close. He was already sixty, old enough to be my father. He looked on me almost like a son; he offered sage counsel, ideas, and money. Without funds, it is impossible to conduct a political campaign. Judge Bingham wrote out a check for ten thousand dollars when I got in the race for governor. Not a loan; an outright gift. That was the largest campaign contribution I ever got.

A large man, more than six feet tall and broad-chested, he was quiet and courtly, always immaculately dressed. He was proud and progressive, intelligent and articulate. Mainly his voice was heard through the columns of his *Louisville Courier-Journal,* the only state-wide newspaper.

The Judge was considered a reformer. Often he took a philosophical stance and was not fond of the nitty-gritty. His chief cohorts were an unlikely pair—J.C.W. Beckham, who as lieutenant governor had been catapulted into the governor's office at age thirty-one by the 1900 assassination of Governor William Goebel, and a raffish Irishman named Percy Haly. Sometimes known as "General," Haly was the son of a Frankfort saloon-keeper, and was a pragmatic political strategist.

Despite wealth and influence, Judge Bingham was no undisputed king-maker in Kentucky politics. Even in Louisville affairs, the Bingham-Beckham-Haly clique had to wrestle the Fourth Street Organization. It was controlled by "Colonel Mickey" Brennan and his protégé, "Miss Lennie" McLaughlin, who took over after his death in 1938. Much of the Fourth Street strength came from Irish, German and other immigrants, most of them Catholic. With hard-learned savvy, homage to the church, and plenty of patronage, "Colonel Mickey" and "Miss Lennie" could be counted on to deliver powerful blocs of votes.

The Fourth Street Organization made strange bedfellows with elitists Bingham and Beckham. Haly, of course, was right at home with them. On many occasions the judge and his men joined forces with the Fourth Street crowd. And in perhaps just as many elections they each backed rival candidates.

The most powerful clique at the state level was a group known as the "bipartisan combine" which sprang up after World War I, representing the racing, coal, textbook and whiskey interests, with the Jockey Club calling most shots. Principal leaders were Maurice Galvin, a Republican lawyer and horseman from Covington, along with Senator Camden from my hometown, another canny racing mogul, Polk Lafoon, and the Democratic wheelhorse who was political boss of Lexington, Billy Klair.

They were reckless and ruthless. If the Democrats insisted on nominating a candidate they didn't cotton to, they would unite behind the Republican—and then concentrate on trying to control his program in the legislature.

That is precisely what happened when "Flem Flam" Sampson was elected governor in 1927 over ex-Governor Beckham. Another clear example of the combine's will-of-the-wisp loyalties and pragmatism was its thumbs-down on Congressman Alben Barkley in his 1923 bid for governor. After beating him, the combine turned around and supported him in his successful 1926 race for the United States Senate. He might do less harm in Washington, they say the combine reasoned, than in Frankfort.

Barkley not only had been a leading advocate of prohibition, but likewise was opposed to parimutuels. So, on moral grounds, was Beckham. Likewise Bingham.

That Bingham would befriend me, and push my political career with his personal influence and publicity, is more than a little ironic. I first caught widespread public attention by booby-trapping parimutuel repeal in the legislature, which he wanted. But the fact is Bingham liked horse racing. He was proud that Louisville had Churchill Downs and its celebrated Kentucky Derby.

What he really opposed was the awesome power of the Jockey Club in Frankfort and its heavy-handed willingness to corrupt state officials. That I had defended the parimutuels didn't bother him; he talked to me plainly. "You're honest, straightforward. You've got principles," he said, with his hand on my shoulder. "You're the kind who can't be bought. You're the kind of public servant this commonwealth sorely needs."

As long as he lived, I had the political support of the *Courier-Journal.* Sadly, after his passing, the newspaper turned slanderously antagonistic. The Judge's son, Barry, seemed civil and friendly. But the malevolence seemed to generate from his wife Mary and an editor imported from Virginia, Mark Ethridge.

As near as I could tell Ethridge was venting his spleen on

me because of his long-running feud with Senator Harry F. Byrd, the grand old man of Virginia. I had first met and admired Senator Byrd when I went back to Keysville to marry Mama. The Byrds and the Watkins were friends of long-standing. Senator Byrd took a shine to me and was my friend throughout his lifetime. He was my ideal and my idol in politics; as near as I could I patterned my principles on his. Ethridge knew of this close friendship.

"I ran the bastard out of Virginia," Senator Byrd said. "Now you've got him."

Once Ethridge took charge, the *Courier-Journal* never let up on me.

It was baseball that first introduced me to Dan Talbott. I was pitching for the Lawrenceburg semi-pros. Dan, a druggist and baseball nut, was managing his hometown Bardstown team. I was impressed with him and he seemed to think I had spark and spunk. But we didn't get together politically until after I began making waves in the state legislature.

When I got Dan I also—fortunately and unfortunately— got his cantankerous father-in-law, "Old Man Ben" Johnson. Not many people were as high-tempered as Old Man Ben. He had been involved in a few shooting scrapes and always packed a revolver.

From 1907 to 1927 Old Man Ben served in Congress from the Bardstown district—ten consecutive terms. Dan managed those campaigns and handled district patronage. Together they built up quite a political organization. When Old Man Ben had enough of Washington and came home he got himself named state highway commissioner. Handling jobs and contracts, he became even more powerful—and irascible. You had to do it his way. If you didn't do it his way, he was going to take his bat and ball and go home. He wasn't going to play.

Dan, on the other hand, was easygoing and astute. He was a skillful manipulator and operator. He knew human nature and psychology. People respected him. His word was good. He made good friends and kept them. He kept Ben Johnson in Congress for twenty years.

But they fell out. A terrible quarrel. A family problem—a nasty one. I got caught in the middle of their break-up. I talked to Old Man Ben, reminding him that Dan was the father of nine of his grandchildren. "Why do you feel like you have to be mean to Dan?" I asked. Old Man Ben was a tough old rascal. He died bitter and wouldn't speak to either one of us at the end.

But I have a letter he once wrote me, in happier times, that I keep in my bank vault. It says something like... "When I think of you, I think you are the noblest fellow I've met in my whole life." I wouldn't part with a letter like that, even from Old Man Ben.

While my political prospects grew, so did our family. On October 17, 1933 our second son was born. We named him Dan—the namesake of both my Confederate grandfather and my political sidekick Dan Talbott. He arrived just five weeks before Mama reached thirty-four. I was already thirty-five. Ben was four, Mimi was just two days past her seventh birthday, and Marcella ten. Our family was now complete; Dan was our last child.

Hard times knocked at everybody's door. Roosevelt began his twelve years in the White House with his "My friends..." fireside chats. "The only thing we have to fear is fear itself...." Despite the Depression life seemed to go on. Mama managed to buy a staticky radio. We heard Walter Winchell begin his Sunday night broadcasts: "Good evening, Mr. and Mrs. America, and all the ships at sea...." And the first soap opera, "One Man's Family." Jack Benny began his radio show in 1933. It also was the end of prohibition—an event which would later give me a political opportunity. (I remember a sign somewhere down in Kentucky that said: "No Near Beer Sold Here— No Beer Sold Near Here.")

In spite of breadlines, bank failures, and staggering unemployment, Americans still were seeking fun. Sally Rand with her fans was the sensation of the Chicago World's Fair. Mae West's "Come up and see me sometime" from the movie *She Done Him Wrong* was mimicked across the land. Mama and I were crazy about some of the wonderful songs coming from Tin Pan Alley, Broadway and the Hollywood musicals: "You're Getting to Be a Habit with Me," "We're in the Money," "Did You Ever See a Dream Walking?" "Orchids in the Moonlight," "Everything I Have Is Yours," "Smoke Gets in Your Eyes," "Only a Paper Moon," "Love Is the Sweetest Thing," "Stormy Weather—Keeps Rainin' All the Time," "In a Shanty in Old

Shanty Town." It seems incredible today that all those good songs have been around for half a century!

The young song and dance man who was to become one of my best cronies, Bob Hope, was starting on Broadway in "Roberta," which ran for about a year. Bob is just as durable as some of those golden oldies. We both are.

Jack Sharkey was the heavyweight sensation, winning his title by kayoing Max Schmeling. And twenty-two-year-old "Dizzy" Dean began a dazzling career with the St. Louis Cardinals, and would lead the National League in strikeouts for three years. And 1933 was the year that Babe Ruth got back at his hecklers. In the third game of the World Series, with the score tied 4 to 4 and two strikes against him, Ruth points to the flagpole beside the centerfield scoreboard and hits the next pitch out of Wrigley Field. His New York Yankees take the series from Chicago 4 to 0.

Ironically, the Depression provided the setting for one of my greatest successes as a financier, or at least as a financial watchdog.

The crash was causing many insurance companies to fail. Here in Kentucky the InterSouthern Life Insurance Company appeared about to go down. I was appointed receiver, through the efforts of Dan Talbott. Dan told Mama that he knew there would be million dollar efforts to get somebody to sell out. "And, Mama," Dan said, "Happy is the only person I know of who would not be tempted by bribery."

He was right on that. People knew I was honest. Nobody— ever in my whole career—offered me a bribe. He would have gotten a broken nose!

I kept InterSouthern from going belly-up by totally reorganizing it from top to bottom. I converted it to a new company called Kentucky Home Life Insurance Company, with new officers and directors and a million or two of new capital.

Not a single policy holder lost a cent. What I did was written up in all the insurance industry magazines as a coup. I'm real proud of that.

10

Life's Most Glorious Moment

A stranger watching Ruby Laffoon lean on his cane and limp down the statehouse corridors might feel twinges of sympathy. The old man wasn't much to look at, either. In his early sixties, he was hulking, unprepossessing, balding, with unflattering big nose and ears. I didn't feel sorry for him. Governor Laffoon was an accident looking for a place to happen.

His own actions brought him ridicule. I was his lieutenant governor, watching firsthand as he turned his administration into a fiasco. The bipartisan combine and his cousin Polk Laffoon had put him in office. Even they couldn't abide his actions. They broke with him and helped turn his final year, 1935, into one of the most turbulent in Kentucky politics.

Governor Laffoon was weak. He never knew where he was. He handed out thousands of Kentucky Colonel commissions. Ruby Laffoon was a former circuit judge from Madisonville, but granted, so I have been told, more pardons than any governor in Kentucky history. A grand jury investigated allegations that convicts were buying their way out of the penitentiary. No indictments were returned. But somebody—maybe not Ruby Laffoon, but somebody—was getting money.

In his bumbling way Laffoon tried to reorganize the state government and help the schools. He proposed free textbooks

and pay raises for teachers. But he waited too late. His plans
were poorly-conceived and botched. He encountered all sorts of
trouble in the legislature and out.

About the only thing he succeeded in doing was to impose
a two percent sales tax. That was his biggest mistake of all.

In Kentucky the governor serves four years, and can't succeed himself. As his heir Laffoon picked his highway commissioner, Thomas Rhea, the powerful western Kentucky boss
from Russellville. They expected no trouble in getting him the
gubernatorial nomination from the machine-controlled 1935
state Democratic convention.

In their overconfidence, they slipped up.

The Depression had states clamoring for relief money. Kentucky squawked it wasn't getting enough. One hitch was that
Frankfort couldn't raise necessary matching funds. That trou-
bled Washington. Also, F.D.R. was concerned his power and
popularity could suffer in Kentucky over resentment of the
machine-controlled state Democratic convention. He sent a
message to Governor Laffoon to call a primary election. He was
aware that a *Courier-Journal* poll showed Kentuckians favored
that process.

Laffoon and Rhea didn't. They affronted the President,
who let them hear from the White House rather vigorously. So
on February 6 they took the train to Washington to explain
their situation to him.

Dan Talbott and I had been closely following these developments. The governor was playing into my hands, for any time
the governor is out of the state all powers of his office fall temporarily to the lieutenant governor. With that advantage, as
soon as their eastbound train crossed the border into West Virginia about midnight, I issued a proclamation summoning the
legislature into special session to enact a primary election law.

Governor Laffoon and Rhea rushed back from Washington. They weren't really afraid of me. They figured there was
nothing I could do that they couldn't undo. I was only lieutenant governor, no threat to them. In a convention I would not
have been. They would absolutely control it, and Tom Rhea
would have been nominated. And probably elected.

Laffoon promptly issued a new proclamation declaring my
call for a special session null and void. That of course raised a

big legal question. Dan Talbott and I took the matter before the Court of Appeals, and it voted 4 to 3 to sustain my special session call.

But Laffoon and Rhea pulled off a clever trick of their own. They persuaded the legislature to enact a law requiring not one but two primary elections—the second, or runoff, in case there were several candidates, none of whom received a majority.

This ploy was deliberately and carefully aimed at former Governor J.C.W. Beckham, whom Laffoon expected to oppose Tom Rhea for the Democratic nomination. Governor Beckham would have been a formidable contender. He had been governor two terms at the turn of the century, serving from 1900 through 1907. He won election to the United States Senate, serving from 1915 to 1921, but was whipped in his bid for re-election.

His Louisville ally, Judge Bingham, was anxious for Beckham to challenge Tom Rhea for the governorship. A Beckham triumph would restore their pride and compensate for "Flem Flam" Sampson's 1927 victory in the gubernatorial election over Beckham.

Laffoon and Rhea thought they would need two primaries, expecting Beckham to lead the first election with Rhea second and others in the field trailing. But in the runoff, with the contest down to two and with the powerful state Democratic wheelhorses marshalling their strength behind the highway commissioner, Rhea expected to win.

They hadn't known it, but I was for Governor Beckham. I was going to give him my support. They thought I made the call to serve myself. I didn't. I wanted to create a situation where Governor Beckham could run for governor and be elected again.

I wanted one primary and they wanted two. I used to say when they got two they *wanted* one and I *needed* two. They got two primaries in order to discourage Governor Beckham. They knew he was sixty-seven and wasn't rugged. They didn't think he would agree to run in a two-primary race.

It is my educated guess that there hasn't been a better governor in this last century than J.C.W. Beckham of Bardstown. He and Mrs. Beckham—she was Miss Fuqua from Hopkinsville—were both lovely, genteel people.

So I went to Governor Beckham and offered to support him against Tom Rhea.

"No," he said. "They've put on these two primaries and, Albert, I don't feel up to it."

They knew that. They were smart. So they didn't get Governor Beckham.

"You run," Governor Beckham said, "and I'll be for you."

That's how I got into the race for governor.

Of course I didn't have any money. Laffoon and Rhea knew that. They had the money. I didn't need very much. Judge Bingham, since Beckham had declined, was for me. He gave me $10,000, the largest campaign contribution I received. He also supported me in his newspaper.

Dan Talbott entered the race for state auditor and we started campaigning together. We went all over the state. Nobody ever campaigned Kentucky like I did. I campaigned it from Amazing Grace to a Floating Opportunity. I went to see everybody.

I hit the road in early Spring. The first primary was coming in late July, and I had a lot of ground to cover. I went straight to the people.

Fortunately everything seemed to click, everything fell in place. I was a child of the hour. People came out to hear me. They listened to me. They liked my smile, my handshake—and what I came to say. I sang songs, and that went over big. I had a straightforward message. I was against the sales tax. It was an unfair burden on the little people. They shouldn't be taxed on the necessities—bread, meat, shoes and shirts.

I promised to work to repeal Ruby Laffoon's two percent sales tax. Just elect me governor and I'd do it!

People recognized me, knew my voice and what I stood for. But I wanted something distinctive as a trademark for my campaign. I kept toying with several ideas—and finally hit on one that was an astounding success.

I began wearing white suits.

I had to be careful. Even then a linen suit would stay clean for only about two days on the campaign trail. I tried seersucker suits a time or two. They weren't all that distinctive. So I bought several white linen suits and stuck to them.

About once a week Dan and I would swoop into Versailles

to pick up fresh laundry. And then it was back out on the road again. Mama kept the home fires burning and watched after the children.

Usually I made a short campaign talk from the back of a truck or a platform, rarely more than thirty minutes. Then I would leap down and work the crowd. That meant shaking hands and talking to people, making friends. Everybody seemed to want to shake hands and have a few words with the candidate.

Crisscrossing the state, going into all one hundred twenty counties, I was staggered to discover that often in a hamlet or small town of five hundred to a thousand population a crowd of as many as five thousand would come out. Of course, many were coming from surrounding counties.

The greatest day I had in any campaign came at Bowling Green—in fact it was one of the greatest days I've had on earth. I spoke to twenty-five thousand and shook hands with most of them after it was over.

It was a hot day, a terribly hot day.

When it was over I was standing in water. My white linen suit was soaked with sweat, my shirt, my underwear, even my socks, and water was standing in my shoes. Lord almighty, I got no business being here after that. I could have died. I wouldn't do that again.

My right hand—my shaking hand—was red and swollen twice its normal size. There was only one thing to do—soak it in ice water. 'Cause next day I had to go out and shake some more hands.

Just as I figured, Ruby Laffoon outsmarted himself by insisting on a runoff primary. Tom Rhea did lead, outpolling me 203,010 to 189,575. But that wasn't a clear majority, since two minor candidates drew a total of 53,911 votes.

One of them was former New York police commissioner Fred Wallis, who had moved down to Bourbon County. Encountering me late in the campaign, he grabbed my arm. "You killed me!" he croaked.

By God, he couldn't talk—only whispered. I never lost my voice or got hoarse. I can't explain that, but my voice always held up. No trouble.

In the runoff, Wallis threw his support to me and so did the other loser, Elam Huddleston. I won that second primary, beating Rhea for the Democratic nomination, 260,573 to 243,124.

Sad to say, both Ruby Laffoon and Tom Rhea were bitter and mean about their whipping.

The Republicans nominated King Swope of Lexington. He was not much of a candidate. Rhea bolted the party and came out openly for Swope. But everybody could see it was just sour grapes. That didn't hurt me.

In the November general election I beat Swope everywhere but on the bottom of his feet, and I'd have done it there, too, if he'd laid down. The vote was: Chandler 556,573, Swope 461,104.

Strangely, at odd moments during that summer campaign in the back of my mind would pop up that prophecy under my picture in the 1917 Corydon high school yearbook, one that had seemed so silly and farfetched at the time:

> Work hard and study while you wait,
> And you'll be governor of your state.

Well, it wasn't silly after all; by some miracle it had come true.

And it became official on Tuesday, December 10, 1935, when I swore in the first time as governor of the commonwealth.

With Mama at my side, I climbed into a victoria for the parade up the streets of Frankfort to the reviewing stand on the steps of the capitol. They say I was the first governor for many years to go by horse-drawn buggy to his inauguration. It was a beautiful sunny day.

I wore a dark business suit with a light gray fedora. Four years earlier when I was sworn in as lieutenant governor with Ruby Laffoon we wore formal cutaways and silk toppers. Considering these hard times, I would have looked ridiculous now in a swallow-tailed coat. I passed by the formal get-up.

It was a great day for my father, who stood with me on the reviewing stand, along with Mama and the children. My old friends were there, too, among them Judge McLeod.

When Judge Clay finished administering the oath to me a great cheer went up from the throng—the largest that had ever witnessed the inauguration of a Kentucky governor.

Oh, but that was a lovely cheer! It was a sound that you

could both hear and feel. And actually almost see! I reached back and seized my father's arm. I pulled him up to the rail beside me. I wanted him to share this high moment. He saw what I saw and felt—that same extraordinary, once in a lifetime exultation. It showed in the surprise on his face in the news photos printed later.

That booming sound from the crowd of twenty-five thousand or so, that lovely, lovely cheer struck the innermost reaches of my heart and soul. I felt unashamed tears welling up in my eyes.

This was the happiest single moment of my entire life! Nothing before or since ever equaled it.

We followed tradition. There was the inaugural ball, and other festivities. But I had little time for savoring the huzzahs. I had made promises. Now I had to get busy and deliver. And I intended to do that with alacrity.

President Roosevelt's recovery programs were beginning to give the country help. At least a glimmer of hope. But the Depression still had a mean grip on Kentucky. State government finances were in deplorable shape. The bureaucracy was fat, unwieldy, inefficient.

Our school teachers were being paid in script. They had to cash it at a discount. That meant their already low salaries were reduced another ten or fifteen percent.

The state had a disorderly debt of thirty million dollars. These vouchers were drawing five percent interest—an outrageous amount for the times. That was a terrible drain on the state revenue. The state was actually broke.

I had promised to do something about this. I remembered the lesson my Daddy had taught me as a boy. You can't spend more than you take in, or you'll go broke. I had talked about that in the campaign, promising that state government would have to get leaner, and better. Above all, the state must not spend more money than it took in. At the same time, it was unfair to saddle the plain folks with a sales tax on their necessities of life. Other sources of revenue would have to be found.

Fortunately I had youthful energy, being at thirty-seven the youngest governor in Kentucky history, aside from J.C.W. Beckham. I'd had six years to closely study state government from the inside. I had some fresh new ideas. I had a lot to do.

But I was comfortable in my confidence that I could improve conditions.

Dan Talbott had been elected state auditor and we had been working out strategy. And I moved fast.

I immediately started clearing out deadwood. By executive order I requested the resignation of all department heads, members of boards and commissions, and all assistants with executive authority that are appointed by the governor. That cut the state payroll by one thousand. And that was just the beginning. We ordered drastic reductions in the highway department. By the end of ten days approximately nine thousand more state employees had been let go.

You can imagine the hue and cry that rose from the stunned bureaucrats in Frankfort. The *Courier-Journal* reported that "these dismissals were followed by appeals, tears, and advice that it shouldn't be done, especially at Christmas time." The newspaper quoted me as replying, "I have read what thou dost, do quickly, and I decided to act." If it were well when it were done, it were well it were done quickly. I've used that quote all my life. I can't take credit for it. I think it's Shakespeare's.

I sympathized with the people who were let go. I told them frankly, "You don't want to be fired, but you don't want to work for nothing. I haven't any money. I can't afford to keep you working. It's that simple."

At that time, while Judge Bingham was alive, the *Courier-Journal* was supporting me, looking on these dismissals as "proof of sincerity" of my campaign pledges "to effect a sorely needed reorganization and reform of state government."

One of my best ideas was to invite university professors to come to Frankfort and help run the government. I thought we had smart fellows over there. We might as well make use of them. I asked the president of the university to give them leaves of absence. They would stay on the university payroll, remain in sort of status quo, and return to the campus when they finished their public service.

Just as noteworthy and effective was my calling on Governor Beckham to head up my task force on reorganization of the government. Governor and Mrs. Beckham moved into the Mansion with us. He set to work with his intimate knowledge of government and put his keen mind to devising ways of streamlining operations. From his work quickly emerged a reorganization act I could submit to the legislature, reducing the state government from twenty-six to only eleven departments.

That was one of the most efficient moves ever made in Frankfort.

Governor Beckham worked closely with Jim Martin, one of my main recruits from the University of Kentucky. It was a lucky day when I found him—Dr. James W. Martin, professor of economics and director of business research. I appointed him commissioner of revenue. He had an uncanny ability to forecast the state's income. Whatever he estimated the state revenue would be, it was that almost to the penny.

Later on I named him commissioner of highways. Some fellow said to me, why do you keep naming this fellow Martin? I said, if I had ten or twelve like him I wouldn't have to move anybody. But I haven't got but one so I put him where I need him most.

Another genius from the university was Dr. Frank D. Peterson. "Pete" helped me refinance the state debt—from top to bottom. The five percent warrants had not been authorized, it was just money the state owed—and I didn't agree to that.

Some of the bond holders were startled when we notified them we were calling the five percent warrants. A few said they wouldn't go along. "That's too bad," I said. "I'm going to pay you!" They didn't believe me; after all, the state was broke and in debt.

What they didn't know was that Frank Peterson had made arrangements with a group of Louisville bankers and brokers to refinance the entire state debt at one percent!

That was, of course, a tremendous savings. Our interest payments on the state debt dropped from a million and a half dollars a year to merely $300,000.

So far, so good. But there was more money trouble ahead. Despite making hard cutbacks, I still needed a budget of about twenty-four million dollars. With the two percent sales tax repealed, as promised, we didn't have that much to spend. The estimated revenue for the next fiscal year was short by an astonishing amount—eleven and a half million dollars!

"Where," I asked Jim Martin, "can we pick up that kind of revenue? We must have it."

I felt a little panicky. But Jim Martin didn't seem at all

flustered. He picked up his pen and jotted down some figures. "I've been thinking of a few things," he said.

"We can't go back on our word," I warned.

"No," he said. "Listen to this approach..."

His program to enhance revenue was ideal—and it certainly didn't fall on the backs of the ordinary citizens. His first idea was a whiskey tax—which translates into a "luxury" tax. Now that prohibition had ended, the distillers were anxious to reopen their Kentucky operations. Jim Martin had devised an excise tax system that would bring in seven million dollars a year. I met with the distillers, and they were agreeable.

Jim had also come up with a graduated tax on personal and corporate incomes and an inheritance tax. There was no trouble getting the legislature to approve the whiskey tax; it was paid by consumers who presumably could afford the luxury of booze.

Martin came up with another "luxury" tax—on cigarettes. That's where we ran into trouble—serious trouble.

When the tax was proposed, growers and manufacturers alike were up in arms. Nearly every rural family in some way was counting on tobacco income, and workers in the Louisville factories and in the warehouses feared their jobs would be in peril if taxes cut into tobacco sales.

The day the measure came up for a vote in the House, four thousand demonstrators filled the galleries and surrounded the Capitol in protest. Frightened, the House rejected the bill.

That was a tax we had to have, so I went on the offensive. I knew who was behind the opposition—and I said so publicly. The warehousemen and the four large tobacco concerns. I called them "selfish minority interests...which can pay their presidents million dollar bonuses, but buy tobacco from Kentucky farmers for as little as they can."

In a radio address before a joint session of the legislature, I warned the legislators against "allowing workers from two Louisville tobacco factories to come up here and stampede you." And that wasn't all.

When the measure came up again for a vote in the House, I pulled up a chair and sat beside the Speaker. That was most unusual, but this was an important moment in my tenure. I think that is about the only time I did that. Other governors also did. Governor Earle Clements went down there and pulled bills out of the hopper. I don't believe the legislature will let governors do that now.

But I sat there beside the Speaker all through the vote and with me sitting there they weren't gonna vote against me. You see, I was keeping tabs. So that scared 'em into line. It was a bit of polite coercion.

The upshot was that in my first fiscal year, the state government operated on about two million dollars less than Governor Laffoon's last year—and didn't take on any new debt.

That was a record no one could criticize.

In this period I consulted frequently with Judge Bingham. He invited Mama and me to dine at his home in Louisville. It was on that occasion he gave me the pistol—that .38 Detective Special—that I still keep in the drawer of my bedside table. If I ever felt like using it on anyone, it would have been Mark Ethridge, who came along as the *Courier-Journal* editor after Bingham's death. But I just got rid of him by outliving him.

The deplorable condition of Kentucky's roads greatly agitated Judge Bingham. There were few paved highways, and the rural roads were dusty in summer and quagmires in winter.

"What you ought to do," Judge Bingham said, "is hire the best highway engineer in the country."

"Why, Judge, I can't do that!" I reminded him that the state constitution placed a "cap" of $5,000 a year on the salary of any state official except the governor, who received $6,500. "I can't hire a really top engineer for five thousand."

"Find the man. Pay him what he asks. I'll make up the difference. It will be just between you and me."

Judge Bingham's proposal flustered me for a moment. He didn't have any personal ax to grind. He just wanted better roads for the people of Kentucky. He was wealthy enough to donate a "bonus."

"It wouldn't be smart," I responded, "to make a secret out of this arrangement. Better that I just announce what you are willing to do. I'll give it a try."

I made inquiries. The best highway engineer in the country was Tom Cutler, then roads commissioner in Missouri. He turned out to be a graduate of the University of Kentucky. My cousin Dean Terrell said he was one of the best students ever to come out of the engineering school.

I sent for Tom Cutler. He said he would come talk, but

wasn't interested in becoming our highway engineer. I told him the job would pay twelve thousand dollars a year. Then he was interested.

Judge Bingham donated the extra $7,000 a year through my term. And his family, after the judge's death, kept up the arrangement for a number of years.

Tom Cutler was the right man. He gave Kentucky a good system of highways. He was willing to try out new methods and ideas. One of his schemes didn't work out too good. Tom got the idea of putting curbs on one stretch of highway. Unfortunately this kept water from running off in low spots. These stretches were slick and dangerous when it rained, and became icy in the winter. Tom recognized the mistake; the curbs were promptly knocked down. But that was just a minor incident. He deserves top praise for the hundreds of miles of excellent highways he built in Kentucky.

11

He-Coon of the Commonwealth

Some outsider visited the Mansion and then came over to the Capitol and quipped: "Those Chandlers must not be bad people—their yard was full of dogs and niggers, chickens and children, you know. They are just old-fashioned country folks."

That wasn't a bad casual-glance summary. We didn't see anything wrong with being old-fashioned, or country. Never did we want the Governor's Mansion to be exclusive or pretentious. It was a beautiful place and we wanted it kept up, neatly kept up. Everybody was welcome. And they knew it. I don't know how many people just showed up. A lot of them we fed. They could see us.

That's a true remark about dogs. I love 'em and always had 'em, if I could. Our four children, of course, were living at the Mansion with us. I can't verify that we had chickens in the yard. But we certainly had the customary retinue of black servants. A whole flock of them—about thirteen.

That staff is one of the traditional perks of earning the right to reside in the Mansion. Convicts, mainly black, were always selected from the penitentiary at Frankfort to be assigned to the governor's household staff, as cooks, maids, yardmen, etc.

Over the years penitentiary officials learned a few things about trusties. They never sent over anyone who had been con-

victed of larceny; they just didn't trust thieves to not steal
again. All prisoners assigned to the Mansion were murderers.
They are considered more reliable. And I have learned that is a
general feeling among penal experts all over the country.

We had a dormitory on the Mansion grounds for our staff
of convicts.

Our son Ben was just then six. He was placed in the care of
a bright, slender young convict named Johnny Russell. They
became great friends. Johnny took Ben to church, and bathed
him, and fed him. He walked him to school and waited to bring
him home.

Johnny wanted Ben to be able to take care of himself on the
schoolyard, so he showed him some of the fine points of boxing.
"Governor," Johnny told me, "I've taught little Ben the one-
two. Now he can whip those fellows who pick on him."

When I took Ben back east with me in 1938 to see the light
heavyweight championship fight from ringside, he surprised
me. Thinking of his friendship with Johnny Russell, Ben began
loudly rooting for the black man, Henry Armstrong. My son
was a good picker at that; Armstrong won.

Dan was only two when we moved into the Mansion. He
was looked after by a black nurse named Nancy we'd brought
with us from Versailles. The little fellow trailed around all day,
hanging onto her apron strings. Then after supper, he'd say,
"Come on, Nancy, let's go home. This is not our house." That's
how young he was.

Nancy watched out like a hawk for Dan. When I made a
trip I'd bring back presents for the children. I never brought
anything for Dan because he was too little.

Nancy would come in and watch while I opened my bags.
"Governor," she would say, "what'd you bring Dan?"

"Oh, Nancy, Dan doesn't know what's going on."

"Oh, yes he do!"

Poor Nancy would get her lip down, and stay huffy for the
rest of the day.

I can look back with pride on my personal and political be-
havior on what is usually identified as the race question. Of
course I was raised in Confederate country. Some people find
great irony in what I did in the Jackie Robinson case. I don't.

We didn't have trouble with black people when I was a boy. My best friend was Bill Blunder, the black boy I spent the summer with loading grain cars. Aunt Nora McClure helped look out for me when I was a little baby. By God, she loved me better than anybody. She was black.

When she went "up north" to Indiana for a while with her husband to work for a white family, they asked her to sit down and eat dinner with them. She said, Oh, she couldn't do that. And the woman up there said, "Your people down there won't let you sit with them at the table."

Aunt Nora said, "Deed dey don't. My folks is quality folks!"

In both Corydon and Versailles, everybody was generally considered to be Confederates. The colored people never made any trouble. They were generally accepted in their place and not out of their place. These towns were completely segregated. The Negroes couldn't go to restaurants. They had their own schools and churches.

In looking back, I feel I was better to the blacks of Kentucky than almost anybody. I followed the law. I said this is the law, I don't make the law, but we are gonna obey it. It's as simple as that and that shaped my opinion and my decision and everything. The governor of all the people has got to keep the law. Understand—he can't justify not keeping the law.

I never had any real trouble with the black question. I was always on their side on public questions. They wanted recognition and opportunity. I always defended their rights to have it.

Just a few years ago a woman senator from down at Louisville, a black, made a silly statement that I had never done anything for the black people, which is utterly stupid.

I wrote her a letter. I burned her up. I never heard from her. I told her, you are refreshingly ignorant. Lord have mercy— only an ignorant person would make that statement because the record clearly shows that in every undertaking where rights and privileges have been accorded the black people, I have defended them.

Even *my* song, "My Old Kentucky Home," has fallen prey to racial sensitivity. Stephen Foster's lovely and sentimental lyrics had the phrase "in the summer, the darkies are gay."

That produced a lot of resentment among the blacks. Now we sing, " 'Tis the summer, the *people* are gay."

Over at Bardstown every summer they put on "The Stephen Foster Story" in the playhouse that I built for them and named for my old friend Dan Talbott. The girl who sings "My Old Kentucky Home" over there still sticks to the original lyrics.

Nobody in Versailles would ever believe any racial prejudice exists in my home. During my second term as governor I was impressed by one of the convicts on the Mansion staff. His name was Porter McKinney, and he seemed very trustworthy and deserving of a second chance. He was a young man. I asked him why he went to prison.

"Governor," he said, "I killed a couple of niggers. If I hadn't, they'd of killed me."

Porter became one of my most trusted friends. He's the best you ever saw. When I left office, I had him paroled, and brought him home with me. Most of those trusties become eligible if they serve well, conduct themselves properly.

And I paroled his wife, Ella V., too. She had killed somebody, just like he did, in self defense. I got Porter a job with the city government and put him on my payroll to take care of things around our place. He can do anything. I used to ask him, Can you do so and so? He'd reply: "Can, Governor, if you say so." No question. He takes care of the whole place here. Don't have to tell him. If it has to be done, he does it. He keeps my fireplace going, keeps the wood in the box, keeps the coal in the bin. He just comes in and goes on about his business. No trouble.

Porter met Ella V. at the Mansion. She was some years younger than he, but she was a great big woman, weighed somewhere around 350 or 380 pounds. Oh, could she make a Sally McGundy pie! We brought her back to Versailles with us, too, and she cooked for Mama. She did everything. She and Porter had their own place in town. They had three children, two boys and a girl, who turned out well.

Porter is self-sufficient. He spent a lot of money on Ella V., who was sick for a long time and finally died a few years ago. Porter is still with me. I don't know how I could get by without him.

Of course, I never was a stranger to work. But in my first

term as governor I really put in the hours. I was accessible—to the people. My office was open to everyone. And I tried to get over there every morning by eight o'clock. I knew by their very nature, Kentuckians wanted a governor they could come talk to.

The average person from the country is a strong individual, he's proud, he's got natural integrity and native intellect, but not necessarily school intellect. It is interesting to realize that prior to World War I, ninety-eight percent of the people of Kentucky were born here. Weren't many outsiders. World War I changed that. Up to then most Kentuckians were home folks and had never been away from home.

Everybody knew I went to the office. Kentucky governors don't make a practice of going to the office anymore, and when they do they don't see anybody. They got people that protect them, from the people. I was available.

I would say to my staff, If this fellow wants to see me, make arrangements for him to see me, and see what he wants. I used to sit in my office and see 'em until noon, and if there were people left outside I'd go out and walk around with a girl with a pad and say to each one of them, What do you want? Put it down.

There's a lot of drudgery connected with that. But I let myself in for that. Some days a hundred people would show up. They'd sit around and wait for me. If they'd wait, I'd see them. Often I was still there at four or five o'clock.

It's awful the way they handle it now. Governor Martha Layne Collins was gone far too many days of her term. That's unbelievable, and unreal, and unnatural—ought not to be. Even when Governor John Y. Brown Jr. went to his office, he wouldn't see anyone or answer the telephone or his mail.

Never in my life have I had an unlisted phone. I usually answer it myself. And I sign all my correspondence. Always have.

Some mornings I might have a breakfast meeting at the Mansion, which flanks the Capitol building, about a block and a half away. I never liked to eat too much, so consequently I've rarely had a weight problem. Don't mind a brisk walk, but I never went in for jogging.

In those days of the thirties the world seemed a saner place. In our little town of Frankfort I never felt any apprehension for my own safety, or for Mama or the children. I never car-

ried that pistol that Judge Bingham wanted me to. Of course
we did have a state trooper on duty at the Mansion. But things
were so quiet around there that the night fellow fell asleep every now and then.

It was smart to be careful. From the time I was elected lieutenant governor I usually had an assistant around you might
term a bodyguard. The first was George Morgan Chinn, whom
I originally saw as a tough little river rat at Mundy's Landing.
Later he played football at Centre College when I coached
there. George weighed about three hundred thirty and was
strong as an ox. He could have whipped Man Mountain Dean.
When fellows knew he was around, they weren't going to take
chances with him. They weren't afraid of me, but they were
afraid of him.

He just saw that I was safely in at night and came over to
get me in the morning and walked over to the capitol with me
and stayed with me during the day. He had access to the whole
place. He did as he pleased. Ran easy. Nobody made him do or
not do anything. Had him nearly all the time I was governor
first time.

When I first hired George Chinn he stayed in Frankfort
only a couple of weeks and then paid a visit to his little farm
down in Mercer County. His wife, Cotton, was surprised to see
him.

"Did you know," he told her, "that a fellow can get a girl in
Frankfort for a ham sandwich?"

Cotton said, "George what did you come home for?"

And he said, "I came home to kill a hog."

George Chinn came to Washington during World War II
when I was in the Senate and wanted me to help get him back
in the Marine Corps. He had been a Marine as a youngster.

I said, "Go home, George. You're over forty years old, you
weigh 330 pounds. You'll get in the way and you'll get killed,
and you'll get other people killed, too. Go home."

"No," he said, "I'm gonna stay here with you and you're
gonna look out for me until you get me back in the Marine
Corps."

"Oh, Lordy Lordy, I can't afford to keep you. I'd have to
board you out because I can't feed you."

I called Colonel Best at Quantico and told him George was in my office. I said, Come get him. And he said, All right. So he came and got him. The first two weeks that George was out at Quantico for the training they give 'em all, they damn near killed him. He said so. But after two weeks, he led them in. He was up front. One of the toughest men I ever saw in my life. Went all through the war and nothing ever bothered him.

George was a gun man. Edgar Hoover told me George designed a gun that was one of the best automatic weapons the Army had. George was a remarkable fellow. He wrote poetry, too. And he came back home and headed up the Kentucky State Historical Society for about ten years.

Had Red Roberts, too, that Centre tackle who was one of the heroes in that Harvard game. Red didn't stay too long. He went someplace else. Also had Joe Burman, the fellow from Rome, Georgia, I played baseball with in the Blue Grass League. He was with me for years, and got to be a major in the Kentucky State Police.

Mama was still in her mid-thirties when she became First Lady of Kentucky. Consequently she injected a lot of vigor and imagination into her role as mistress of the Mansion. She had to. It was a full-time job. She had servants, of course. But she had to ride herd on four young children. She usually did that; not me. And importantly, she had to make certain the Governor's $6,500 salary covered the household and living expenses. That took a lot of stretching. There were always guests to entertain and feed. Mama worried about the cost of food. I think she sort of envied Governor "Honest Bill" Fields. He was a mountain man and a farmer. The first thing he did when he moved into the Mansion in 1923 was to build a chicken house. He had his own flock of hens and fryers. I guess the Fields never went hungry. Somebody said one of the early governors had a pig pen out behind the Mansion. I don't know about that.

When Earle Clements was governor later he must have encountered something of the same food problem. He put in a big vegetable garden on the Mansion grounds, and had such a tremendous harvest that Mrs. Clements was always handing out baskets of squash, tomatoes, radishes and green onions to her friends.

Mama has a hard time hanging onto a dollar; she's not the most frugal woman in the world. But she had to be in the Mansion. As they say, necessity is the mother of invention. What she did to stretch her food dollars was to hop in her car and whip over to Lexington and buy at the wholesale markets. That worked out fairly good. But not well enough. For in our first four years in the Mansion we had to dip into our savings and spend about $20,000 over and above the pay I got as governor.

Usually I was able to let her know if we were going to have more than a couple of guests at a meal. But there always had to be enough on the stove for unexpected company. Mama had some of those good old Virginia recipes, especially a carrot ring that everyone thought was quite tasty. Naturally we had lots of ham and chicken. And that southern favorite, spoonbread.

Of course, we entertained important guests in the Mansion, people like Jim Farley, Senator Harry Byrd, business and horse racing tycoons, Hollywood celebrities—important folks. Mama thought it would be nice to keep a list of our guests so she got a little register and had them sign in.

She was proud of that little book. Until one day she made the stunning discovery that a page had been ripped out. Someone had decided to pilfer a famous autograph! She kept trying to safeguard her little guest register, but she couldn't. More pages were ripped out. So she just gave up the whole idea.

All her life Mama has been an avid bridge player. She had a couple of clubs that met in the Mansion. Three tables. Friends of hers. They met most Wednesdays and Fridays. I used to play bridge. But I gave it up—I guess rather dramatically down in Florida when I was baseball commissioner. We were playing a game with some baseball people and I bid seven no-trump, which my opponents doubled. I immediately redoubled. Then the play started.

I made the bid. Then I got up and said that was about as good as I could ever do, and so I was giving up bridge. I never played again, and I don't really miss it.

There never was a better mother than Mama. As I say, practically all of the raising of our children fell to her. I usually was not around home when I could have been of some help.

Remember Mama as a teenager rode bareback lickety-split

down Main Street in her hometown of Keysville, Virginia. And when she got behind the wheel of an automobile her juices started flowing. She had a heavy foot.

I think she was finally stopped for speeding in every county in Kentucky—but she might have missed one. Most of the state troopers knew her and they'd give her a sign and slow her down. But not all the cops recognized the First Lady.

Mama was taking her mother and some of the children to Louisville for some important dinner. They were late. Mama was stepping on the gas pretty good when they whizzed into the outskirts of Louisville.

She was spotted by a city cruiser, which turned on its siren and pulled her over. The policeman got out his book to write a ticket.

Mama was irate. "I'm Governor Chandler's wife," she snapped. "And I'm late for a dinner. I wouldn't have stopped, except that I thought you were coming out to escort me in."

The cop was skeptical, but he got on his radio and checked the state police post. "Describe her," said the trooper on duty. The Louisville cop did.

"That's her," said the state trooper. That was an incident I had to straighten out later.

Even little Dan was a bad influence on his mother. He used to stand up on the front seat beside her, his eyes bright, and urge: "Go *hast*, Mama. Go *hast!*"

Finally I decided something had to be done. I got a mechanic to install a governor on Mama's car. It held down her speed to a safe limit.

Of course she didn't like that. One evening she was trying to pass a truck going up a hill when the governor cut in and slowed her down.

"Oh," she cried, "the damn governor is going to get us killed!"

That remark mystified little Dan. "Why, Mama," he exclaimed, "the damn governor isn't even here. He's at home."

Incidentally, it was just about that time that I decided to quit driving an automobile. As governor I didn't have to get behind the wheel because I always had a driver. And ever since then I've always had someone who was willing to drive me.

When people ask why I quit driving, I usually say: "Well, there were too many drivers on the road anyhow. One less won't hurt."

I haven't driven a motorcar in over fifty years.

The best driver I ever had, a fellow who drove me it seems about a million miles, came to me obliquely through University of Kentucky's immortal basketball baron, Adolph Rupp.

I was lieutenant governor when I first met Rupp. I knew all about him, what he had done with Phog Allen out in Kansas. He came down to Kentucky as basketball coach and in his first year won the Southern Championship.

Dr. Ligon and Dr. Cooper were running the athletic program. They weren't much interested in basketball; what they wanted was a winning football team. They called Rupp in—and offered him a one-year contract.

He was stunned, and of course disappointed. We were friendly and he came to me for advice.

"If they offer you a one-year contract when you win," I said, "what do you think they're gonna offer you when you lose? Go back and tell them you don't want the job. And I'll give you a better job than that until you get on as a coach somewhere else."

He was getting $2,800 a year. Think of that.

My offer made him bold. He went back to the University and told them he didn't want the contract. Well, they thought that over and gave him a three-year contract and he took that and never had any more contract troubles. For forty-two years he stayed there.

Rupp had those qualities you've got to have in order to be a good coach. He was wise. He knew the game better than anybody. And he knew how to recruit, knew what to do with 'em after he got 'em. He was a special fellow. He won 890 games and lost 190. He was way ahead of all the rest of 'em.

I've got his autograph in a book that I keep that says I was his best friend throughout all the years. Every now and then he got his tit in a wringer, and I got it out. Most of those were personal problems; it's better to let his troubles die with him.

During the latter part of his life he drank some, I'm sorry to say. That caused him some trouble. I worried about that a whole lot, but there wasn't much I could do. Once or twice I remonstrated with him. But he didn't want anybody to tell him what to. He was hard-headed and wanted to do what he wanted to do.

His wife Esther was a lovely girl, and I think they got along well. He had only one child, a boy. And the baron had one grandson, Chip, who played basketball at Vanderbilt.

Through Rupp I developed my lifelong friendship with John "Frenchy" DeMoisey, an outstanding high school center in Northern Kentucky who came to U.K. and made All-America under Rupp in 1934.

Frenchy came from an absolutely marvelous family up at Walton. His father had been a sailor and a boxer and became a preacher. His mother was a championship basketball player in high school. Frenchy turned out to be one of my best friends. He stayed with me for many years through politics and was very helpful while I was baseball commissioner. When he died in 1963, his younger brother Foxy became my main man. He usually drives me on all important trips, although he has an important full-time job as a drug company representative. Foxy DeMoisey looks out for me pretty good.

Frenchy was about six feet eight inches tall. He was outstanding in baseball as well as on the basketball court. He was a good strong-arm pitcher with one hell of a fastball. When he graduated the University, the Cleveland Indians organization wanted him. Walter Johnson came down to Lexington and signed him up with a $1,500 bonus, which was pretty good money for those times.

The Indians used him in a couple of late season games in Cleveland. But somehow he hurt his arm. Perhaps he suffered a chill in that bleak weather up there by the lake. Anyhow, he couldn't throw his fastball any more. So he went to sidearm stuff, curves and so forth. The Indians had him pitch some for the Louisville Colonels. In the winter he coached basketball at Grayson, Kentucky and later at Harrodsburg.

Frenchy thought he was about to make a comeback as a pitcher. He resigned as coach at Harrodsburg, and started packing to go south for spring training with one of the minor league clubs. There was snow and ice on the ground in Harrodsburg. Frenchy was putting some gear in his car when his feet slipped and he came down hard. He landed painfully on his right elbow, cracking it.

His pitching days were over. He came to see me at the governor's office.

"I need a job," he said.

"Is that all the trouble you got?" I asked.

"Yes."

"That's over. Think of something else."

I took him on right away. He was an outstanding fellow, with real ability in many fields. I took advantage of his skills in sports and as a motivator by assigning him as superintendent of the Greendale Reform School for Boys.

We traveled a lot of miles together. He was a careful driver. I used to tell DeMoisey to be careful. "Listen," he'd say, "I'm in here, ain't I? I'm not going to hurt me."

Frenchy liked nicknames and when we were in Versailles he called me "The Squire of Woodford." Over at the state capital he referred to me as "The He-Coon of the Commonwealth."

Of all the duties a governor faces, the worst is having to sign death warrants.

Just keeping prisoners in the penitentiary never bothered me. I made it a point to go down there and get the inmates together and talk to them. I wanted them to know that the laws were going to be fairly administered.

I told them straight out that I wouldn't hesitate to give a pardon if a fellow had not been properly tried and properly convicted—if there had been a miscarriage of justice.

"I'm not responsible for you being here," I told them, "but I am responsible for keeping you here. You've got a chance to earn parole, earn it by the way you conduct yourself. In a reasonable time you can earn parole, but you earn that. Look at each other, and understand one thing clearly—nobody's gonna walk out of here because somebody paid somebody. None of you are going to get out that way."

There had been all that talk in the Laffoon administration that a prisoner could get sprung for a thousand dollars. The grand jury looked into that and nothing came of it, but some people thought it was true. I did.

There was not even the slightest rumor of that kind when I

was in the governor's office. A fellow down at the penitentiary said, "Well, Chandler's in now and if you had a million dollars you couldn't get anybody out."

It's terrible to hold the power of life or death over one of your fellow citizens. That's awesome. It was up to me to hear the prayers and petitions of those people, boys and girls, mothers and fathers. I had to listen to that. And they told me this was a good boy. They begged, Commute his death sentence. . . .

I saw to it that every case on death row was fully investigated. I wanted to know two things—that they had a fair trial, that there were no extenuating circumstances, no justification or excuse for the crime.

I signed thirty-six death warrants. I never found any unfair trials, no extenuating circumstances.

It never bothered me at all to sign the death warrant for a rapist. The law was that we hanged them in the courthouse yard in the county where the crime was committed. I didn't hesitate a minute on that. Let the women folks of my state be safe in the streets. And during my time, the record will show, we were pretty safe. They didn't do it very often.

Down in Casey County there was one particularly horrible murder case. The victims were a father and son, just ordinary peaceful farmers. They were killed and their bodies wired together, weighted down with rocks, and thrown in the river.

When the killers were arrested next day they were ghoulishly wearing their victims' overalls.

When I came into office one of the killers was on death row. His sister came to see me to beg that his life be spared. I had to listen to her. And I told her I'd make the proper investigation.

When she came back for my answer, she brought along the convict's two little boys. I felt sorry for them—and her. But I couldn't bend.

"If it wasn't for your brother and these two boys' father," I told her, "that man and his son would still be living on their poor little farm down in Casey County. They weren't bothering anybody. I don't know whether it's right for the state to take the lives of its citizens, but it's the law. And I'm sworn to enforce the law.

"The court says he had a fair trial and there were no extenuating circumstances. The court says he's going to the electric chair. He's going."

The woman leaped up, doubled up her fists and gave me a terrible look. "You'll pay for this!" she shouted. "You'll pay! I'm gonna pray for the devil to take you . . . to do something awful to you!"

That kind of a scene will shake you up. But when the time came, I signed his death warrant. And then I put my head down on the desk and cried. I'm not ashamed to say that.

There was a peculiar aftermath to that case.

The night before that Casey County murderer went to the electric chair he called for paper and a pen. He wanted to write a letter to the governor.

His body already lay in the morgue when his letter was brought to my office next morning. I studied my name scrawled on the envelope. I hesitated to pick it up and open it. I had no idea what sort of message he was sending.

Finally I tore it open and read his note. It was only a line or two. He said he appreciated the clost consideration—I'll always remember that he spelled it that way, *clost*—that I had given his case.

"I've made my peace with the Lord," he wrote, "and being with Him means it all.

"I was your inherited prisoner and I'm guilty. I don't want you to blame yourself for doing what you've done, because you had no alternative under the circumstances."

12

Mystery of the Poisoned Ice Water

From the Oval Office I stepped out into the reception room at the White House and beckoned Major Burman.

"Joe, come in and meet President Roosevelt."

"Is he for us?"

"I don't think so."

"Then," Joe Burman said, "I don't want to see him. Let's go."

It was late January, 1938. I had gone to confer with F.D.R. about the race for Senator Alben Barkley's seat. I had a reason for wanting to oppose him. Barkley had already announced for re-election. Roosevelt said he wanted him to stay in the Senate. Barkley had been elected Majority Leader, and thus was pivotal in guiding New Deal programs through Congress.

The President asked me to be patient and "wait." He pointed out that I was young and promised he'd take care of me.

"I'm very concerned and intrigued," I responded, "that you're solicitous about my future and you're going to look out for me. But I'm afraid that won't do. I'm self-reliant and I've always looked out for myself."

To a degree also I was being guided by a voice from the grave. Judge Bingham had urged me to oppose Barkley's re-election. The Washington press kept referring to Barkley as "bumbling" and as a "party hack." The Judge and I shared that assessment of "Old Alben." Judge Bingham didn't like

Barkley. He was right about it, too. It was a mystery how he could sell himself to so many people. He did have a lot of support among people who thought he was just going to *do* for them. And he didn't give a damn about 'em.

Sadly, Judge Bingham had just died—suddenly, in December 1937. His death, of course, brought in a new regime at the *Courier-Journal*, which had always supported me politically. I remember riding to Judge Bingham's funeral with the British Ambassador. As our limousine passed a white horse I automatically wet my thumb and "stamped" it. "Good luck," I explained. The ambassador had just "stamped" his own palm. "That's one of my pet superstitions, too," he said.

"Well," I said, "back when I was playing baseball we had another. We'd pick up hairpins. Each one meant we'd get a hit. That worked pretty good." I didn't bother to tell him that Mama had an even stronger superstition: All her life she'd walk a mile to avoid crossing the path of a black cat.

But stamping white horses and finding ladies' hairpins did not preserve my good luck in having the support of Bingham's heirs. They turned his newspaper against me.

Fortunately by that time I had a good grip on my governorship. I thought I knew where I was going.

A few state officials fought my government reforms. The attorney general, Beverly Vincent, called in his staff and told them he was going to break with the governor. When he asked them to choose up sides, he lost. He was a knothead. He didn't know how he got there.

He complained loudly that I was "trying to set up an oligarchy the likes of which Huey Long never dreamed." I whipped him pretty good, and he got back in line. Agriculture Commissioner Garth Ferguson gave me some trouble. I stepped in and fired eight of his top assistants. He accused me of "vengeance and vindictiveness." I knew how to keep my administration on track.

My enemies moaned that I was trying to build up a political machine. That was true. I had built a pretty good political machine—proof of that was that we had just won the governorship.

I was proud of my accomplishments. And they were visible to the people—like the reorganization that totally streamlined the state government. I appointed the first woman ever to serve as trustee of the University of Kentucky, naming Paul Blazer's wife Georgia. Paul was chairman of the Ashland Oil and Refining Company. Mrs. Blazer proved to be an outstanding trustee and I reappointed her during my second term as governor.

I have always had a certain philosophy about political jobs. I could give someone a job, but it was strictly up to him to do the work and keep it.

I had one fellow I've known all my life. Worked for the highway department. Got drunk and wrecked an automobile. Came to see me and said, "I want you to think of my family, Albert."

"Well," I said, "I've been thinking of 'em. That's the reason you've got a job. I want you to think of 'em. I'm going to give you another chance. Don't do it again."

He did it again.

Did it another time.

He came back and said he wanted me to think of his family.

"I've been thinking of them," I said. "And now you're through. You're not going to drive another state car, and you're not going to work here. Go get a job someplace else. You're through."

You have to do that. I gave him a chance—and he didn't appreciate it.

I didn't believe too much in state jobs for kinfolk. I was proud of my father's attitude. He didn't want a state job. He didn't want me to be criticized for giving him a job. That was an unusual situation. My daddy had plenty of character. He didn't want me to do anything that could be interpreted as lack of principle or violation of law. I agreed with him on that. I told all my people: Check the law. If it's legal, we do it. If it's not legal, we won't.

My Daddy told me, "You're not supposed to look out for me. I'm supposed to look out for myself."

And he was strict about that. I never could get him to let me buy him a new car. Once in a while I'd send him a check. He didn't even want me to do that. He wanted to be self-sustaining. And he was. He never acquired much of the world's wealth. But when he died he didn't owe anybody anything.

My cousin Robert Terrell sent his daughter to me about getting a state job. Cousin Robert had been the first highway commissioner the state ever had. At that time he was, I believe, city engineer of Danville. The Terrells never had treated me very well. I told the girl I didn't have anything for her, and I didn't think I ever would. Not all the Terrell clan were mean to me. My cousin Carrie Terrell Bray was the sweetest one to me of all. She lived to be ninety-six. Two years ago I went over there to Trimble County and helped bury her.

Loyalty has two sides. I made arrangements once to appoint a county judge. I had known the fellow many years and held him in high regard. The word got out I intended to name him, and a delegation of fifteen or twenty people from his hometown called on me at Frankfort.

"Governor," said their spokesman, "this fellow is not very popular up there among our people."

"Well," I said, "he'd better get popular—because I'm going to appoint him."

I sent them all back home.

In my home county of Woodford, I appointed a county judge who lasted forty-four years on the bench. He managed our affairs fine, decently.

As soon as I appointed him, I went to see him. I said, "Hey . . . Everybody knows I appointed you. Some of them are going to come—if they get a speeding ticket—to see if I can use my influence with you to get 'em off. Sometimes I'm gonna ask you. But first I'm gonna ask 'em if they were drunk. If they were, I won't ask because if you let them out they may kill someone next time they're drinking. If a fellow is going seventy when he ought to be going sixty, I may ask you to pass that by."

Well, for forty-four years that was our bargain. I kept my word. He let some people go. Just take the ticket and tear it up. That wasn't so bad. But I never asked him to let a drunk driver go. I wanted him to be a good judge.

In the summer of 1936 Mama gave me one of the worst scares of my life.

It began as a sore throat. It got worse, and she called her new physician, Dr. Branham Baughman, to the Mansion. A graduate of Centre College and University of Michigan medical school, he was just getting his practice started in Frankfort. Mama met him in her bridge-playing circle.

Her ailment was strept throat, the physician decided, and put her on the new sulfa drugs.

That proved a terrible blunder. Mama has always been very allergic to many drugs. She can't even tolerate aspirin. She suffered a violent reaction to the sulfa. Before he realized she was allergic to it, Dr. Baughman had given her so much she broke out in *giant urticaria*, commonly called dinner-plate hives because they are that big.

She was so instantly consumed by the hives that it looked like she had been burned all over. The doctor began giving her first one new medicine and then another. She developed a high fever. She started having all kinds of side effects that were simply terrible. Her organs began to swell. Her spleen became so enlarged that it seemed on the verge of protruding through her side.

Dr. Baughman, frantic with worry and puzzlement, consulted other physicians. Their suggestions helped little. Mama was confined to her bed, in real torment, with a registered nurse at her side.

The children and I, as well as her mother who was then visiting, hovered around, frustrated and worried. The hours dragged by with her condition no better.

Finally she broke out with a hard chill, so severe that she literally shook the bed. The doctor grabbed a hypodermic and gave her a shot of morphine in the hip. He prepared two additional hypodermics with injections of heart stimulants before departing.

Minutes later, Mama suffered a terrible reaction to the morphine. Her breathing almost stopped. The startled nurse said her respiration fell to five, when normal is around twenty-four. Quickly the nurse injected one of the hypos. The poor woman was just about paralyzed with fear. In a minute or two she injected the second.

It looked like Mama's circulation had virtually stopped. Both injections stayed almost static in her arm, bulging up like two little marbles. Her circulation didn't seem to be taking up the shots at all. The doctor rushed back, and called in practically every doctor in Frankfort.

But Mama went into a coma, and we began to think we were losing her.

I got down on my knees in the hallway, with the children and Mrs. Watkins, and we prayed. We prayed that God would spare her.

In the sick room I could hear the nurse's frantic cries: "Breathe, Mrs. Chandler! Breathe...breathe...!" She was trying to reach Mama through the coma. The doctors resorted to every trick they knew—including the old-fashioned coffee enema.

The reporters had gathered outside because word was out that she might not last the night. The *Courier-Journal*, I was told, held its final edition until almost dawn expecting a bulletin.

Mama had been given so much strong heart medication that the physicians were fearful any sudden loud noise might throw her into a fatal seizure. Everyone crept about inside the Mansion, and traffic was stopped for the night all around the Capitol area.

One automobile defiantly roared up and down in front of the Mansion two or three times, loudly blowing its horn. That was a little ironic sidelight of my years of off-and-on political feuding with John Y. Brown Sr., who had been both friend and rival since we were in the legislature together. At this time we were on the outs for some reason. John Y. Senior got it in his head somehow—he was given to strange reasoning—this was a fake medical crisis blown up to create some vague sort of political sympathy for me.

By daybreak, Mama passed the crisis and began to emerge from her coma. The doctors consulted and wisely decided to suspend all medication. Expecting to be printing her obituary, the *Courier-Journal* had in type a just-written account of the First Lady's life. They accurately reported she was still hanging on, but printed the "obit" anyway. Mama always said it was the most glowing and flattering article ever published about her.

Within a few days she began to pull out of it. But it was weeks before she regained her health. I took her to the resort at French Lick, Indiana, carrying her through the door in my arms, for a long recuperation.

"Don't blame poor Dr. Baughman," she begged. "He just didn't know how allergic I am." She kept her faith in him, and called him in to see after the family health all the years we were in Frankfort. Not long ago he passed away at eighty-three.

A terrible weather tragedy hit Kentucky just at the beginning of 1937.

I was in Washington in late January with Mama to attend President Roosevelt's inauguration. Hard rain started falling up there. For several days it rained cats and dogs, as they used to say. I didn't know that it also was raining all over the country—especially in Kentucky.

Water spilled over the dam in Frankfort. The rivers came up and quickly inundated the whole town. The penitentiary was in downtown Frankfort. Lieutenant Governor Keen Johnson got me on the phone and said the situation back home was desperate. Mama and I had been invited by Senator Millard Tydings of Maryland to go for a cruise on Marjorie Merriweather Post's yacht. Our good friends Senator Harry Byrd of Virginia and his wife Cindy also were going.

I abandoned all my plans and rushed to the Union Station. Rain was still coming down and the floods everywhere were getting worse. Mine was the last train to come through from Washington to Lexington before high water shut down the Chesapeake and Ohio railroad.

I found the flood in Frankfort unprecedented. Water was six or seven feet deep inside the main prison building. Huddled there were three thousand men, and a few women prisoners. They had to retreat into the cells on the second floor. They were frightened to death. I don't blame them.

The first thing I did was get in a rowboat and go through the front gate and talk to the prisoners. I had Major Burman with me, also the state adjutant general and some others. There had been reports some prisoners had drowned, and I wanted to check that out firsthand. It wasn't so.

I stood up in the boat and asked the prisoners to be calm and patient. "I'll get you out of here. I promise." They broke out in a cheer.

"I'm not responsible for the flood," I said. "But I feel responsible for your safety. This is not something I anticipated or expected, and you-all didn't either. Now just all of you take dead level rest, just belly up here to this place and be patient and I'll get you out—and I won't put you back in this hole!"

I was thoroughly sick of conditions in the penitentiary anyhow. It was horrible. There was no worse place in Ceylon. It was damp and filthy and old. It was one hundred years old. It was overpacked—three thousand prisoners on twenty-seven acres of ground.

Immediately I got a tent city erected on high ground, guarded by the militia. And I tore that old prison all to pieces and built a new state office building there. We built a new modern penitentiary at LaGrange.

For several days I toured the flood disaster areas of the state with a party of officials checking conditions and organizing relief and repair. In Paducah I waded into the lobby of the Irvin S. Cobb Hotel. The water was up to my knees. I also was knee-deep in flood water in the opposite corner of the state, in a bank in Hazard.

It took months to fully repair the damage and get things back to normal.

Political historians are pretty much in agreement that my 1938 campaign for the Senate was perhaps the most signal misadventure of my career.

Even today I look on that race with a certain amount of wonder and amazement, and a great deal of mystification.

It began simply enough. Judge Bingham pushed me as early as 1936 to go up against Alben Barkley. "He must be removed from the Senate," Judge Bingham told me. "He is a cipher in Washington. He is a bad influence. He is not serving the interests of the people of Kentucky."

The Judge favored President Roosevelt and most of his New Deal policies. Likewise he understood F.D.R. counted on Barkley's help as Majority Leader. But the Judge knew well enough it wouldn't be hard to find another Senator more qualified for the leadership post. As a matter of fact, Barkley had become majority leader by just one vote. And the record shows he was pretty much a bumbler in his job.

So Judge Bingham had made it crystal clear to me that he wanted to unseat Barkley.

Then, unfortunately—in just a matter of weeks after we had finally agreed that I would challenge Old Alben—the Judge passes from the scene. I am deprived of his wise counsel and the extremely potent and critical support of his newspaper. His son, Barry Bingham Sr., is a strong and loyal supporter of Roosevelt policies.

So I know if Roosevelt asks Barry Sr. for help in the Senate race, the *Courier-Journal* will go all out for Barkley.

I felt I must go on, even though the reigning god of national politics tries to dissuade me, asks me to wait and promises to look out for me later.

I am not foolish. I am not unwise. I know my strength, or think I do, with the plain and honest people of the commonwealth. So I plunge into the fray.

Then the fireworks begin. I do not know at the outset that F.D.R. will take the train and come into Kentucky to throw the weight of his national prestige against my effort to win a Senate seat. Nor how fierce will be the onslaught of "dirty tricks" and the use of federal relief funds to try to influence votes for Barkley.

Nor—most of all—that there will be a deliberate attempt to kill me to keep Alben Barkley from being knocked out of office.

That campaign turned out to be a real dogfight. It all happened fifty years ago. And I don't waste much time mentally rehashing it. But political historians do. They're still analyzing it, as one recently said, because it was "the focal point of a national political struggle over the New Deal" pitting as opponents "two of the most powerful Kentucky politicians of the twentieth century."

I tore into Barkley. Newspapers reported my references to "fat, sleek senators who go to Europe and have forgotten the people of Kentucky except when they run for re-election." I said he had become a stranger to the state and gave us the absent treatment. It was time for "a man of action to replace a man of words." The people knew which man was which.

Barkley campaigned with his same old tired, stodgy, long-winded speeches. I talked briefly, sang smartly, and shook hands. I made only promises that I could keep. I took my "Happy Days Are Here Again" bandwagon all across the commonwealth from Paducah to Pikeville. I didn't miss anybody.

I knew Roosevelt was popular in Kentucky. He had carried the state by over one hundred seventy thousand votes in 1936. But I had to express dissatisfaction with some of the policies that were emanating from the national capital. "Contrary to the beliefs of some," I said, harking back to the philosophy I learned at my Daddy's knee, "it isn't possible to spend your way to prosperity."

In a lot of speeches, I gave this opinion a homespun twist. I told my listeners that the father of success is work, the mother of success is ambition, and the oldest boy is common sense. Some of the other boys are honesty, foresight, and perseverance. The oldest daughter is character; her sisters are sincerity and economy. The baby is opportunity.

"Get acquainted with the old man," I said, "and you will get along with the rest of the family."

The President was working diligently to "purge" opposition to his New Deal in the upcoming elections. He made a fireside chat declaring his "right" to intervene "in those few instances" where there was a contest between liberal and conservative candidates. That was his declaration of full-scale war against me.

Mr. Roosevelt had decided to come to Kentucky and make speeches endorsing Old Alben. His administration was getting some flak from the national press for "playing politics with human misery" for permitting the relief rolls to be manipulated to re-elect candidates he supported.

With the national focus falling on Kentucky, Washington reporters came to see for themselves how the battle was being fought. Tom Stokes of the Scripps-Howard Newspapers wrote a series of stinging articles detailing how the WPA was deep in politics for Barkley. The accuracy of his exposé was so universally respected that he won the Pulitzer Prize for it.

In the poverty-blighted mountains where people were desperately hungry, the Barkley forces struck one exceedingly low blow. They distributed sacks of food bearing the printed legend: "This food was donated by a friend of Senator Alben W. Barkley."

The fact that Roosevelt was coming all the way to Kentucky to try to derail me put me in the spotlight in the national media. *Time* magazine made me a cover-boy and featured the Senate race.

Roosevelt's swing through the state began the first week of July with a rally at Covington's Latonia Racetrack. I was on hand to greet him, as a governor should when the president enters his state. Some scurrilous comment was made that I leaped uninvited into the President's car and wedged myself between him and Senator Barkley.

That is a bald-faced lie. I have good manners. The President asked me to ride with him in the motorcade, and said, "The Governor here," pointing next to himself, "and the Senator there," indicating the left hand seat.

It was clear to me, as to every one of the twenty-five thousand in the race track throng, that Mr. Roosevelt had come to urge re-election of his Majority Leader. Yet in retrospect from this great distance it is interesting to see how much he tempered his remarks to remain friendly to me. In the most widely quoted paragraph of his speech, he said:

> I have no doubt that Governor Chandler would make a good Senator from Kentucky—but I think he would be the first to acknowledge that as a very junior member of the Senate it would take him many, many years to match the national knowledge, the experience and acknowledged leadership in the affairs of our nation of the son of Kentucky of whom the whole nation is proud, Alben Barkley.

I didn't pass that by. In a few later speeches I referred to the President's remarks. "He says he is my friend, and I have made a good governor, and I'll make a good senator—and that's enough for me."

But in his speeches in Louisville and Bowling Green, F.D.R. made it clear Barkley was his choice in the contest. He posed arm in arm with Old Alben, and said Washington needed men with national experience "because of the great national problems."

Now the race was just about to hit the home stretch down to the wire. The polls still showed Barkley ahead. But I didn't believe them. I was confident that I would unseat him. And I believe he was getting worried—and his campaign managers were actually desperate.

There is no other way to account for what happened next.

On July 23 I was in a room at the Kentucky Hotel in Louisville delivering a state-wide campaign address over the radio. This was before the days of air conditioning. It was a hot night—terribly steamy in the little room.

With me were several others, among them Major Joe Burman, Dan Talbott, and Ted Lee, who was the past state commander of the American Legion.

A waiter brought in a pitcher of ice water. I sweat easily and copiously in hot weather and I always drink a lot of water. I poured myself several glasses out of the pitcher, before and during the broadcast. Dan Talbott drank a glass or two. So did Ted Lee, and my driver, a state trooper, drank one.

Nothing seemed at all out of the ordinary until I awakened in the middle of the night wringing wet with sweat. My pajamas were soaked. I got up and changed—twice. I felt feverish. I knew there was something wrong. I was rugged, you know. I never had been sick at all, and I didn't just get sick by accident. I rang for the hotel doctor and he came, a Dr. Clybaugh.

"You've gotten some poison somewhere," he said. "Somebody's poisoned you." He gave me something to make me throw up. But my fever shot up, and water just kept pouring off me all over. My pulse was racing, something between 140 and 170. Two other physicians were summoned, Dr. J. W. Bryan and the state commissioner of health, Dr. Arthur T. McCormack.

They were all afraid I was dying. For several hours it was touch and go. Mama was notified and rushed over from Frankfort. I was becoming cyanotic and going into shock. I heard Mama ask: "Is he going to live?" One of the doctors answered: "It's all going to depend on how healthy his kidneys are. Right now they're paralyzed. He's bleeding on the inside."

Dr. McCormack thought I'd been fed arsenic. The physicians began to suspect that the drinking water I'd drunk during the broadcast had been poisoned. They were certain of it when they learned that Dan Talbott and Ted Lee had also become nauseated with similar stomach cramps, though not as bad as mine.

Immediately they tracked down the hotel waiter, a black man, who had brought in the pitcher of water. It was just a regular pitcher of ice water, he said, and had not been tampered with in any way that he knew.

It was not possible to make any tests for poison because by this time the pitcher and the glasses had been routinely washed in the hotel kitchen. To rule out some accidental cause, Dr. Bryan questioned the hotel manager and examined the hotel plumbing, and found nothing amiss.

I was too weak to even stand. The doctors kept me in bed at the hotel for another twenty-four hours and then moved me by ambulance to Frankfort to my own bed in the Mansion. I was put on a light diet and began slowly recovering.

I think somebody tried to kill me. I never accused Senator Barkley. I didn't think he would have countenanced anything like that. But someone working in his campaign—somebody who feared I was going to win—could have bribed somebody . . . . Arsenic could have been put in that drinking water, even without the waiter knowing it.

They knew I drank a lot of water. The only thing that saved me is that I didn't drink more because Dan Talbott and Ted Lee drank part of the pitcher. I'm certain that the poisoning aggravated Dan Talbott's health problems, and consequently shortened his life.

The Louisville police department was openly skeptical. No one investigated the case very much because the officials over there weren't for me. The district attorney called the incident a bedtime story. But later the Grand Jury made an investigation and concluded that I had been poisoned by "persons unknown."

Some newspapers carried headlines that I had been poisoned but luckily escaped death. Dr. Bryan was quoted as saying I got more than half of a fatal dose.

Barkley sent a wire of condolence to the Mansion, "sorry" that I was sick. But on the stump he tried to turn the incident to his political advantage.

Look who's broken down first, he cracked, not the "old" Barkley but the "youthful" governor. They say that in his autobiography—which I never read, and don't intend to— Barkley had great fun with The Case of the Poisoned Ice Water.

His campaign manager, with an elaborate flourish, formally announced that in this treacherous campaign climate Barkley had been provided with "an ice water guard" and a trusted "food taster."

This ridicule reached silly extremes. Barkley on the stump would pause during a speech. He would bring a glass of water to his lips. Then instead of taking a drink, he would come to a dramatic pause. He would hold out the glass, study it warily, and then with a shudder set it aside.

Perhaps he thought his audience enjoyed that pantomime. It wasn't the least funny to me—somebody deliberately had put arsenic in my drinking water. You don't joke about that!

While I was laid low, Mama undertook to fill some of my speaking engagements. Fortunately, she was pretty popular. She could sing and she could play the guitar. In addition, she had gone with me to so many stump speechings that she knew my philosophy and how I expressed my views.

I was practical and conservative. I never did see how they were going to run this country by giving it away. Spending money you haven't got and nobody else has got, and going into debt. I never practiced that. Lots of times when I was a boy there were lots of things we didn't have that we wished we had. But nobody gave us anything. In fact, if they had, we wouldn't have liked it. We all worked.

Even Marcella and Mimi went out and made appearances for me during the period I was sick. They were spunky kids.

Mama had one bad experience, which she explained to me: "I went over to Louisville where all the candidates were on the platform. There must have been fifteen of us, because all the alderman candidates were there. I was worried about you and worn to a frazzle. But I stepped up to the mike to tell them you were still sick and I was taking your place and doing the best I could.

"When I got up to speak I want you to know my brain actually sat down. I couldn't think of the first thing to say. I stood there just as blank as can be for a minute and then I said, 'I am having difficulty getting my wits together and I'm gonna sit down, and if I can get over this little spell I'll get back up.'

"So the rest of them went ahead with their speeches and sat down. By then I had my wits back and was able to stand up and make my little speech. All those people were nice. They gave me a big round of applause when I finished."

After about ten days I was able to get back out on the campaign trail myself.

In the last days it turned into an uphill battle for me. Those speeches Roosevelt made for Barkley came back to haunt and hurt me. I told some folks: "If I lose, well there are worse things. If you want to send me back to the country, all I can say is I still know the way."

A long time ago I learned—and resolved—whatever the circumstances therewith to be content.

When the votes were tallied Barkley had 294,562 and I had 223,690.

It was a pretty bad beating. I sent the senator a wire: "I bow to the will of the majority."

Then I just wiped that loss off the slate, and moved my digger. I was still governor of Kentucky and I had work to catch up on.

When that winter rolled around I was handed a unique diversion—leading a junket to Hollywood.

It turned out to be a festive excursion, but producing unexpected sidelights that would soon trigger a rupture in my principle that every family must have a permanent base.

Our base was at 191 Elm Street, Versailles. In 1934 I had acquired the handsome three-story dwelling that had graced the corner for sixty years. It was a depression bargain for us, only $6,500. It had been built in the late 1800s by prominent Woodford County lumber people. It was master-crafted, solid, strong.

We were happy to have so much space we could spread out for a change. There was a full basement for storage. The attic was so spacious that we used to hang country hams from the rafters to cure. There was one major drawback—with three floors and children to look after, Mama was in for a lot of stair-climbing.

"Every family ought to have a base," I told Mama. "This is ours."

It has been. We are still on the same corner of Elm Street after all these years.

But the Hollywood junket caused us, ironically, to desert that base for nearly two years. Fortunately, it was just a temporary thing.

Our trip to movieland came about because Twentieth Century-Fox had produced a feature film called *Kentucky*. Much of it was shot on location in our state, and naturally as governor I was of considerable assistance.

The studio invited me to bring my family and about a dozen friends to Hollywood for the premiere of *Kentucky*. I took Mama and our two daughters. Both boys, in school and

too small to enjoy the event, remained behind. Others in my
party included the mayors of Louisville and Lexington, some
horse racing people, and a group of newspaper men, and wives.
I was proud to invite Bo McMillin, then coaching at Indiana
University, to bring his wife Catherine and come with us to Tin-
seltown.

In addition to the stars of *Kentucky*—Loretta Young,
David Niven, Walter Brennan, and Richard Greene—we met
about a hundred movie stars during the round of parties associated with the premiere showing. With many we formed lifetime
friendships—Bing Crosby, Robert Taylor, Spencer Tracy, Clark
Gable, Joan Crawford, Robert Montgomery, Greer Garson, Al
Jolson, for example.

At a party at the Coconut Grove, I joined Rudy Vallee's orchestra and sang "When I Grow Too Old To Dream." Then I
sang, I thought appropriately, "My Old Kentucky Home." I
had hardly finished that number when Sid Grauman rushed up.
"I've never heard that song sung better," he beamed. "And
you're hearing that from a showman!"

But the star of the entourage from Kentucky turned out to
be our daughter Mimi.

Though not yet thirteen, Mimi was vivacious and outgoing. She was what I call whipping-smart. She was pretty, and
she could sing like an angel. And she was a dancing fool.

Hollywood wanted to sign her up as a "starlet." Mama was
initially hesitant. "She's just a baby," she protested. But some
of the producers we'd become friendly with insisted she could
continue her schooling while she made movies. Other young ac-
tresses were doing that, they pointed out.

The offer was tempting—one hundred fifty dollars a week.
Mama and I talked it over with Mimi. At length, and several
times. We didn't come to any conclusion before returning home.

In the end, the Hollywood adventure for our beautiful and
talented little "starlet" was to become the rock on which our
home base was broken.

Fate and the gods of politics would have taken care of that
anyhow. For abruptly—despite being vanquished by Barkley
and the White House—I was suddenly on my way to Washington to take my seat as Senator from Kentucky.

Our junior senator, Marvel Mills Logan, died suddenly in the fall of 1939. I quickly struck a deal with my lieutenant governor, Keen Johnson, who had already won the Democratic nomination as my successor. I resigned on October 9, 1939, with two months remaining of my term. Johnson, of course, automatically stepped in as governor.

His first act was to appoint me to fill out the unexpired portion of Senator Logan's term.

"Won't old Roosevelt be one surprised human being," I told Mama, "to see Happy Chandler showing up in the Senate!"

13

"Cactus Jack" and "Uncle Daddy"

Our two boys came back to the Mayflower Hotel with bulging pockets. Their eyes glittered and they grinned like they knew a secret. Ben, who was eleven, and Dan, seven, began digging out handfuls of spent sub-machine gun cartridges. Mama, beaming, watched as they piled them up in mounds. They had a couple hundred empty brass hulls.

"We've had such a good day sightseeing," she told me. "Your friend Edgar Hoover was so nice. He let the boys go down in the basement of the Justice Department and practice shooting with the FBI agents." She swept her hand across the bullet casings. "These are their pistol range souvenirs."

On brocade tapestry chairs, Marcella, eighteen, and Mimi, fourteen, struggled to learn to lace their own ice skates. Mama got the skates and introduced the girls to the ice rink. Nearly everything else bored them. They grew homesick.

On Capitol Hill, Mama got restless watching the Senate in session. I caught her as she left the gallery. "Get back, woman," I ordered. "Senator Joe Bailey of North Carolina is up next. He's a Baptist preacher. If you miss him, you've missed it all. He's the best we've got."

Mama went with me to a White House reception. President Roosevelt, with his Georgia politeness, paid her smiling and gracious attention. The ladies of the press fell in love with

Mama. "Isn't she the cutest thing?" I heard one say. "And such a darling, darling hat!" She did look stunning, and she charmed everyone—especially F.D.R., which was a skill apparently beyond me.

But living in the hectic nation's capital in a little hotel apartment with four rambunctious children didn't seem to work. We were too crowded. Mama tired of it after a few weeks and packed up in early 1940 to return with the children to Versailles.

"I'm going back to the home base," she said. "I don't think I'd ever be satisfied living here."

"Well," I crowed, "what if I'm elected President?"

Mama smiled. "That's different. The White House is plenty roomy. Suit the kids and me just fine."

A few times—but not many—Mama brought our brood back to visit Washington. On one occasion I rented expensive roomier quarters on DuPont Circle. But a Senator's pay—then $10,000 a year—only stretched so far. It was difficult to maintain a Washington home and a Kentucky base. For me a single room at the Mayflower was only six dollars a night.

When I put them aboard the Kentucky-bound George Washington at Union station, Mama kissed me. "Go do whatever you have to do," she said. "Remember who you belong to, and come home when you get ready." This girl has never made any trouble for me in her whole lifetime.

But she's a hardhead. She's the most independent woman that I ever saw in my life. She's an unreconstructed rebel and she learned it that way. She doesn't want anybody on earth to tell her she can't do something. She's not a coward, and she's not afraid of anybody.

Oh, we've always had friendly differences. Once in a while there flared up the question of who was going to get a knuckle sandwich. She always said I'd *get a receipt* if I harmed her. For years she has told about what happened one morning at the Mansion during my first term as governor. We were in the family dining room, kids on both sides with noses buried in their oatmeal, Mama at one end and me at the other. We were having an argument—I don't remember what it was about—and I told her to shut up. "Or I'll come over and shut you up," she remembers I said.

She wasn't about to stop talking. I jumped up—according to her story—and came around, lifted her out of her chair onto the floor. We were wrestling around. Abruptly she jerked her thumb toward the pantry door. Our convict kitchen servants had cracked the door and four pairs of wide eyes, whites gleaming, stared in amazement at this unseemly tableau. Mama says I got up, dusted myself off, and calmly resumed the meal.

"I know," she told me later, "you were just trying to prove that you could do what you said you'd do. You were no more anxious to get that receipt than I was to give it ... But, Happy, wasn't that whole episode a kick!"

Well, Mama would be fair and say I've treated her well, and tried—for a Scotsman—to be generous. On our tenth wedding anniversary, and our twenty-fifth, too, I bought her a mink coat.

On our fiftieth Joe Cronin took us down to friends in the garment district in New York, and I fixed her up with a beautiful sable. She still wears two of those coats.

When Governor Johnson appointed me to succeed Senator Logan I made a short acceptance speech and promised to "help Roosevelt keep the United States out of war." I thought that was what he wanted to do. Later I found out that I don't think he did. I think he wanted the Japs to give him some excuse to join the British in the war. You see, he was a million percent British. He out-Britished the British. Churchill played on him like a flute. And Churchill was so much smarter than he it wasn't even close.

The *New York Times* tried to take an unkind jibe, predicting that the new senator from Kentucky, to quote them, "is as wily as a squirrel and as amusing as Artemus Ward's kangaroo.... For a time at least he is likely to be a terrible infant let loose among wax figures...."

Well, they tried to make it appear that I was wild. I wasn't wild. I was full of energy, and I was full of life, but I wasn't wild. I wasn't out of gear. They thought I had a disposition to be reckless and wild. I wasn't any such thing. I was sober and they underestimated me badly.

You can imagine how Barkley reacted to my arrival in Washington. He was in a position to make trouble for me in the Senate. And he did. Not only as senior senator from Kentucky but as Majority Leader, a powerful, powerful post. Barkley blocked me every way he could.

In the Senate I was the freshman, seated in the last row. They made me see right away that I was Number 96. Barkley tried to keep me off committees that I wanted. Senator Harry Byrd helped me. He didn't like Barkley, thought he was too liberal. I thought the same thing. Old Alben wanted to give the country away.

I did pretty well. I got on two important committees, military affairs and judiciary. At forty-one I was the youngest member of the Senate. Charlie McNary, the floor leader, called me, "My dear boy." I have always had the knack of making friends. And I kept them. I never deserted a fellow. One thing I have been criticized about: they say I *stayed* too long.

Nixon had the same trouble. That was his trouble, trying to help out some stupid fellows. He didn't know anything about the Watergate thing. That was one of the worst things that happened in my lifetime. He went to the defense of a lot of fellows for doing a stupid silly thing. Anybody killed in Watergate? Anybody take any money from anybody at Watergate? What's it all about? They went to get some information they didn't get. And they put the President out for it.

I think that's a damned outrage. I never have reconciled to that. It was one of the worst things we have done in the history of this country. He was a good fellow. One of our better presidents. Now they are taking his advice on foreign policy. If it wasn't for him we wouldn't be in China. I know Henry Kissinger contributed a lot. *Qua facit per alium, facit per se.* That's my Latin maxim—What a fellow does through another, he does through himself.

Not surprisingly, I was a workaholic in the Senate. I answered all my mail, sitting up nights to sign every letter. And it was just four or five years before I was getting more mail than all but five or six senators. Another senator asked me how that happened. "Well, I sit down and answer their letters . . . then they write back."

Senator Richard Russell of Georgia was the smartest parliamentarian in the Senate when I was there. I sort of patterned myself after him. I paid attention and watched how he did things. I was not an expert but I had enough skill to get along. I was able to take care of the floor occasionally. I didn't have any bad experiences. My years of presiding in the Kentucky Senate had helped prepare me for this. Back in Frankfort I had picked up a lot of pointers. I was well versed, too, on Roberts Rules of Order. I handled everything that came along. They never had to send up somebody to get me out of trouble. The Senate has a right to appeal the decision of the chair. None of mine was ever appealed.

Vice President John Garner proved to be a good friend. He was a truly unforgettable character. He finally broke with Roosevelt over the third term. He was the cutest little fellow you nearly ever saw in your life. I used to preside over the Senate for him. I got a letter from him—one of the treasures I keep—that said I was one of the best presiding officers he'd ever seen, and that was an art seldom acquired by people.

Garner used to call me to his office. He knew I didn't drink, but he did. "I know you won't join me," he'd say, "but I'm going to strike a small blow for liberty." He'd fill a glass three-quarters full of red whiskey. No water. And just drink it down. Chugged it right down, and just shook his head. But I swear to goodness he was absolutely courageous and correct. Superior to F.D.R. in character.

I know this story about Roosevelt and it happened over and over again. The President and Jim Farley called a fellow in and gave him a big cock and bull story. When the visitor departed, Roosevelt turned to Farley and said, "Well, we fooled that son of a bitch, didn't we?" One of the fellows in that meeting obviously had to tell me that story. It wasn't Roosevelt. I never cared much for calling in a person for a talk aimed at fooling or misleading him.

Garner talked often to me in confidence. He told me he was going to leave Washington, and wasn't coming back. His wife left for Texas ahead of him.

"Do you ever play poker?" he asked me.

"Nope."

"Well, I've made one hundred thousand dollars since I've been in Washington playing poker."

"How'd you do that?" I asked.

Garner chuckled. "Well, I always put three thousand dollars on the table in front of me. The blue sky above me is my limit. If I don't like the way you look, I push it all in."

The old man suddenly looked quizzical. "What would you do?"

"Lordy," I blurted, "I'd turn the table over!"

He kept saying I'd be welcome. But I never had a card in my hand while I was in Washington. John L. Lewis said that "Cactus Jack," as Garner was known, was a poker-playing, whiskey-drinking, evil old man. He was one of the best fellows you ever knew, but he did play poker and he did drink whiskey.

"We're gonna have fun tonight," Garner said one evening. "John Y. Brown's coming. He thinks he can play poker, and we know he can't. Scott Lucas is in the game. So we're gonna have fun."

My nemesis in Kentucky politics had been—his one and only time—elected Congressman. Garner said they always fleeced John Y. Brown Sr. He was a gambler. He was just like his boy. Old Man John Y. gambled away a fortune. I expect he made several million dollars. And when he died he didn't have, as the British would say, even an 'erb.

Later when I was baseball commissioner Garner and I kept in touch. I bought him shirttail shirts like I wear; he didn't have any of those. He owned downtown Uvalde, Texas. He bought all the buildings in that little town. He had a key to everybody's gate. I went out there and visited him and Mrs. Garner. He was good to me, and in the Senate I was somebody he could count on.

It was in the office of the Secretary of the Senate, a fine Virginia gentleman named Edwin Alexander Halsey, that I first met Bob Hope. Halsey invited Bob to lunch in his private dining room to meet four or five senators. Halsey was leading him down the line, making introductions.

"This is Senator Chandler from Kentucky," Halsey said.

Bob grasped my hand. I gave him my regular stout handshake.

Hope took a couple of steps forward, stopped, and turned back. He shot me a perplexed look. "No senator with muscles . . . !"

He was impressed by the fact that I had muscles. And he always has been. The other day he said, "My God, you're the stoutest man alive!" He grabbed hold of me. "Happy, how do you keep that way?"

"Bob," I said, "I earned that in the tobacco patches of western Kentucky. Worked hard all day—sun-up to sundown. And I never lost it."

From our first meeting we were great friends. We played golf together—everywhere. He is one of the few fellows I can beat. I played a lot of golf with Bing Crosby, too. I couldn't beat him. Every time Bob comes to Kentucky he'll call and we play. A few years ago I took Bob and his wife over to Mercer County, where my Scotch friend Bucky Blankenship owns a golf course—beautiful and well-kept. Then we all had dinner at the famous Beaumont Inn. Bob and I have kept in close touch for— well, seems like a hundred years.

We called the Senate secretary's offices "Halsey's saloon" because many of the senators went back there to drink. I didn't. And I never approved of that—senators drinking during the day. Some of them appeared on the Senate floor carrying more whiskey than they ought to have taken in, and consequently they were not responsible for what they were doing and made a bad out of it. I knew who they were and I had no great enthusiasm for them.

I've had Senators come to me and ask what happened at a committee meeting we both attended. Just had too much to drink and couldn't remember what he or anybody else had said. That was terrible.

One I didn't care for was Harry Truman. I was in the Senate with him for seven years. All he did was drink whiskey and play cards. He wasn't even the best senator from Missouri— Champ Clark Jr. was. And he drank too much whiskey, too.

Jim Farley got shabby treatment from Roosevelt. Farley wanted to be president. I thought he overreached and don't think he had any chance. He broke with Roosevelt because Roosevelt wouldn't support him. Roosevelt wouldn't support anybody but Roosevelt. He didn't envision any successor. And he picked old Truman because Truman had a passion for anonymity. Nobody knew Truman. Nobody gave a damn about Truman and they gave him that investigating committee to get him acquainted.

Truman was in his office one evening bent over papers on his desk when I passed his open door with my friend Frank Peterson, who had dropped in from Kentucky on a Washington visit.

Looking up, Truman hailed me and invited us in. He looked Peterson over.

"Senator," Truman said to me, "is he a real Kentuckian, or is he like you?"

I gave a little laugh. "I believe he would," I said.

So Truman poured Peterson whiskey in a glass. "What do you want with it?"

"You probably say branch water," Peterson responded. "Down home, we say sprinkle it with stump water."

We chatted a while. I told Truman I was taking Frank around to the Senate chamber to show him my seat. Truman looked at his watch. "The janitor's probably gone by now," he said. He fumbled in his desk for a ring of keys. "Come on. I'll go unlock the door for you." And he did.

Washington has always been an intensely social town. Evelyn Walsh McLean was noted for her exclusive parties. She often invited Senators. One of her quirks was to seat people who didn't speak to each other at the same table.

One evening when I went to the table in the next chair was Mrs. Eleanor Medill (Cissy) Patterson, owner of the *Washington Times-Herald* and the most successful woman newspaper publisher of her day.

"Darling," she said, "do I speak to you?"

I told her who I was. She said, "Oh, I love you."

"Well," I said, "I must be a lucky fellow."

Mama and I got well acquainted with Cissy Patterson and other important people in newspaper circles.

When I'd get fed up with Washington I'd run up to New York for a weekend. I've always been a fight fan, and I got acquainted with Jack Dempsey. Somewhere along the line I invited him to speak before the legislature in Kentucky. Jack stood up at the speaker's rostrum and said: "I can whip any man in the House."

There was a rumble in the back row. Jack and I saw a big legislator from the mountains wiggle out of his chair and start down the aisle. Lordy, he looked like he weighed three hundred and fifty pounds.

"That is," Jack interposed, with a quick smile, "any fellow who can make my weight."

One year when Mama and I were visiting New York, Jack invited us to dinner at his restaurant. It was a fun evening. I was sitting there when I began to feel something wrong with my foot. It was getting hot—it was burning. I looked down and saw a blazing match wedged in at the sole. Jack started laughing his head off. That son of a bitch had given me a hot-foot! Mama, too, got a big laugh out of that episode.

From Washington, I didn't write many letters to Mama. I remember one, however, after I'd been to the fights in New York with a lot of photographers around. I told her: "You're going to see in the newspapers a picture of me at the fights, and there's a very attractive woman seated next to me. She just happened to be there. Don't read anything into it."

Living a "bachelor" life in Washington was a little strange. I never was a lonesome fellow. I went to a ball game if I got lonesome. I went and played golf. I managed to take care of my time pretty well.

Besides, my home base was just an overnight train ride away. I could get on the Chesapeake and Ohio limited, the George Washington, at six-thirty or seven in the evening and next morning at eight o'clock be in Lexington. Mama was always there to meet me.

The normal eight-to-five daddy comes home in the evening and rules his roost. But not me. Much of the time our children were growing up, I was an absentee father. Politics required that. The day-to-day raising of our youngsters fell largely to Mama. And I must say she did splendidly at that task. And it can be a task, as every parent knows. I wasn't completely out of the picture. I got in my licks too—and they were *licks,* woodshed variety.

Once I was switching little Ben at age five or six. He screwed up his face and confronted me not with tears but a look of defiance. "I like whippings!" he said.

Dan was more clever. He knew the whipping would stop as soon as tears came. So he boo-hooed the first moment.

Definitely I was rough on 'em. Dan misbehaved and I ordered him upstairs. He didn't move very fast. I stood by the stairs and helped boot him up. "I'm introducing my shoemaker to your tailor," I told him.

They were only mischievous, never bad boys. Usually discipline descended on them for something like shooting BB's at birds. Mama got irate if they did or said anything that would cast a reflection on their father. I think Mama may have been overprotective. She was always following Ben around worrying about him, sticking a thermometer in his mouth. He was as healthy as an ox, and strong, and always has been a good athlete. I think he could have gone to the major leagues. He's sort of shy now in crowds. He has no interest at all in politics.

Since they're grown-up we had a lot of discussions about those years when they were children. Ben says they used to think of me as "Uncle Daddy." He was reminiscing not long ago: "When I think back about who taught me to write a check, fix a flat tire, or about the birds and bees, it was never Daddy because he was not around for that. He seemed like just a weekend visitor in our home until the time I was married. Of course, he was in an active political career."

Mama still points out that I didn't spend time passing on to the children my love of singing and poetry. She upbraided me, too, because I didn't take them hunting or fishing. And I felt like they ought to stay home most of the time we took trips. I did take Ben fishing a few times.

Out in our big back yard I played baseball, basketball, and football with the boys. I wanted them to develop as athletes, and be strong and healthy. Dan remembers me as "a tough competitor," considerably more mature and quicker than youngsters who were just growing into themselves. Playing with them led to a celebrated and explosive episode that's still the talk of the family.

It happened when Dan was about thirteen. We were playing softball in the back yard. I hit one solidly and somebody winged it in from centerfield, but it was good for a three-bagger.

Instead of stopping at third, I charged on toward home, trying to stretch it into a homerun. Dan, holding the ball, stood guarding home plate, waiting to tag me out.

I barrelled into Dan just like they do in the major leagues. Dan was knocked one way and the ball flew the other. And I was safe at home.

The back screen door burst open and Mama, white-faced with anger, came rushing out. Dan was picking himself up.

"Poor little Dan, you've killed him!" she screamed. "Why did you do that?"

"Mildred, nobody else is gonna get out of his way and I want to teach him a lesson."

Her eyes kept flashing fire.

"The thing is that Dan's got to hold onto the ball, and take care of himself, and tag the runner out. If he loses the ball, the fellow is not out. Nobody's ever going to just let him win . . . not in this life."

As young and little as he was, Dan saw the point. Recalling the incident—for the jillionth time—Dan told me: "It was helpful that you treated me like a grown-up. You taught me how to meet the man, look him in the eye, listen to his name, and give him a firm handshake. Those are little things. But you showed us how important they are in the game of life. I know that you can always get by if you're strong person-to-person, in demeanor and bearing."

Dan was impressed as a kid by what I taught him about being aggressive and competitive. To a friend he remembered: "Growing up I had enthusiasm and intellectual curiosity, but I didn't have the killer instinct. I could get the ball down inside the ten, but I just lacked the drive to get it over. You know Daddy would take it into the end zone and right on through. If anybody ever had the killer instinct it's him!"

There was never any trouble between our boys and our girls. Mama was the disciplinarian for the girls. Dan recalled in an interview recently: "If Daddy had a weak spot it was with the girls. He babied them—still does. At times it was like I had three mothers. They were always criticizing everything. Finally Daddy would break in: 'Let him alone.' Of course, that made me a little independent."

Once when Mimi gave her mother some sass, Ben said: "Mama, do you want me to hit her?" Mimi was sassy—still is.

Marcella, in a tape-recorded recollection for my oral biography over at the University of Kentucky library, said I told her never to say anything she would mind seeing in newspaper headlines the next day. I did tell her that. I told the whole family. Lots of times people talk when they ought to be listening. I had the same strong feeling of the old Chinaman who said he never had any reason to regret that on public occasions he said nothing.

Ben will never forget one little tragedy that occurred when he was playing basketball in school. I was too busy to attend games, but somehow managed to tear myself away from the governor's office to watch this one. Ben made a grand play. He got the ball and dribbled all the way down the court and sank the ball—in the wrong basket. Ben says he'll never forget that as long as he lives. Mama says everyone thought it was funny . . . but to Ben it was a highlight tragedy.

I was out in the back yard on Sunday, December 7, 1941, on our little baseball diamond with the boys hitting pepper.

Mama opened the back door and yelled I had a long distance call.

I went in. In a few minutes I came back outside, and told the boys: "That was the White House. I hate to break up the game but I've got to rush back to Washington. We're going to declare war in the morning."

14

Flying High on "The Guess Where 2"

On a Spring morning in 1942, our stripped-down B-24 roared off the airstrip at Nome, Alaska into blue sky. The weather seemed ideal. But everyone aboard felt edgy. We were not going to a picnic. The pilot turned southwest—toward the war zone in the Aleutian Island chain.

I headed a Senate subcommittee venturing out to check on our military efforts to stop this perilous Japanese thrust toward the American mainland. West of Dutch Harbor, the yellow men held every island in this chain. Our plane was heading for Dutch Harbor or Umnak. It was a dangerous mission. We were unarmed. To avoid enemy detection, we had to maintain radio silence. That forced us to guess about the weather ahead.

Unfortunately, the weather fooled us.

I was not eager anyhow to make this trip. The subcommittee had come up by train from Los Angeles to Spokane, Washington. With me were Senators Mon Wallgren of Washington and Rufus Holman of Oregon.

Major Henry Myers met us. "Senator Chandler, I'm flying your party." He shook hands firmly and looked me straight in the eye. "I'll get you there—and back." I liked him right off. He was from Tifton, Georgia. Somebody told me he had a lot of medals for bravery and flying.

On the Pacific edge of the Aleutian range, the B-24 turned almost due west. Barely an hour later the weather abruptly changed. The sky turned black; fierce winds slammed and rattled the plane. We had hit the edge of a typhoon. We all looked at each other and got tense. The B-24 was shaking like a wet dog.

Of a sudden, the bomber was caught in a giant updraft and hurled in breathtaking seconds at least twenty-five hundred feet higher. Through the porthole I could see us hurtling toward the towering rocky face of a snowy mountain. It looked less than ten seconds away!

This is the end, I thought. I glanced around. Everybody thought we were gone. Eyes were wide with fright. Faces were white.

But we didn't crash. The pilot skilfully guided us over the mountain crest. A minute later we broke out of this Pacific Ocean storm into blue sky over the Bering Sea, as if by lucky magic.

Major Myers gave the controls to his co-pilot. He came back to check on his passengers. "Everybody okay?" He gave a little shudder. "I don't want too many that close." Senator Holman, big, fat, and the oldest man on board, was still scared. "I thought our time had come," he muttered.

It sure as hell frightened me. I began to think that maybe God intended for just birds to fly. And that flying and praying went hand in hand. I started turning "anti" on air travel. I had to fly during the war. But now I won't take a plane; if I can't get there by train or auto, I stay home.

We landed on the American airfield at Umnak. And the strangest thing happened. Ozzie Colclough stepped up and greeted me. Even in khakis, I recognized him at once—we were classmates in Harvard Law School. I hadn't seen him since 1922.

The war, and its sidelight surprises, caused a great upheaval in the placid Chandler family routine. Things didn't settle back to normal for three or four years.

Senatorial duties consumed most of my time. After Congress declared war against Japan on December 8, 1941, and three days later against Germany and Italy, I started feeling I ought to be in uniform, as I was in World War I.

Joseph Chandler, Happy's father, in an 1895 photo.

Chandler with his younger brother Robert, who was fatally injured in a fall from a tree when he was fourteen.

Above. Chandler (left) working in the Lee County oil fields in 1922. *Below.* Chandler (right end, second row) as the football coach of Versailles high school in 1928.

Above. Fred Vinson, congressman from Kentucky and future Chief Justice of the U.S. Supreme Court, speaks as Chandler does what comes naturally on the campaign trail in 1935. *Below.* While a law student at the University of Kentucky, Chandler coached the girls basketball team in Versailles.

The white suit campaigner of the thirties giving another of his inimitable speeches.

A tall order for the new governor of Kentucky in the tall hat at his inauguration in 1935.

bove. In a scene typical of American political campaigns of this era,
handler delivers a speech from the front porch of a supporter in 1935.
elow. Chandler's hero Uncle Charley Moran (the umpire) watches
ardinal pitching great Dizzy Dean score a run in St. Louis in the thirties.
Russ Maxwell, East St. Louis Journal)

Chandler in the governor's mansion reviewing a campaign poster in the thirties. *(Eugene Smith-Post)*

The youngest governor in America is all smiles on his inauguration day in 1935. Mama is to Chandler's left and beside her is his father, Joe.

A reflective moment for the governor and Mrs. Chandler.

Chandler, family and friends pose in front of a marlin he caught on vacation in the thirties. *(Burwell Photos, Ft. Lauderdale, FL)*

Above. Chandler at the 1938 Kentucky Derby won by Lawrin. Included in the group are his daughter Mimi Chandler and the winning jockey, Eddie Arcaro (second from right). *Below.* Two colorful personalities meet on Chandler's 1938 trip to Hollywood: The governor and Mickey Rooney.

The celebrated incident at Latonia Racetrack during Chandler's 1938 senate campaign against incumbent Alben Barkley (climbing into car) when the governor was accused of riding in President Roosevelt's car uninvited.

Rudy Vallee interrupts the governor's dance with Loretta Young on Chandler's 1938 junket to Hollywood for the premiere of *Oh Kentucky*.

Above. Major Joe Burman (right), a long-time friend and golf partner, spends a day with Chandler at the links.

Opposite page, top. Mama prepares herself to fill in for Chandler on a radio broadcast after he was poisoned in the senate race.

Opposite page, bottom. The governor singing at a picnic of the Kentucky Colonels in 1938.

Right. Escaping from the travails of his office, Chandler enjoys a day at the shooting range in French Lick, Indiana in 1937. *(Edgar C. Schmid, French Lick Springs, IN)*

Above. War time senator Chandler addressing troops at Santa Anita Racetrack in 1943. *Below.* The congressional tour of American installations during World War II stops at Kun Ming, China. From left: Chinese official, Claire Chenault, James M. Mead, Henry Cabot Lodge, Chandler, Chinese general, General Joe Stilwell, Richard B. Russell, Ralph Brewster, John Elliott Rankin.

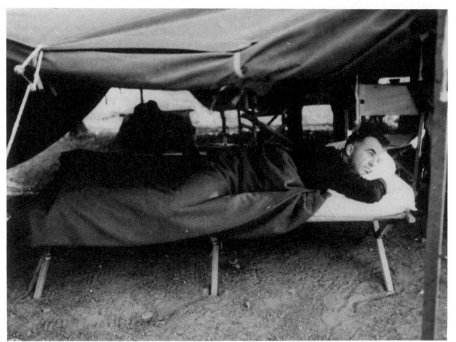

Above. The morning sun in Australia shines through the tent of Senator Chandler during his 1943 war tour. (Signal Corps Photo) *Below.* The newly appointed junior senator from Kentucky hands Vice President John Garner (middle) and senior Kentucky senator Alben Barkley a twist of burley tobacco as a "down home" souvenir in 1939. *(International News Photo)*

Above. Chandler with Major Stanley Black (middle) and aide looking through opening in Dover castle toward Calais on war tour in 1943. *(Signal Corps Photo) Below.* Senator Chandler touring hospital with New Guinea native and Lieutenant Lilla Anderson in 1943 outside of Port Moresby, New Guinea.

Chandler displays his pitching form shortly after being named baseball commissioner in 1945.

Connie Mack—the winningest manager in baseball history—and Baseball Commissioner Happy Chandler.

Right. Chandler with President Truman and New York Yankee owner Del Webb on opening day 1948 in Washington between the Yankees and Senators. *(AP Wirephoto)*

Below. Baseball Commissioner Happy Chandler visits with Charlie Cronin (left) of the Philadelphia Phillies at a game in Cincinnati.

Above. The Leo Durocher of the eighties, Billy Martin, with Chandler in 1984. *(Richard Collins, Pt. Washington, NY)*

Left. New York Yankee outfielder Dave Winfield congratulates Chandler at Cooperstown on being elected to the Baseball Hall of Fame. *(Richard Collins, Mineola, NY)*

Above. Chandler being sworn in as governor of Kentucky for the second time in 1955. *Below.* Seats were hard to come by at Chandler's 1955 inauguration.

Above. The boom for the White House started during the 1955 inauguration. *(Herald-Leader) Below.* An enthusiastic crowd greets Chandler at the 1956 Democratic National Convention, where he was seeking the nomination for president. At his back: Art Buchwald and his trademark cigar.

Two old pals, Chandler and one of his favorite dogs, Champ.

Above. Elizabeth Taylor and Montgomery Clift take a break from the filming of *Raintree County* in Kentucky to meet Mama (right end).
Below. The Chandler family gathers for dinner at the governor's mansion in the fifties.

Above. Four Kentucky governors at Demo rally. From left: Julian Carroll, Ned Breathitt, Chandler, and Bert Combs. *(Steve Mitchell, Frankfort, KY) Below.* On their European trip in 1957 the Chandlers and Colonel John Gottlieb and his wife Betty meet Pope Pius XII.

Above. Chandler family at the 1955 Inaugural Ball. From left: Dorothy Epes (Mrs. Chandler's sister), Marcella Chandler Miller, Thomas Miller, Mimi Chandler Lewis, Virginia Watkins (Mrs. Chandler's mother), J.J. Lewis, Mildred Chandler, Lee Gregg (Marcella's daughter), Governor Chandler, Davis Miller, and Cathe Gregg. *Below.* Jack Lemmon and Peter Falk take time out during the filming of *The Great Race* to share some laughs with Chandler.

Above. Selling a pig at a livestock auction in Paris, Kentucky, stockyards in 1942 is auctioneer-for-a-day Happy Chandler. *(Signal Corps Photo) Below*. Chandler reading in the library of his sumptuous two-story guest house behind the main house.

Above. From left: Baseball Commissioner Bowie Kuhn, Hall of Famer Bob Feller, Chandler, and Vice President George Bush at the 1981 All-Star game in Cleveland. *(Richard Collins, Mineola, NY) Below.* Accepting an invitation from the people of Hyden, Kentucky—a long-time Republican stronghold—Richard Nixon makes his first public appearance after his resignation with Chandler in 1978.

Above. Christie, the artist, working on a portrait of Mama. *Below.* The Chandlers with boxing promoter Don King (third, left), Joe Namath (second, right), and others at Happy's roast in Lexington.

Above. Canadian Premier Pierre Trudeau and Chandler at the 1982 baseball All-Star game in Montreal. *(Richard Collins, Pt. Washington, NY)*

Below. Bob Hope and Chandler take a break during a charity golf match at Bright Leafs Golf Club in Harrodsburg, Kentucky in the seventies.

Above. Chandler on Lexington television in 1988 explaining his alleged racial slur. *Below.* Chandler enjoys a quiet moment with his newspaper during the height of the Watergate scandal in the early seventies.

Two music buffs, jazz musician Al Hirt
and "soloist" Happy Chandler.

Chandler and Rosalynn Carter campaigning
for her husband in Lexington during the
1976 presidential race.

Opposite page, top. Muhammad Ali precedes Chandler
into a press conference where the former boxing great
defended Chandler after his controversial remark at
a University of Kentucky trustees meeting in 1988.

Opposite page, bottom. The former baseball commissioner
poses with two of the games greatest, Willie Mays (left)
and Roy Campanella, at Caesar's Tahoe in 1984.

The former governor, senator, baseball commissioner, and current University of Kentucky trustee and Mama—married on November 12, 1925.

I phoned Secretary of War Henry L. Stimson and reminded him I held a reserve officer's commission in the Judge Advocate General's Department of the Army. "When do you want me to report for duty?"

Secretary Stimson listened quietly. In a moment he said, "What I need now more than another captain in the JAG is a Senator who's working full-time at his job. Stay where you are, Senator Chandler. You're helping win the war."

In floor debate I found myself challenging the basic Allied strategy of the war. The United States should shift more forces to the Pacific theatre. Else, I argued, there was grave danger the Japanese might string together enough island victories they could directly attack our West Coast. I knew I was speaking for a substantial segment of American opinion.

I laid out my views in a three-hour Senate speech. None of my colleagues refuted me. But Winston Churchill appeared next day before a joint session of Congress, and took an oblique poke at me. "Lots of people can make good plans for winning the war," he growled, "if they have not got to carry them out." Then he came over to my side, at least tacitly endorsing my argument. "Britain," he promised, "will fight on against Japan as long as blood flows through our veins."

While I was tied up in Washington, Mama took our two daughters and lit out for California. Marcella was just at the age to fall in love with a man in uniform. She got herself engaged to a pilot. Mama and Mimi went with her to the West Coast for the wedding, a few weeks before her husband was expected to ship out with his B-29 crew.

Hollywood once again wanted Mimi to take a screen test. Buddy De Sylva called her a triple-threat—singer, dancer, and dandy little actress. She deserved her break. So Mama rented out our house in Versailles, parked Ben and Dan at a ranch school in Arizona, and went to Hollywood as Mimi's chaperone. I think Twentieth Century-Fox would have signed up Marcella, too, if she hadn't been too involved in being a wartime bride.

"Happy, I think I'll see you as often in California as I do here at home—three or four times a year," Mama told me, explaining her Hollywood decision. I couldn't argue about that; and it turned out I got to California on Senate business every now and then. In addition to the Alaskan trip, which included a few days in Los Angeles, I was in charge of a survey of the treatment of Japanese-Americans interned on the West Coast. That also gave me a chance to visit her.

Mimi and Mama attended a lot of movie star parties. Cary Grant sat down next to Mimi at Elsa Maxwell's place when she was playing the piano and singing. "Gee," he said, "you ought to be in pictures." Mimi gave him her dazzling smile. "I am."

She appeared in several films, starring as the teenage girlfriend in the Henry Aldrich series. She had a good role in *And The Angels Sing*. Mama got a Hollywood job, too, contracting to read books and hunch Twentieth Century-Fox on possible movies from the novels.

A wartime romance interrupted Mimi's movie career. She, too, fell in love with an aviator. She met him at the Palm Springs Air Force base where he was a fellow pilot of Marcella's husband. The studio forbade Mimi, their budding starlet, to get married. She's a feisty one; never in her life had she been stopped by the word "no." She chucked her contract, and at seventeen married her pilot. When her husband's squadron was shipped out to the Pacific theatre, Mimi and Mama came back to Versailles. Sad to relate, neither of those two marriages lasted very long.

I had a steady stream of visitors from Kentucky, naturally. Every now and then came my friend Joe Burman, the state police major.

We were having dinner together one evening at the Mayflower Hotel. He left the table for the men's room and was gone so long that I went to see what happened to him. I discovered that plenty had.

Joe suffered from an enlarged prostate. A year or two later that developed into cancer and took him quickly. That night he was making water slowly. Some drunk was in the men's room, staring at Joe.

"You son of a bitch," said the drunk. "You should have gone to the ladies' room."

"What did you say?" said Joe.

"Don't you understand English?"

"Yeah, I do . . . but would you mind repeating that?"

The drunk did.

"I thought that was what you said," said Joe.

He reached over and took off the fellow's glasses, took hold of his tie and hit him in the nose. The drunk collapsed on the floor. Joe lifted him up gently, measured him and smashed him in the nose again.

I arrived about that time. "Please, get me outta here," the drunk begged. "He's gonna kill me!" Joe smashed his nose again. The broken nose was gushing blood. That incident took a little smoothing over. The assistant manager helped me get the guy in a cab, and I paid his restaurant tab. Nothing more came of it.

Major Burman was small but tough. "I could have whipped Jack Dempsey in there tonight," he observed. "Didn't I ever tell you I'm the best little shithouse fighter in the United States?"

At the Mayflower I developed a close friendship with Colonel John Gottlieb, who was a graduate of West Point and came from a family that had trucking and laundry interests in Chicago. He was a fine Jewish boy. Ordinarily I didn't cotton to them, but he was living at the Mayflower and we were together a lot. His wife was in Florida and mine was in Kentucky so we often went to dinner, especially across the street at Fan and Bill's.

He knew people everywhere. He was wealthy and lived the role. He was on excellent terms with Chicago newspaper writers, especially Irv Kupcinet. He was a close friend of Phil Wrigley, who owned the Chicago Cubs. He knew the Comiskeys, also baseball people.

Colonel Gottlieb was more responsible than anyone else, I believe, for first suggesting that I ought to be baseball commissioner. I know he put that bug in Larry MacPhail's ear.

I had gone to Washington, of course, as merely a temporary senator. My appointment to succeed Senator Logan was only until an election could be held back home for the unexpired portion of his term, two years. That election, in 1940, was easy. I whipped Louisville Mayor Charles Farnsley in the primary and swamped Walter B. Smith in the general election, 561,151 to 401,812.

But in 1942, when I ran for a full six-year term as senator, the campaign was hectic and seemed much tougher, coming right in the middle of the war.

My old political adversary John Y. Brown Sr. jumped in and filed in the Democratic primary. He set out to unseat me any way he could.

We've had a curious Damon and Pythias relationship over the years. We were contemporaries in age and sprang from the same hard-scrabble heritage in western Kentucky. John Y. bragged about being born on the wrong side of the tracks. He was smart and clever, and became probably the greatest criminal lawyer Kentucky ever produced.

That didn't keep him from being nasty in politics. He scrambled around to try to find any kind of ammunition that would knock me out of my Senate seat.

I was in Washington when the reporters came in and hit me with the hot issue he had found—the swimming pool in my backyard in Versailles.

Old John Y. wanted it to be a big scandal. It wasn't. To hear him tell it, this was the second battle of the Marne, and we were losing.

The facts were simple. Ben Collings and his wife went to school with me. He was a contractor in Lexington. We've always been friends. They didn't have any children and I had four. Ben and his wife would come visit us here, go with us to the games at the University. His wife had money. One day he told Mama: "I'm going to come up here and build a pool for your kids." It was about the only pool in town, and usually was overflowing with neighborhood youngsters.

Ah ha!, said John Y., Collings used restricted war materials in building the pool.

I called that bluff, suggesting that the Truman Senate Investigating Committee make a formal inquiry into these purely political allegations.

I went to Senator Hatch, chairman of our ethics committee. "If I have done anything wrong," I said, "you won't have to convict me of a damn thing, I'll resign. Find out!"

The *Courier-Journal* went crazy. You'd have thought I'd stole the capitol.

Of course, nothing ever came of it. The Truman committee found that Collings' men had used restricted materials—five or six brass lane markers that cost about a dollar and a quarter apiece!

"You can have 'em" I said. "Take 'em out. Let old John Y. take 'em out."

That ended that. It was the only issue in the campaign. John Y. carried only one county in Kentucky in that primary. They counted him sixteen votes ahead of me in Letcher county. I didn't believe that. I know they stole that county; I believed it then and I believe it now. But it didn't matter. I just washed him out.

And I didn't have any trouble at all in the November general election. I swamped the Republican, Richard J. Colbert.

When we weren't feuding over politics, John Y. Sr. and I were pretty good companions. We've visited a lot over the years. My boy Dan and his son John Y. Jr. were thrown together so much as youngsters they developed a strong friendship that has lasted into adult life.

Lot of tragedy in life for John Y. Sr. His wife divorced him three times. Each time she'd sell all the furniture. She came from a family that seemed to produce odd people. Unfortunately she also had a problem with the bottle. His pretty and daring daughter tried in the 1960s to fly the Atlantic in a balloon and disappeared over the ocean. Oddly enough, his son, John Y. Jr., achieved the goal that eluded the old man—a term as Kentucky governor.

Some mornings Mama and I would sit down at the breakfast table and see John Y. Sr. parking his car and coming for an unannounced visit. He was articulate, interesting, a crack storyteller. He came often. One night a few years ago he stopped by for about an hour to chat. Next morning we got news he'd wrecked his car and was in bad shape. He was better than eighty then, and he was hurt so bad they couldn't pull him through.

In a peculiar way in 1942 I became the newspaper publisher in my hometown. It was a little weekly called *The Woodford Sun* that had been in the Bowmar family since the late 1800s. People used to joke that it was so skinny you could throw the paper up in the air and read it all before it hit the ground. It had been run by brothers Dan and Atcheson Bowmar for sixty years. Atcheson lived across Elm Street from me.

He came over one evening not long after his brother died.

"For sixty years," he told me, "I have been at the same

place. I have been folding those papers through the window to Dan, and I still keep doing it, but he's gone. I've got to get away from that place. I want to sell the paper to you."

I said, "Mr. Atchie, I can't run the paper. I'm in the United States Senate, and I'm not a newspaperman anyhow. I tell you what I'll do. I'll buy it if you'll run it for me."

"I'm sorry. I can't do it. I want to get away."

"All right, what do you want for it?"

He said $12,500 and I bought it. The same year I bought a similar sheet at Midway, *The Bluegrass Clipper,* for a thousand dollars. It was not easy to find an editor and manager, but we kept the *Sun* going. It was only a little proposition; maybe a thousand subscribers. Finally I gave all the stock to Mama. She split it between our two sons. Luckily, Ben about 1955 took over running the paper and has made a real go of it. He bought out Dan's stock in the seventies, and now controls the whole operation. He's developed it into a million dollar proposition.

Mama may have hung on to a share or two of stock for sentimental reasons. And she keeps her hand in at the *Sun* by writing a weekly opinion column. Some of her talent seems to have rubbed off on Ben, too. He's a fine newspaperman.

In recollection, it seems that I had many visits and conversations with President Roosevelt. I was not a blind follower of him. When he said "my friends" a million suckers jumped in the pond. He fooled a lot of folks.

Once Roosevelt told me he was not going to run for a third term. "Somebody else ought to run," he said, "but I ought to be Secretary of State. I know more about foreign policy than anybody else living."

"Mr. President, I don't blame you. Keep going like you are now, it'll kill you. This is a frightful job. It's an awesome responsibility and you're not rugged. You haven't got rugged health. Takes a fellow who's a glutton for punishment and a rugged character, you know, to put up with this. I think you are right. You ought to make arrangements with your successor to be Secretary of State, if that's what you want."

He was just talking. He wanted to be President. As the facts show. Never envisioned any successor. The fourth term, and then how many more, if he had lived . . . .

One evening F.D.R. invited me to the White House while Winston Churchill was visiting him. We got together in the upstairs apartment and talked for about an hour.

The Prime Minister held a glass in his hand, looking pleased.

"Your President has taught me to drink Old Fashioneds."

He was dribbling ashes from his long, black cigar. I thought he looked like he had been through the rough. And he didn't give a damn either. He didn't care. But he held your attention. He was an instant character, like John Nance Garner. He was compelling. If he talked to you, you wanted to listen to him. And you couldn't tell what he was going to say next. He didn't know either, but whatever he was going to say, he was going to say it.

Churchill wasn't a military genius but he was the toughest fellow for his side that I ever saw. He handled Roosevelt easily. Roosevelt was the most ambitious man that I've met in my life and Churchill made him think he was going to be President of the United States of the World. And he thought he was going to be, too.

Churchill always depreciated his own efforts and magnified Roosevelt's in public speeches and everywhere. Like saying, President Roosevelt did this, and I was his lieutenant. Sir Winston always put himself down. I don't blame him, because the British were living on their wits. I never permitted anybody in my presence to criticize Hitler for not invading England. He thought of fifteen ways to land an army in England, but he didn't see any way to feed them after he got them there, or to get them out.

England was prostrate. They couldn't stop anybody. Hitler decided to pick up all he had and go and fight the Russians, and he was right about that. But the Russians strung him out and burned the ground ahead of him, and he just didn't make it. But if he had made Stalingrad, he would have turned around and said, "I've got you!" And it would have been all over. We wouldn't have gone into the thing. It wouldn't have been effective. We couldn't have kept the British from going under.

Beyond doubt my greatest Senate experience was being assigned to accompany four other Senators on a round-the-world warfront inspection. Our purpose was to secure firsthand information from the various theatres of operations as to provisions being made for the health and well-being of our troops, as well as finding out what the men were thinking and talking about, the conditions of their morale, the suitability of the tools of war being produced at such great effort and expense, and the general effectiveness with which the war was being prosecuted.

We scheduled a take-off from Washington on July 25, 1943, expecting to travel about forty thousand miles and return in sixty-three days. Others designated as committee members were Dick Russell of Georgia, chairman; Henry Cabot Lodge Jr. of Massachusetts, James M. Mead of New York, and Ralph O. Brewster of Maine.

Imagine my surprise when our pilot met us at the plane. He walked up, greeting me with a friendly big grin. It was Major Henry Myers again! The decorated pilot who had saved our skin on that stormy flight out to the Aleutian Islands. Was I ever relieved to see him in charge of our airship. And it was quite a plane—a four-motored converted Liberator bomber named "The Guess Where 2," and called by the Army a C-87.

I had managed to get the War Department to assign another Kentuckian to the flight as assistant surgeon general. He was Brigadier General Fred W. Rankin of Lexington, a cancer specialist and son-in-law of the famous Dr. Charley Mayo. Dr. Rankin had just been promoted and I had the pleasure, at thirty thousand feet over the North Atlantic, of pinning on his star.

Ours was a dramatic flight—every leg of it. From Washington we flew via Presque Isle, Maine, to an air base in Newfoundland; thence we proceeded to another airfield in Labrador. From that frozen base we flew across the awesome ice caps and peaks and glaciers of Greenland to Iceland. Then on to the United Kingdom, where we spent several days, much of the time with our Eighth Air Force.

Prime Minister Churchill arranged for us to call on him at Number 10 Downing Street. It was a conference we were all looking forward to.

The night before at our London hotel I ran into Bob Hope.

"You picked a funny time to move back home," I laughed. I knew he was born in England, with meager poor-folks prospects before he came as a boy to the United States, worked hard, and finally got his first break as a vaudeville song-and-dance man.

"I'm just passing through," Bob said. "We're putting on USO shows for the troops. Got a lot of fine musicians and"—he gave an exaggerated sly wink—"lots of Hollywood starlets."

I laughed, and then turned serious.

"Do you know Winston Churchill?"

"Know Churchill? You gotta be kiddin'! A shanty mutt like me!"

"Okay," I said. "I'll introduce you. We're meeting him tomorrow at ten. Be ready. I'll have the military aide pick you up. I'll take you along."

Wisely, I didn't mention to United States Ambassador Winant that I was adding an unofficial supernumerary to our contingent. He would have cancelled the arrangement. He wouldn't let me bring Bob.

But when we formed up in the receiving line at the Prime Minister's house, Bob was right with me. Churchill's aide was making the introductions.

"Mr. Churchill, this is Senator Chandler from Kentucky."

"Oh, yes, I remember him well."

We shook hands.

"Mr. Prime Minister," I said, pulling Bob forward, "this is Bob Hope."

"How do you do, Mr. Hope?" Churchill said courteously. And then he took a startled second look, like what the hell was this fellow doing here.

While the official Senatorial delegation repaired to the garden for about an hour's conference with Churchill, Bob was adroitly shuffled into Sir Winston's office to wait for us. When I saw him later, he said: "I had a fine time. I amused myself trying on Churchill's hat for size. Sat in his chair. Geez, he's messy for a bigwig—got cigar ashes sprinkled all over everything. Hey, I stole a souvenir—one of his little note pads."

From a gigantic airport in southwest England, "The Guess Where 2" took off at midnight for Marrakech, in Morocco. We spent more than a week in North Africa, visiting all of the important cities and troop concentrations on the Mediterranean, as well as the scene of the terrible desert fighting just weeks earlier. One soldier handed me a battlefield souvenir—a German helmet still marked by blood stains. I brought it back to Versailles as a memento.

One morning in Tunis, I emerged from our quarters, a cottage on the beach, and spotted General Jimmy Doolittle splashing in the surf. With him was another man in bathing trunks. I recognized him instantly.

I filled my lungs and began singing loud so they could hear me. "You'll never know just how much I love you....You'll never know just how much I care...."

That was as far as I got before Bob Hope turned around.

"Happy," he screamed. "What are you doing here?"

"Still inspecting. Talking to the GIs. The brass. Looking everything over...And you?"

"Our troupe's putting on a USO show tonight. Do these GIs eat it up. You'd think they'd never seen legs before! Do you know General Doolittle?"

The general nodded, sticking out his hand. "Oh sure. We got acquainted in Washington. Good to see you, Senator."

Bob grinned. "Old Happy here was singing our theme song. I don't know which of us started it. But whenever I hear 'You'll never know...' I know all right. It's gotta be Happy!"

Bob put on a great show that night for the soldiers. He picked out one little dancer on stage, dragged her up to the mike and said with his fake leer: "Honey, that's enough dancin' for tonight. You go on back there to my dressing room, slip into something comfortable, and freshen up....I'll be along bye and bye."

His all-male audience roared with delight.

One thing I can say about Bob, he never told smutty stories. And he was a good family man. Mama and I are crazy about his wife Dolores. Bob likes a ribald story, and tells them well. But never have I heard him descend to smutty humor. That's not true of a lot of entertainers. I was once trapped at a Las Vegas show, jammed in where I couldn't get out. Johnny Carson was on stage. Unfortunately, he had a filthy mouth. I can't go that. Thank goodness Bob doesn't either.

Leaving Cairo, we travelled across Arabia to Basra and Abadan on the Persian Gulf. We talked to our men who were assembling and delivering to the Russians vast quantities of war materials under lend-lease. I don't know how they could stand the torrid weather. The thermometer was way over one hundred at midday, and it didn't cool off much at night. I was afraid the older senators might keel over.

Next stop for "The Guess Where 2" was Karachi on the west coast of India. We flew on to New Delhi. There I met an old friend and a new enemy. The friend was Colonel Gottlieb, my Mayflower Hotel companion, who was now on active duty in India. The enemy was a bug, an intestinal virus. All of the senators came down with it. They call it Delhi Belly.

Usually my stomach is made of cast-iron, but it seemed hard to find anything to eat in India that wouldn't upset you. Colonel Gottlieb came to my rescue. He had a case of American-canned grapefruit juice. I drank it all—the whole case. It got me through India.

At the airport as we prepared to depart and fly over the Burma "Hump" into China, I gave Colonel Gottlieb a goodbye handshake.

"Don't leave me here, Happy," he said. "Take me back with you."

"Why, Colonel, if you're assigned here—that's bound to be where the Army needs you."

"But, I want to go home."

"Sorry, my friend."

"All right," Gottlieb said, laughing. "From here on out you'll have to rustle your own grapefruit juice."

We stopped in Kunming and Chungking. Naturally we conferred with Generalissimo Chiang Kai-shek. He didn't make a large impression on me. Of course I had a delightful and intimate conversation with Madam Chiang, whom I knew back at Wellesley college in the 1920s as Mei-ling Soong. She was gracious and beautiful. She asked how many children I had and gave me exquisite Oriental souvenirs to take to them and to Mama. We then touched down at Calcutta on the east coast of India before proceeding on across the Bay of Bengal to Ceylon.

From that point "The Guess Where 2" was readied for an historic flight. No land plane had ever flown across the Indian Ocean. Barrels holding hundreds of gallons of reserve gasoline were loaded aboard, crowding us a trifle. Then we took off for Carnarvon, on the west coast of Australia.

Our crossing took fifteen hours and forty-five minutes. That long in those hard seats put kinks in our backs.

From Port Darwin and Townesville, we flew across the Coral Sea to General MacArthur's headquarters in New Guinea. His personality was dynamic, and winning. As ironic as his fate became, in the summer of 1943 he made a large impression. In my official report to the Senate I observed:

> The most pressing problem that confronts the people of the United States today, in my opinion, is the war in the Pacific. Last Spring we asked that greater emphasis and more consideration be given to the war by our master strategists. There is no question but that up to that time the Pacific has been treated as secondary and as a holding operation. The Japanese are our toughest enemy. Their strength was greatly underestimated by the American people. They were strong on land, at sea and in the air. Their production of ships and planes has been greatly underestimated.
>
> General MacArthur, in his campaign in the Pacific, is on the offensive, but is limited by supplies and equipment, and needs more support. General MacArthur, according to some of our ablest military leaders, is a great commander. He knows where he is going, and, if he is given material and equipment, he will bring about a victory for us sooner than we would otherwise gain it.
>
> The operation in the Pacific seems to be one operation and should be co-ordinated under one head. MacArthur seems to be the best qualified man to lead the offensive, and, by his courageous exploits so far, he has shown himself entitled to the respect and support of the American people.

We stopped again in Australia, and went on to New Caledonia. We headed home across the Pacific, stopping at Fiji Islands, Samoa, Christmas Island and Hawaii on our way to Los Angeles.

Everybody knew that flying never really has been comfortable for me. Dick Russell observed with a wry grin that I was always the last one to come aboard "The Guess Where 2" and the first one off when we landed. That was about right, but I did have a lot of confidence in our pilot. He was a steady man.

When our big Liberator rolled to a stop at the Long Beach flying base, Major Myers caught me as I was starting out the door of the plane. He popped off a snappy salute. "Well, Senator...Once again I got you there and back—safely."

"That's wonderful...wonderful." I was hardly listening to him. I was craning my neck, looking eagerly all around the tarmac.

Abruptly I grabbed his arm and flashed him a happy smile. "Hey....Come out here with me. Meet somebody who appreciates your being a safe pilot as much as I do....Major, you'll probably get a big kiss!"

I had just spotted Mama standing at the hangar door, waiting for me.

15

Goodbye Senator—
Hello Baseball Czar

My office got an urgent call from Cleveland in the late afternoon of February 25, 1945, and sent a Senate page to summon me from the floor. At about four o'clock I picked up the phone and heard Larry MacPhail of the New York Yankees say hello.

"Senator, we've just unanimously elected you high commissioner of baseball, and they told me to call and ask if you would take it."

"My Lord, Larry . . . ." I hesitated. This offer did not come out of the blue. Larry had mentioned the possibility. We sometimes visited, went to a game or the races together. I had met him years earlier when he was running the Cincinnati Reds. Judge Landis, who was commissioner twenty-four years, had been dead just four months.

The major league owners were just then convened at Cleveland to try to solve war-time baseball problems and see if they could settle on a successor for Landis. Many prominent national figures were considered. Larry had put my name on the list.

"Larry, the war's not over yet. I know America will win—on both fronts. I just don't know when. But I can't quit, I can't leave the Senate until we whip our enemies.'

MacPhail was ready for that. "Well, Senator," he said, "we'll make arrangements for you to take the appointment and let time pass and see what happens. As I told you, the salary is fifty thousand a year, and expenses."

No question about it—money was important to me. As a Senator I received $10,000 a year. The governor's office paid $6,500. I had never made any big money in public service. This was a rare opportunity to build up a nest egg for my family. I didn't want to pass it by.

So I accepted the offer—with the understanding that I would not actively serve until I could in good conscience resign from the Senate. That was all right with the baseball owners.

I didn't know, unfortunately, I was stepping into a snake-pit.

My decision to leave the Senate turned out to be more emotional and traumatic than I had anticipated. They say the United States Senate is the world's greatest club, and it certainly was that for me. There I developed deep, sincere and enduring friendships with some of the noblest fellows who ever served their country.

When I stood on the Senate floor to announce that I had accepted the baseball offer, making sort of a farewell speech and thanking everybody, my voice got a little husky, they say, and I know my eyes were misty. There were friends there I hated to leave; and a bunch of them got a little emotional too, standing up to commend my service in the Senate. I remember high tributes from Harry Byrd and Carter Glass of Virginia, and Hiram Johnson of California, and quite a few others. I was touched by Harry Byrd's unusual gesture of friendship; he leaned over and kissed me on the cheek! Lordy, Lordy . . . I'll never forget that!

Hiram Johnson walked off the floor with his arm around me. His wife was waiting, as she always did, at the lobby door. She told me that she was sorry I was leaving the Senate. She stepped over and hugged me. "You have always been so good to Senator Johnson," she said. I saw tears in her eyes; she was a luv. I did greatly admire Senator Johnson, who became frail and finally died in August while I was still in the Senate. The next time I was in California I went to his grave and knelt and said a little prayer.

Senate affairs kept me heavily occupied into the summer of 1945. However, I knew that the war would not last much longer—and I knew exactly why. I was one of the few who knew the government was desperately working to create the atomic bomb. That was one of the best-kept secrets in American history.

My involvement came through Jimmy Byrnes. He was a great public man—Governor of South Carolina, United States Senator, Associate Justice of the Supreme Court, a position which he resigned to become War Mobilization Director. He was F.D.R.'s strong right arm, especially on Capitol Hill.

President Roosevelt requested a special appropriation of four billion dollars for something known as the "Manhattan Project." The President had classified it Top Secret, and said the nature of this giant expenditure was too sensitive to tell. He had imparted the secret only to Senator McKellar of Tennessee, chairman of the Appropriations Committee, and two or three other legislators.

The White House knew I was a pay-as-you-go advocate, and quite vocal on the Senate floor about the war. Roosevelt expected me to raise questions about such a tremendous expenditure—four billion dollars!—for something we couldn't be told about. Not even given a hint.

I didn't like the pig-in-a-poke mystery. "Jimmy, do I speculate on the safety and security of the American people if I don't vote for this?"

"My dear boy," said Byrnes, "I very much fear you do."

Still I had reservations. "You don't have to be in doubt," said Byrnes. "The President trusts you to keep it secret. He gave me authorization—if it had to come down to this—to tell you."

He then in private filled me in about the atomic bomb project. Naturally, the awesomeness of such a powerful weapon staggered me. Imagine a bomb with the explosive power of twenty thousand tons of TNT! It was hard to visualize—but it came as no surprise to me later when it was revealed that "Little Boy" flattened four square miles of Hiroshima, killing one hundred thousand Japanese outright, and a like number later from burns and radiation sickness. Frightful—but necessary, as everyone knows, to bring the war to a close.

"I'll go along," I told Jimmy Byrnes.

Byrnes clapped me on the back. "I'd like you to tell the President." He quickly got F.D.R. on the phone, and I gave my pledge. The four billion item was adopted in McKellar's appropriation bill.

As we know from history, the Manhattan Project scientists were able to assure Roosevelt just before he went to the Yalta conference in February, 1945, that they had solved their problems and could now construct the nuclear bomb. It was barely two months later, April 12, that Franklin D. Roosevelt died at Warm Springs, Georgia.

Though definitely determined to hold my seat until both the Japs and the Nazis surrendered, I had not too many deep regrets about leaving the Senate, except for missing close friends. I had grown somewhat weary and unenthusiastic. There were ninety-six senators. You never could do anything by yourself; you had to take a dog-fall. I still sat on the back row.

Back home as governor, I could get things done—*at once.* There were plenty of people to lend the Number One man in the commonwealth a hand, do his bidding. I rode in a limousine with a state trooper at the wheel; on Washington's teeming streets I had to compete with government clerks to flag a taxicab, and that was never easy.

By May the fighting stopped in Europe. In August President Harry Truman ordered the atomic bomb dropped on Hiroshima, and three days later the second on Nagasaki. The Japanese promptly surrendered. That was in September.

On November 1, 1945, I resigned from the Senate. I did not go on baseball's payroll until the first day I took over actively as high commissioner. No double salary. That was quite a contrast to my predecessor. When Judge Landis was named commissioner, he was making $7,500 a year as federal judge. He must have had some doubts about whether he would like the change. At any rate he did not resign from the federal bench for two years, and accepted his government pay, although he deducted it from the $50,000 organized baseball was paying him.

While I was waiting—from Spring until Fall—I closely monitored the baseball world. It dawned on me that the baseball club owners actually wanted to clip the wings of Landis's successor. I knew Landis. I had spent time with him in Chicago.

He was good for baseball, actually *necessary*. But he really knew little about the game. He didn't know a baseball from a bale of hay.

He was a tough federal judge, the essence of social and political conservatism, and they needed him after the 1919 White Sox bribery scandal. The baseball owners were impressed by the fact that he fined Standard Oil eighteen or twenty million dollars. Never collected, by the way. And that he threatened to extradite the Kaiser to the United States for having sunk the *Lusitania.*

They needed a straight arrow because public confidence in the integrity of baseball—imagine players throwing a World Series!—was at a low ebb. Judge Landis even looked mean. He believed everybody had some larceny in his heart. People were scared of him. I think he made some mistakes. He should not have banished Shoeless Joe Jackson. That was a grievous error. As time passed, everyone saw that.

The owners were screwing around to diminish the new commissioner's authority. I didn't know that. Their idea was that the commissioner would merely be the administrative executive; they would do the legislating, make the rules. A lot of them were plain greedy. Looking out only for Number One, their own bank accounts. Some owners were decent and fine, men like Connie Mack and Clark Griffith, two stalwarts who come first to mind.

On July 12, 1945, the owners gathered at the Mayflower Hotel in Washington—while I was, of course, still in the Senate—to informally talk things over with me. That session began to take the scales off my eyes. And give me at least a glimpse of storm clouds on the horizon.

Alva Bradley, owner of the Cleveland Indians, cornered me. He began talking about how they had to live by their wits and bend the rules.

"We all cheat, if we have to," Bradley said, brazenly. "This fellow cheats, that fellow cheats. I cheat, too... In fact, we all cheat."

"Well, Mr. Bradley, I wish I'd known that before I signed on for this voyage because I didn't agree to leave the United States Senate to preside over a bunch of thieves... If I catch you, be prepared to belly up. I won't be easy."

The Cleveland owner didn't seem to be listening very well.
He went right on, "You've just got to learn to wink at rule
breakers."

I gave him a sharp look; probably something like Judge
Landis might have done.

"There are sixteen teams in this game," I said evenly. "If I
wink at one, I'll have to wink at fifteen others. That's not a
wink, that's a twitch . . . . When you get caught, don't crybaby.
Just come on up and take your medicine."

Sadly, I found that there were a lot of cheaters. Not the
true benefactors of the game, the great grass-roots types like
Mack and Griffith, but corporate raiders like Del Webb, Lou
Perini, Dan Topping, and Fred Saigh. More about them later.

There was such an overabundance of avarice that the majority of owners didn't want to let any stray dimes slip out of
their grasp. They wanted to deprive the commissioner's office
of control of discretionary funds earned from World Series re-
ceipts.

At the Mayflower confab, I stood up to them.

"I don't want to handicap you," I said, "but neither do I
want anybody to get the impression that I am going to let
down the bars. The rights of the players must be protected. The
stake of the fans in our game must be recognized."

They now were listening closely.

"I am going to be helpful but tough. I am going to be understanding but also firm. I was elected unanimously. When I
accepted I assumed I would have full powers and I insist upon
having full powers, and nothing short of it."

They knew, and I knew, that they had agreed in 1920 to accept every action and decision by Judge Landis without challenge, even if they believed him wrong, and to refrain from
public criticism of him, or of each other.

They made Landis the baseball czar.

I wanted the same thing. I looked at this as a lifetime job.
All my days I have been straightforward, and candid, and not
afraid to stand up to wrongdoers, and willing to say what I
think. Surprisingly, I discovered quickly that not everyone connected with organized baseball appreciated having a stand-up
guy in charge. Even while I was finishing out my time in the
Senate, and waiting to go on baseball's payroll, some secret enemies among the owners undertook a smear campaign against

me. Apparently they didn't like the idea that I'd crack down on cheaters and would not tolerate crybabies or mistreating of the players. I had been pretty candid about that—I guess they thought too outspoken.

Anyhow, in October 1945, barely six months after I'd been unanimously elected commissioner, newspapers carried a story that a few owners were proposing to buy up my contract for $350,000 and get themselves a new man—a commissioner who would not be a czar but somebody more pliable. There were supposed to be three ringleaders of this scheme to decapitate me before I even took control. They were not named, but I was beginning to get an idea of which clubs didn't want the kind of commissioner they could see I intended to be.

Even at that early stage I began to get criticism from some of the sports writers, especially the New York crowd. But I had some defenders, too, on the sports pages. Joe Williams, the well-respected columnist for the *New York World-Telegram,* was critical of the anti-Chandler smear. "There is something malevolent about the attacks on him," Williams wrote. "Is this a calculated attempt to drive Chandler out of baseball scarcely before he enters it? . . . He's been around long enough to know what small minds with envious souls will attempt. Today he has the best job in baseball. What rankles is that others wanted it and didn't get it."

After fingering the evil of jealousy, Joe Williams ridiculed the owners for taking cognizance of the rumor my contract might be bought up, writing:

> They issued a formal denial. They did it with characteristic stupidity. First, they admitted the rumor was ridiculous, and then proceeded to dignify it with a denial.
>
> But it was probably a healthy thing at that. It will help to put an end to such silly speculation. If Chandler needed a new vote of confidence, this was it.
>
> I'm on Chandler's side for two reasons: (1) I don't believe he got a square deal up to now; (2) I feel he has the stuff to make a fine commissioner. . . . He's got everything Landis ever had, plus forthrightness in public and genuine friendliness. Give the guy a chance.

Of course, I had plenty of sports page critics, but there were many going to bat for me. Columnist Vincent X. Flaherty in the *Washington Times Herald* welcomed me like this:

> Baseball is to be congratulated because Chandler, I am certain, will write a new and golden chapter for it, surpassing anything and everything that has gone before- . . . . Chandler will not be another Landis. . . . I conscientiously believe Happy will be a greater influence on the game. . . . Happy is no stuffed shirt. He is a brilliant, vibrant, indefatigable young man of 46 and behind those smiling blue eyes there is a great, vivid and wonderfully balanced mind.

By the time the sharpies opened fire on me, Vince had moved on to the *Los Angeles Examiner,* where his column protested: "Chandler will do all right. He has a keen mind, tremendous energy and a wonderful enthusiasm for baseball. Give the guy time."

The owners made one change that I couldn't do anything about. They revised the method of electing a high commissioner. This had been accomplished by majority vote; in the future, election would require approval by three-fourths of the owners, in other words twelve affirmative ballots.

That change set up my Waterloo.

Soon after Landis died in November, 1944, the grapevine sprouted a long list of possible successors—Jim Farley, J. Edgar Hoover, Fred Vinson, Fiorello La Guardia, even Ford Frick, president of the National League. One reason Larry MacPhail put me on the list was because he felt organized baseball needed someone who had influence and knew the ropes in Washington. Wartime restrictions were pinching all of us, businessman and citizen alike. But the government closely scrutinized baseball, many officials regarding it as just a pastime, and not essential.

Teams were struggling along with old men and 4-F youngsters—some of whom were being reclassified as fit for military duty. The travel ban was tight. Ever present was the threat that the major leagues might be shut down for the duration. I spoke out against any such action, saying: "It's foolish to discount the value of baseball as a morale factor."

I had demonstrated my Washington influence in 1943 by getting President Roosevelt to invite a delegation of baseball owners to the White House so they could have their say. In his best day, would old New Deal-hater Landis have done something like that?

There was no reason to keep the baseball commissioner's office in Chicago. It was there just because that was the judge's hometown.

I selected Cincinnati as the new site. I took a modest suite of three offices on the twenty-sixth floor of the Carew Tower. My window had an inspiring and beautiful view. Directly across the Ohio River, I could see "the promised land"— Kentucky, where my heart will ever be. I had my big oak desk placed catty-cornered across the back end of the room so that every time I looked up my eyes were feasting on the Kentucky landscape.

Just at the start of 1946—when I had been on the job barely two months—all hell broke loose.

Within six months I was scrambling to cope with three critical challenges to my baseball czardom.

The rich and colorful Jorge Pasquel saw the post-war upheaval when baseball veterans were coming back from the military as an opportunity to grab American players for his Mexican League. He was handsome, canny, articulate, and eccentric enough to sometimes go around wearing a silver encrusted gaucho gunbelt with two gleaming pistols in his holsters.

Bringing satchels of greenbacks and his four brothers, Pasquel swept north across the Rio Grande for his great "beisbol" raid.

Mexico was "beisbol" crazy. Hiring American stars would not only be a business coup, Pasquel thought, but also a political boost for his friend Miguel Aleman, who had just been elected president of Mexico.

Typically the Pasquels would summon a player like Stan Musial of the St. Louis Cardinals to their hotel room and toss piles of hundreds and fifties on the bed. "We want you to play in Mexico," Jorge would say. "Name your price, señor."

Unfortunately, we were not then paying our big-time players enough. Stan Musial was getting $13,500 a season. The lure of big bucks had to be tempting to a lot of our fellows.

They say Jorge Pasquel got Ted Williams up to his room and handed him a blank check. "Fill in how much you want," said the Mexican multimillionaire.

Williams, according to the story, studiously looked over the check, front and back. He was laughing up his sleeve.

"Wait a minute," said Williams, "what about letting me take four strikes, instead of three?"

Jorge didn't even blink. "Si, si."

Smiling, Ted Williams handed back the check. "Just joking. I really am not interested in playing in the Mexican League."

But about twenty Americans were. One defector was Max Lanier, the Cardinals' leading pitcher; he jumped south of the border in the Spring, and threw a scare into the St. Louis drive for the National League flag. Vern Stephens, the Browns' shortstop and one of the hottest batsmen in the majors, jumped—and jumped back after only two games. His was an unusual case, because being involved in a contract dispute, he was not signed when he took off for Mexico. I learned later why he came back—their diet of beans and tortillas and their casual lifestyle was too much for him. He complained that the Mexican spectators thought nothing of relieving themselves against the outfield wall. Other defectors included Danny Gardella and Sal Maglie from the Giants, along with Fred Martin and the redoubtable Mickey Owen.

Poor Mickey. He was a real star for the Dodgers, one of the best catchers who ever put on a mitt, a durable fella and a good guy. But jumping South of the Border was his second big mistake. He was already the "goat" of the 1941 World Series, having let a last-out third-strike slip by him in the fourth game. His blooper permitted the Yankees to go on and take the series from Brooklyn.

The Pasquels installed Mickey as player-manager of the Vera Cruz team. It didn't turn out to be what he expected. At the end of the year they fired him, and he was out on a big limb.

They were playing crazy baseball in Mexico. Not the same kind of rules we use. The Pasquels just made a show out of the game.

The Mexican League brazenly juggled its outstanding players. One week one team would be on top and another on the bottom. The Pasquels would take the stars off the top team and exchange them for losing players. Their idea of "beisbol" was simply stupid.

These raids were serious. Mickey Owen, just out of the Navy, jumped to Mexico strictly for the money. I knew a lot of other major league players were tempted.

The high commissioner would have to stop these raids. So I faced up to my first crisis. I had to be tough enough to defuse the Pasquel enticement. Somebody suggested slapping all the defectors with a one-year suspension from organized baseball.

"I'm afraid that wouldn't work," I said. "Some of these fellows would take a gamble. They'd only risk losing one season in the United States. That might not stop them."

Finally I made the decision: "Any player who breaks his contract and violates the reserve clause is herewith suspended for five years."

That may have been harsh. But it was effective. The defections seemed to stop. Of course, it remained a volatile and touchy situation. The Pasquel brothers were totally outlaw operators, and were not at all interested in what was decent and beneficial for the major leagues in the United States. Being a realist, I had some people in Mexico trying to get the Pasquels straightened out.

Just then Sam Breadon, a hardhead and owner of the St. Louis Cardinals, took it on himself to play the Lone Ranger. True, he had some of his best players lured by Mexican bucks. But it was not an individualistic or selfish proposition; it was an evil that affected all of organized ball.

I had no idea of what Breadon was doing until I got a call from Ford Frick, president of the National League. I was in New York, attending a game at Ebbets Field. What he said startled me.

"Did you know," Frick asked, "that Sam Breadon is in Mexico?"

"No. That's news to me. Did you know about it?"

Frick said he didn't know in advance Breadon was going to Mexico, and suggested that we ought to meet with Breadon in Cincinnati on the following Monday. I agreed and sent a summons to Breadon. Frick was there on the appointed Monday, but Breadon was not.

I called Breadon. "Be in my office tomorrow," I said.

There was a pause on the telephone. "I'm not coming, Commissioner. I can't. I've given my word to the Pasquel brothers that I did not represent organized ball. If I came now, it would give the appearance that I was such a representative."

I was angry, I admit. "You should have thought of that, Mr. Breadon, before you stuck your nose into this situation and meddled. There's no telling how much damage you have done. I'm doing my best to eliminate this problem, and you have only made it worse. I don't know what the Pasquels are thinking now. The situation was looking encouraging, but I am afraid your visit will be interpreted as a sign of weakness and fear on the part of organized ball, and thus give a wrong impression. You will be hearing, sir, from this office!"

And he did—promptly.

For his refusal to report to my office I fined Breadon $5,000, suspended him from privileges of the rules for thirty days, and barred him from attending the joint league meeting scheduled to be held July 8 in Boston. Pending payment of his fine, I embargoed $35,000 which was due the St. Louis club from funds held in the commissioner's office.

Those penalties set the St. Louis owner squirming. He did not pay his fine, but showed up at the July league conference in Boston, trying to get back in good graces. He had Ford Frick and the National League legal counsel, Lou Carroll, running interference. They brought him to see me, and Breadon muttered some lame drivel about "a misunderstanding."

I looked the St. Louis owner up and down.

"Mr. Breadon, you have been a club owner and a vice president of the National League for a long time. And you know it would be impossible for the commissioner to operate his office unless his summonses are respected. I want to see you in my office next Tuesday!"

This time he didn't pussyfoot. He showed up, meek as could be. Not only that, he sent his check for the $5,000 fine. I did the best I could to straighten out his thinking. I will say that he displayed a better attitude, and so I remitted the fine, and tried to get back to the main problem—how to deal with the players who had jumped, and those that might be still tempted. One of the owners most livid over the Mexican raid was Clark Griffith, the seventy-six-year-old president of the Washington club. He was literally steaming about the Pasquels, telling reporters their attempts to sign name stars were "cheap publicity stunts." Griffith went on: "Those bush league Mexican parks can't support any such players, and you can say for me that any Washington player fool enough to fall for their propaganda deserves to end up in the outlaw Mexican League."

Just then the word was that the Mexicans were offering half a million dollars to Cleveland ace Bob Feller. He was smart enough to turn them down. They went after Hank Greenberg, the Tiger star—likewise with no success.

But of course pressure began at once, and continued, to get me to abolish the penalty I had imposed on the defectors. I felt sorry for Mickey Owen when he came back home, under suspension. His wife, a great lady, even appealed to me to reinstate him. I always admire a wife who fights for her man, but I couldn't do that.

The Mexican League mess hung on for a few years. Lawyers got into the thing. Danny Gardella went to court to challenge his banishment. So did Max Lanier and Fred Martin. Danny, who had violated his reserve clause with the Giants, sued for $300,000. Finally a United States Court of Appeals turned down Gardella's request for automatic reinstatement, sending the case back for trial on its merits.

I felt that vindicated the action I had taken. And now that the Pasquels had abandoned their foolish raiding, I could afford to be forgiving. The suspensions had been in effect three years. That was a stiff enough penalty. So on June 5, 1949, I let all the players come back.

In announcing my decision I observed that I was "tempering justice with mercy"—and that's just what I meant. But some sports writers snorted with glee that I had unlimbered an ancient platitude, a bromide, a cliché. Their chortles didn't bother me in the least; some old sayings are still pretty good. No matter how many times they have been uttered, they do the job. I couldn't help wondering if any of those reporters had spent much time reading Shakespeare or the Scriptures—and how hard they would have to work to *improve* those oft-used immortal words!

Unfortunately, Ford Frick didn't give me much help in the National League with the Mexican "beisbol" crisis. It was a time to be strong and brave. Frick and a few of the National League owners were cringing and cowering, so panicked by the damage suits of the Mexican jumpers—which ran up to close to three million dollars—that they wanted to settle out of court.

But I wasn't about to cave in—and finally came out on top. At least that was the opinion of one of the most knowledgeable

and respected sports scribes in the country, Shirley Povich of
the *Washington Post.* In a magazine article, Povich wrote:

> That's when Chandler solidified himself with most of the
> club owners—by his handling of the whole Mexican situa-
> tion. He accepted the whole responsibility at a time when
> most of the baseball men were panicked and were glad to
> lay the problem in his lap. He handled it smartly, never at
> any time permitted baseball to lose face, was willing to take
> the rap, by-passed baseball's own attorneys, got the counsel
> of John Lord O'Brien.
>
> Right then and there, Chandler earned his salary for
> the whole seven years. In lawyer O'Brien, he chose wisely.
> At a time when baseball was being sued as a trust, Chan-
> dler was hiring the man who was famous for working the
> other side of the fence as the Government's No. 1 anti-trust
> man, who knows both the questions and the answers.

Challenge Number Two came at the outset of my commis-
sionership. It developed into a problem that I never could solve.
It was as much responsible as any other factor for my being
fired.

What happened was that the New York sports writers declared open season on Happy Chandler.

Not all of them. But most of them. John Kiernan of the
New York Times and Joe Williams of the *World-Telegram* were
decent and friendly and fair. So were some others.

The baseball writers started this feud. I didn't. I was not
about to roll over and play dead. That's not my style; I'm a
fighter, partner. So I couldn't do much about their quarrel. And
their vicious attacks on me continued to the day I left the commissioner's office.

For a while I didn't understand what was happening. I always got along with the press. Not that I've always gotten a
fair shake. Even so I can count as some of the closest friends
over a long life a few outstanding reporters and editors.

The New York chapter of the Baseball Writers Association
of America invited me to speak February 3, 1946, at their banquet in Newark, New Jersey.

It hadn't occurred to me yet how the enormous contrast between myself and old Judge Landis was sending some baseball
reporters into a tizzy. I knew Landis well. He wasn't normally a
friendly fellow, but he was very friendly to me. He was hired to

look mean, and he played the part. I don't think he liked going to ball games, and didn't go very often. But I've seen pictures of him and the cameraman always seemed to catch him in the same posture.

Landis's fist would be under his chin, his white hair ruffled and flying, his face creased in an ugly scowl. Precisely what he saw going on out on the field, I can't say. I'm not sure he knew much about the game. He might have been sitting there just puzzling.

The judge didn't have much truck with reporters. And they pretty well steered clear of him.

Then along comes his successor, a man named "Happy." Happy Chandler does not frown. He smiles. He doesn't try to look mean. He laughs. Oh, he's different, all right. And perhaps the biggest and most shocking difference is that Happy sings! That floored 'em.

It all started when I stepped up to the mike at that Newark banquet, which was supposed to be in my honor. I made pretty much my usual kind of informal, down-home speech. I told how much I love Kentucky and her wonderful people, talked about the good fishing, my days as a barefoot school boy, working the tobacco patches, my experiences as a player in the minor leagues, and as an umpire in the Blue Grass League.

Of course I talked about Versailles, my home, and Mama and the children. That seemed natural. They'd invited me; they must want to know something about my ideas and background.

I was gazing on this crowd of pretty intelligent-looking men when an impulse hit me. It wasn't anything startling or new. I told them that I would wind up my remarks by singing. Of course, I have always loved to sing, and I'm a better than fair hand at it. My choice that night was *My Old Kentucky Home.*

Well, that put a chill on. My Newark appearance went over like a lead-stuffed balloon. Instead of pleasing, it antagonized.

Sitting out there, beginning to sneer at me, were a sharp-eyed lot—the Red Smiths and Arthur Daleys and Dan Parkers. They could see I was a Southern country fellow, and New York reporters look down their noses at Southern country fellows.

New York writers know, of course, that milk comes from

wagons and anything west of the Alleghenies is Indian territory and that only a clown would sing at his inauguration. Could anyone imagine Judge Landis doing such a thing?

They never let me forget it. They started their ridicule at once. They changed my name to "Sappy." they called me "Playboy" and "a windbag." When I said I loved baseball, they laughed.

The mean ones tried their best to make trouble for me. They took issue with everything I did. I didn't know anything about baseball and I was a country bumpkin. They called it a mistake to set up the commissioner's office in Cincinnati. They said it ought to be in New York.

I just took it in stride. I had a job to do. I did it. I usually issued announcements through the secretary. I didn't call press conferences. I wasn't looking for any publicity or notoriety. I didn't have anything that I wanted to keep from the sports writers. Anything that they ought to know that I knew, I was willing to talk to them about.

If they asked me something that was none of their business, I just said that's my responsibility, not yours. You make whatever you want out of it. I don't care.

Their sass made me say some sharp things to them, too. "I always thought a sports writer had to know something," I said. "I was wrong, I see. All you need is a pad and pencil, and no brains."

It took me a while to recognize a couple of other reasons for their disenchantment with the new baseball czar.

The New York writers wanted the job to go to Ford Frick. He was an old sports writer—one of them. He was already climbing in baseball, having made it to president of the National League.

Secondly, they were afraid I'd do something about their freebies. In those days the baseball owners subsidized most of the team newspaper coverage by providing transportation, room and board, and valuable gratuities around Christmas. The writers cottoned to people like Del Webb of the New York Yankees because of what they got from him. And of course his team got good publicity.

I didn't furnish them anything. Webb did, though. And Del

Webb was the most refreshingly ignorant sonofabitch I ever met in my life.

A lot of those sports writers didn't live off their pay. They lived off the privileges they got from the owners. I knew that. That was none of my business.

I am glad to see that's all changed now. The newspapers woke up to a little question of ethics. They pay all the expenses when their sports writers make out of town trips these days. That's decent, it's honest; freebies weren't.

Mama says that I have never been a very forgiving fellow. She says that I can't get a basket big enough to hold all the heads of enemies I've lopped off.

When some bastard in the press box got terribly rough on me, I just bided my time until he stuck his toes out where I could stomp 'em. Bill Corum of the *New York Journal-American* got nasty as he could be. Then the radio people put his name up to be one of the broadcasters for the World Series.

The commissioner had to approve everything about the Series—radio announcers included. I said I would not approve Bill Corum. Just flat no.

J.G. Taylor Spink of *Sporting News* interceded. I wouldn't budge.

"No dice on Corum," I said. "If he wants to be mean to me, let him be mean on his own time, not on mine."

Those sports writers were a sad lot. They didn't question my honesty or my integrity. They just thought I didn't know how to be commissioner. They didn't know that I wasn't just hatched. I was born and I had a father and a mother and a grandfather and a grandmother and I'd spent seven years in college and I had been governor of my state and once appointed and twice elected to the United States Senate.

To show how Fate turns, several years later when Colonel Matt Winn died, they wanted Bill Corum to succeed him as head man of Churchill Downs, home of the Kentucky Derby. Then I was back in the governor's office—my second term. The man who succeeded Colonel Winn had to have the governor's blessing.

Bill Corum came to see me at the Governor's Mansion. He thought I was going to turn him down. That old boy was so nervous he was shaking. He hadn't expected this encounter. He tried to indicate he was sorry he had been a bit rough on me.

"We were rough on each other," I said. "But you started it."

"You understand, Governor," Corum said, "that if you object to me, Churchill Downs will not give me this job."

"Yeah, I know they won't. I appoint the racing commission and I can go as far with you as I want to. I can keep you out of this job."

"Well," he said, "much obliged."

"As far as I'm concerned," I said, "it's over. I don't owe you anything and you don't owe me anything. I don't care who runs the Kentucky Derby for Churchill Downs. If you want the job, take it."

I'm sure that surprised hell out of Bill Corum. I was out of baseball then. He wasn't any threat to me.

Bill Cunningham of the *Boston Herald* was another nasty one. He started ridiculing me before he ever laid eyes on me. I never thought much of him, but he changed his opinion of me. I met him during spring training at St. Petersburg once in my final year as commissioner and he said he thought I was doing fine.

Dan Parker of the *New York Mirror* was supposed to be a pretty big name in sports. I wasn't impressed with him. He was a blow-gut. I wrote him a letter once. I called him ulcer-belly. He published it and I didn't care. Red Smith was just as mean to me. He wrote for the *New York Herald-Tribune*. They say he was the greatest writer. To me he was just a damn drunk. Almost every time I encountered him he was soused to the ears. Red Smith was one of the commonest men I ever saw. The last time I saw him he was in a cab in front of the Waldorf Astoria, drunk. I don't drink and I didn't associate with drunks.

Of course this feud with the sports writers did not escape public attention. I found a lot of people taking my side. One friend, Frank Murphy, former governor of Michigan and at that time an Associate Justice of the United States Supreme Court, wrote: "Don't let the critics bother you. Each day you're growing stronger in public esteem and that is because you are a man of character and good judgment. Only the game fish swims upstream and you're that sort."

Oddly enough, my third major crisis of 1946 was caused by a man named Murphy—Robert Murphy of Boston, a former examiner for the National Labor Relations Board. Incidentally, he was a Harvard-educated lawyer.

Robert Murphy decided to single-handedly unionize big league players. He established the American Baseball Guild. His goal was to secure for players a guaranteed minimum salary, spring training expenses, a pension plan and union recognition. Murphy talked to players in spring training camps. They agreed they felt entitled to most of what he was asking.

The Baseball Guild warrior picked his first target—the Pittsburgh Pirates. He reasoned that since Pittsburgh was a strong union town he would generate helpful support from the thousands of steelworkers and other unionized workers.

Executives of the Pirates resisted his demands for a contract. I knew the Pirate people. William Benswanger, president of the club, was the son-in-law of Barney Dreyfus. The Dreyfuses once had that ball club in Louisville before transferring it to Pittsburgh. The Benswangers were as sweet as could be. Bill Benswanger was a wonderful musician, wrote pieces for the Pittsburgh Symphony Orchestra. He came to visit me in Versailles over the years and I was very fond of him.

When the Pirates refused to recognize the Guild, Robert Murphy threatened a player strike. That wasn't taken too seriously. Sports writers would crack jokes about "Second Basemen's Local 307" and the prospect of paying overtime for extra inning games.

It was even good for a laugh at the White House. President Harry Truman was asked by the *New York Times* if he would seize the Pirates if the players struck. Of course old Truman was a Missourian. So he told the reporters: "If I do have to take over baseball, I'll make sure St. Louis has two good teams."

It was not a laughing matter in Pittsburgh. Reports circulated that Murphy had ninety-five percent of the Pirate players signed up in the Guild, and a majority of at least five other clubs.

I was opposed to a baseball union. And I certainly did not intend to permit players to go on strike if I could prevent it. If they had just demands, they'd have to get them some other way. and I was willing to help them.

But no strike! Any player who walked out I would immediately suspend from organized baseball.

I dispatched John "Frenchy" DeMoisey to Pittsburgh to

keep an eye on the situation for me. He was one of several people I had brought along with me into the commissioner's office. As I indicated earlier, he knew baseball; he'd been a pitcher in Minneapolis before he ruined his arm. I just called him a special assistant. He did a lot of things for me, and was a top hand.

Frenchy phoned me that Robert Murphy had called a strike to take effect the night of July 7.

"Can he pull it off?" I asked. "Will the players walk?"

"I can't say right now," Frenchy replied. "Not all of them."

"They know I'll suspend them?"

"Yes."

"What I want you to do," I told Frenchy, "is round up any players you can. If there's a strike, field some kind of a Pirate team. I won't tolerate stopping baseball."

"I think I can do that. I know Frisch will play. So will 'Rip' Sewell and Honus Wagner."

Frankie Frisch, one of the greats, was the Pittsburgh manager. Frankie was nobody's dumbbell, and the reporters seemed to figure he was sort of caught in the middle of a labor-management confrontation. But you can't get a college degree and become a Hall of Fame second baseman, as he was, without knowing the score. So he was loyal to the owners, but at the same time gave his players every opportunity to talk and listen. Wagner, of course, was another old-time star who was a Pirate coach. He must have been seventy. Sewell was an outstanding pitcher, who seemed to baffle the batters with what he called his "eephus" ball, a high, arching change-up. As near as I know he got that name from a lacrosse term. But his "eephus" throw didn't fool Ted Williams in the 1946 All Star game. Ted whacked it for a home run.

The Pittsburgh strike crisis went right down to the wire. Frenchy was keeping me posted every few minutes by telephone. Murphy kept demanding that Benswanger negotiate, but the club owner steadily refused. It got to ninety minutes before game time. Frenchy called: "Frisch has kicked Murphy and the other outsiders out of the clubhouse. Now the players are going to take a vote."

Everyone got a chance to have his say. Sewell made no bones that he was against the strike. He was so worked up that he jumped up on a bench or trunk and loudly warned his teammates that they didn't know what they were doing. "If you are determined to take this strike vote," he argued, "be dead sure. If you are going to walk, don't settle for less than a three-fourths majority!" That seemed to the players sensible and fair. They settled on that requirement.

Frenchy and Frisch were ready to field a make-shift team. It might not have been much, but they would be in Pirate uniforms.

I waited anxiously. Frenchy finally called. "They've just voted. Only twenty voted to strike." With thirty-six players on the roster, that meant the Guild lost. "They're going out to play. There's no strike!"

That was a mighty fine thing "Rip" Sewell did—hopping up there and turning the tide of what would have been a disgraceful episode by the Pirates. I wanted him to have a momento of his heroism, and a token of my personal appreciation. As soon as I could find one I thought quite handsome, I sent Sewell a gold watch.

That close call on a strike, plus the Mexican jumpers, was sufficient to alert the owners they had some fences to mend. Larry MacPhail got up an advisory committee. These executives gave the game the most searching analysis baseball had had in thirty-five years.

Their report recommended needed reforms for the players. They enacted a new uniform contract, set a minimum salary of five thousand dollars, agreed to pay spring training expenses, grant some player representation, and establish a pension plan.

I knew that pensions were badly needed. That was impressed on me one day back in Lexington, Kentucky, when the House of David came through barnstorming. They had on their team two baseball greats—Grover Cleveland Alexander and Dazzy Vance. They called me and I took them to dinner at the country club.

What a shame for people of that character to leave baseball with no money and have to go around making one-night stands. I felt as sorry as I could be that such stars would have to scrounge for money just to live on. While I was feeding them that night, I made up my mind if I ever got an opportunity I would try to get a pension for baseball players.

So in a way, Robert Murphy and his abortive Baseball

Guild—which was reminiscent of a short-lived effort to form a Players' Fraternity about three decades earlier—did the game a good turn by bringing to a head some conditions that were overdue for attention. Murphy rather mysteriously faded from the scene. I often wondered whatever became of him.

But all was not serene in the baseball world. The high commissioner himself was heading for more trouble—with the owners. Spelled with a capital T.

16

Leo the Lip and Other Troubles

"Happy, some woman just called and said you were her lover," Mama said by long distance from Versailles. "And that you deserted her!"

I was sitting in my hotel room in New York. I just about dropped the phone.

"Why, Mildred! What did you say to her?"

"I said, 'Get yourself a lawyer. Don't bother me with it.' "

That was Mama, all right. That was my girl! It didn't ruffle her. Couldn't be anything like that going on. She didn't believe the woman.

Mama had suggested earlier that my living a sort of bachelor life in Washington might inspire unwarranted gossip. She warned me: "Now, Happy, let me tell you, there are some things that I have read about in Washington you'll have to watch out for. You may be liable to some very serious difficulties. But don't ever let anybody scare you into thinking I'll believe whatever tales they put out."

My so-called jilted lover was about the worst of any tale that reached Mama's ears.

The woman called Mama from New York several times over a period of a few months. She was wasting her time. Mama didn't pay her any mind.

It was a weird episode. And it ended with a sort of mystifying denouement.

Eventually the woman telephoned me at the Sherry-Netherland Hotel in New York. I said, "Where are you?"

"In the lobby," she answered.

"Please just wait there at the desk. I'm coming right down."

Two detectives were in my room. We were discussing baseball business. I asked the detectives to go down with me. "I don't want you-all to do anything, but just observe."

When we emerged from the elevator I saw a handsome, dark-haired, stylish-looking woman standing by the desk. I figured that must be my trouble-maker. I walked straight to her.

"Did you ever see me before?" I asked.

The woman studied my face intently for a bit. Then she shook her head. "No, sir. There's been some mistake."

"Lady, there's been a bad mistake. You've been calling up my wife. You've been telling her that I've been with you and I've deserted you and I've left you without money. Did it ever occur to you that you might make great trouble for me?"

"I'm sorry," she repeated. "There's been some mistake."

The woman turned and walked away. She never called again. We heard no more of her.

Mama is a pretty good detective—at least she knows how to add two and two. And I think she finally solved the mystery. It was a freak case. One of the New York papers carried a story about something I had done as commissioner, and printed a picture of a man about forty-five with dark, combed-back hair. It had my name under the picture. But it wasn't me. Matter of fact, the face was too grim or mean. I didn't fret about the mistake. I couldn't see it did any real harm.

Then somebody said that was a picture of Joe Adonis, the Mafia gangster. He was a real ladies man, so Mama concluded he was the one who jilted the woman. "He's probably had a thousand different women," Mama said. "I guess that's why she didn't know his name."

There has never been any strain on our marriage. I was a faithful husband and Mildred was true-blue, a loving wife and fantastic mother. Of course we hold many differing opinions—even about baseball. Though she was a college athlete who won three letters—tennis, track and basketball—she hates baseball.

I put my foot in it once. I had her bring the boys and come up to Cincinnati for lunch and to see the Reds play Brooklyn. The boys and I had a great time, but Mama was miserable. The game went nineteen innings! The record is twenty-six.

"I feel like I was born in this seat," she told me, disgustedly. "You're not going to do this to me any more." Except for her danged bank overdrafts, she's been a wonderful partner to go with down life's road for sixty-some odd years.

But living in peace and harmony with me did not seem to be a priority item with the whole passel of the baseball club owners. A few of the skunks started picking fights with their new commissioner before the ink was dry on our contract.

Lou Perini of the Boston Braves tried to run over me, and when he couldn't, thought he was clever enough to make an end run. The conflict was over the option rule. A lot of owners were trying to cheat on it. The rule is sound and makes sense. It prevents a powerful club, like the New York Yankees used to be, from continually optioning worthy players to minor leagues and thereby denying them a fair crack at the big leagues.

Perini fought me over a promising youngster named Jack "Lucky" Lohrke. The Boston Braves had already sent him down to the minors on options three times.

"Three times is the limit," I told Perini. "You know that. The owners keep the books, the players don't. You've got to play fair. If you try to option him again, I'll declare him a free agent."

When the commissioner declares a player a free agent, he can sign with any team that wants him. If he's hot, he could get a big bonus. Once I made the Detroit club release a player and he got $40,000 to sign with somebody else. After that he called me Uncle Happy.

Perini came to the annual meeting at my office in Cincinnati. I told him: "I don't know if Lohrke is going to be a major leaguer or not, but this is his day. He's eligible for free agency. I'm putting him in the common draft today." Perini's face flushed with anger.

He stomped around the table fuming a few minutes and then an idea struck. He requested an opportunity to say something before the draft roll-call. I told him to go ahead. He stood up at the table.

"I want to make a statement to my partners," Perini said,

with a smug survey of his colleagues. Even though the clubs
are furious competitors, the owners look on themselves as partners in business. "I want you to all pass on Lohrke." He sat
down.

I told the secretary to call the roll. Horace Stoneham of the
New York Giants got first crack because his team finished last
the previous season.

Stoneham raised his hand. "I'll take Lohrke."

Perini was stunned, and never forgave me. That didn't
bother me. The Boston Braves were a common, ordinary set.
Perini later got some notoriety he didn't relish. He was included
in the book on America's Twelve Outstanding Tax Frauds by a
famous government agent.

Lohrke didn't prove to be a great athlete. He lasted only
four or five years. But I gave him his chance. And in the process
turned Perini into a permanent enemy. A lot of the owners were
a sorry, greedy set. They mistreated the ball players. "When I
catch you mistreating a player," I said, "just belly up, don't
squawk."

Not all of them were crybabies. Walter Briggs, the Detroit
owner, was a square man. Players charged his manager, George
Trautman, with mistreatment. I held a hearing. Trautman was
a miserable creature. He asked me not to mention his name in
my findings. "That's ridiculous," I said. "This is a hearing
against you." He had mistreated ten of his men on their farm
clubs. I made them free agents. Briggs wrote for a copy of my
report. He sent me a copy of his one-line letter to Trautman:
"Handle the players right, and the commissioner won't take
them away from you."

Do you think a green youngster still in high school ought
to be yanked up to a major league team and permitted, or
forced, to throw out his arm in two or three months?

I didn't. We had a rule that they couldn't sign a fellow until
his high school class graduated. If a fellow is going to be a good
baseball player, two things are essential: he ought to be mature,
and he ought to be smart. Mature he will eventually be. Smart,
maybe never. But you must give him a chance for both. You
don't pluck him before he's ripe.

High school coaches around the country tried to develop
these players, bringing them along gradually. For them it was a
labor of love. They tried their best to train young fellows as

they matured so they would grow and qualify. They were disgusted to see the big leagues lure an immature student and cover him up and try to get away with it.

I strongly opposed grabbing these green players. The owners took the attitude: catch me if you can!

I caught Del Webb of the New York Yankees. He was too indignant to even talk to me. He had his partner, Dan Topping, call me. Dan never lifted anything heavier than a knife and fork; he had been married several times, once to the skater Sonja Henie.

"Dan," I said, "you've signed a boy you shouldn't have signed. It'll cost you five hundred dollars. And you've lost the player. Send me a check."

"Suppose I don't send the check," he said.

"I can be rough."

That prompted Del Webb to call for an appointment. He came to my room at the Sherry-Netherland, bringing his entire board of directors, five or six men.

"This is an honor," I said. "You still lose the boy—and the five hundred dollars."

The Yankee owner blew up and stomped out, trailed by his directors. But he paid the fine.

The crybabies were in sharp contrast to a stand-up fellow like Bill Veeck. Bill used circus razzle-dazzle to fill his baseball stadiums. He put fun and excitement into the game. He bought the Cleveland Indians in 1948 and set an attendance record. He was the first to put players' names on the back of their uniforms and to let an exploding scoreboard signal a home run.

Bill Veeck sometimes broke a rule. I caught him. "Bill, belly up," I said. Veeck didn't whimper. He just accepted his punishment. I like that kind of a fella. Later for a time he owned the St. Louis Browns and the Chicago White Sox. He would have made a good baseball commissioner.

If I had remained commissioner, I would have banished both Del Webb and Fred Saigh, owner of the St. Louis Cardinals, from organized baseball.

Webb started life with a hammer and a nail and ran it into a fortune. His biggest coup was building the Flamingo Casino in Las Vegas for Benjamin "Bugsy" Siegel, the Mafia overlord who reportedly was rubbed out by gangland hit men.

Reports kept circulating that Del Webb had been given an

interest in the casino as part payment for constructing the place. I had to know the truth about that. Baseball could not afford any more gambling scandals.

To investigate Webb I assigned my executive secretary, Walter Mulbry. I thought he was my most trusted man. I found out different. I went back a long ways with Walter Mulbry. He and I were in college together, graduating from Transylvania in 1921. He took me down to his house in Sadieville in the lower end of Scott county to meet his parents, fine people. We went to church together.

When I became governor I wanted a smart fellow. Walter was a copy-reader on the *Kentucky Post* up in Covington, making $2,000 a year. I hired him as my executive secretary. He thought he was better than that. He wasn't better. I had two of those in my time, and I made a mistake on both of them. I don't know, they get delusions of grandeur. They resent the fact that people used to bring me presents. Mulbry would ask, "What did you bring me?" And of course that embarrassed my visitors.

I hate to mention this episode. Mulbry is gone now. So is his wife. They had two fine sons. I sent both of them to Annapolis. Pretty good free education. When Mulbry left me he was making $30,000 a year. I have to console myself on a bad choice by saying the Lord made people like this and sometimes even He had off days.

When I assigned Mulbry to investigate Del Webb I had no notion he would turn disloyal. But apparently he saw a chance to do something for himself. So he tipped Webb off!

It's unbelievable, but I did not find out about this treachery until I left the commissioner's office. I'm a hardhead about loyalty; I suppose too loyal to my own people for my own good. Of course, outsiders who smell a rat usually hesitate to tell you about it while the dirty work's going on.

Webb and his crowd played Mulbry for a sucker, making him think he was going to be president of the American League, or even commissioner of baseball. He wanted my job. Of course, when you get a guy like that it's a damn shame.

When it all came out Frenchy DeMoisey was furious. "Give me permission," he told me, "and I'll kill him!"

I think he meant it seriously. He was that loyal.

My abortive investigation of Webb's reported Las Vegas connections, of course, turned him flatly against me. In the end he teamed up with Perini, Saigh, and other skunks to put me on the skids before I could get them.

Fred Saigh first fell out with me over Sunday baseball. He wanted to play a Sunday night game. I wouldn't let him. "We've got to do what people generally approve of," I explained. "That is, have a game after church in the morning and before services in the evening. That's been the rule for years and years. Keeps down trouble."

Saigh wasn't satisfied. He began finding a lot of fault with the commissioner's office. Gambling talk kept cropping up. The situation warranted careful investigation. I asked J. Edgar Hoover to recommend a good man, and he suggested a former FBI agent, Robert E. Boyle. I sent him down to St. Louis and he brought back a detailed report. Fred Saigh was a no-good, but I didn't get him, the government did. He was found guilty of tax fraud and spent a few years in prison. But not before he helped do me in.

I had a gambling confrontation with Dizzy Dean. I summoned him to my office in Cincinnati from St. Louis where he was broadcasting the games. He had been a great pitcher and a swashbuckler and he had the cutest little wife you ever saw. She always tried to protect him and look out for him, and God knows he needed it. Miss Patricia—she came with him into my private office.

"You like to broadcast the games?" I asked Dizzy.

"Oh, yeah."

"Can you broadcast them if you don't see them?"

"No, sir."

"You're sending bets by the clubhouse boy to the saloon on the corner. You're broadcasting the game and you're betting on the game. Make your choice. Quit betting, or I'm taking you out of the broadcast booth."

"I'll quit betting," Dizzy said.

"I'll see that he does," said Miss Patricia.

Then they wanted to know what I intended to say to reporters who were waiting outside my office. "I'm not going to say anything. It's nobody's business. If I were you I'd not say anything."

When the door opened and reporters crowded up, Miss Patricia said: "Gentlemen, we will have no statement."

Dean poked his finger in the chest of the leading fellow. "We're not talking, pal, see."

I never heard of him betting again.

Professional gamblers constantly lurked around the major leagues. I kept my staff on alert to catch suspicious signs. Baseball certainly could not afford another black eye like the 1919 World Series scandal. Professional gamblers could buy tickets just like plain John Doe and watch the games from the bleachers or the best box seats. They could take sides and bet among themselves, and in some parks these little coteries of so-called sportsmen staked out their own areas. They would make wagers in advance on certain plays or moves, for instance, how long a pitcher would stay. They could be seen passing money back and forth, paying off. Naturally that wasn't good, and most of the clubs took action to discourage it. I backed them up as strongly as the law and baseball rules permitted.

Where I came directly into the gambling picture was in watching for contacts between members of the gambling fraternity and the officials and players of organized baseball. In some places the professional gamblers had access to the clubhouses and locker rooms, and were socializing—drinking and playing cards, shooting pool, and partying—with baseball people.

I did not intend to permit that fraternization to continue. It had to always be looked on as suspicious, and it certainly could lead to scandal down the road. To protect the integrity of baseball these professional gamblers had to be put off limits and kept there. I don't think I was seeing spooks; there have always been weak people who can be corrupted by the promise of big money. The 1919 scandal proved that. And the threat and temptation was there every day for some of the players.

Why, barely three or four years after the Black Sox scandal, the great spitball pitcher for the New York Giants, Shufflin' Phil Douglas, tried to rig a game. This one was important, the St. Louis Cardinals coming to the Polo Grounds for the match-up that would decide the National League pennant in 1922.

Douglas had the idea—probably planted by some gambler friend—that the Cardinals would be crippled by the timely disappearance of their hottest outfielder, Leslie Mann. So Shufflin' Phil took pen in hand and blatantly wrote a letter to Mann saying it would be worth his while to "go fishing" the day of the crucial game.

Fortunately, Mann had gumption enough to report the bribe offer to his manager, who happened to be Branch Rickey, and Commissioner Landis was notified. Shufflin' Phil Douglas was thrown out of baseball—for life!

The end of World War II somehow seemed to bring on a new surge of gambling fever in American sports. I can't explain it; maybe because so many men had been risking their lives, and hoping the odds were in their favor where Jap or Nazi bullets were flying, that they yielded on return to the homefront to sports betting for its innocent thrill.

This gambling climate, especially insidious in New York, finally led to my celebrated 1947 confrontation with Leo Durocher, the manager of the Brooklyn Dodgers. Nobody in baseball, I don't believe, gave me more problems and headaches as commissioner than Durocher.

Unfortunately, Leo was a general all-around bad actor. He didn't get his nickname "Lippy" by accident. He was a brash loudmouth, who could be one minute caustic, ruthless, pugnacious and the next amiable, charming, flirtatious. He was a dude and strutting clothes-horse supposed to have a wardrobe of seventy-five tailored suits, thirty sports jackets, seventy-five pairs of slacks, half a dozen tuxedos, thirty alpaca sweaters, a closet full of topcoats, monogrammed shirts, and probably silk drawers. The story was he changed his underwear twice a day.

That didn't keep him from being dirty and dangerous. He was too ready to use his fists. He picked all kinds of fights— with umpires, fans, players, his bosses. His temper was so hairtrigger that it finally reached the point where I thought he might kill somebody. I'm not kidding about that.

His career started when he was about twenty, with Hartford in the old Eastern League. Some scout for the New York Yankees liked him, and farmed him out for a couple of seasons. In 1928 when the Yanks brought him up he sashayed into the clubhouse where the big stars were Babe Ruth, Lou Gehrig, Bob Meusel, and Waite Hoyt. They say Leo was so feisty he came in just like he was as much a superstar as any of them. He got to be a pretty consistent pop-off. Ruth, then at the peak of his form, wouldn't give Leo the time of day. Durocher was better at popping off than he was at hitting or fielding. So he bounced and wound up playing shortstop with the St. Louis Cardinals in time to help win the 1934 pennant and World Series.

That was the year he gave the Cardinals their odious nickname, by cracking to a sports writer that American League clubs wouldn't appreciate St. Louis because "we are just a bunch of gas-house players." Another time, Leo, apparently trying to justify his own rough-and-tumble—actually dirty— tactics on the field, made the crack that "Nice guys finish last!" They say that line was picked up and credited to him by *Bartlett's Quotations*. It's not in mine; maybe I've got an outdated copy. Looking back from this time in life, it seems the Durocher "thing"—as everyone seemed to call it—happened a hundred years ago. But I remember it all clearly, and I often think how quirky Fate was in lining up the principal players in that drama, Larry MacPhail, Branch Rickey, Durocher, and me.

Leo finally wore out his welcome with St. Louis and Larry MacPhail brought him to Brooklyn and the next year, 1939, named him manager. Of course, Larry was a quirky guy, too. Even before spring training started, MacPhail phoned up Durocher down in Hot Springs, Arkansas—where they say he had just won $750 at bingo and had a fistfight with a golf caddy. "You're fired!" Larry snapped. Out of the blue.

While I wasn't then too well acquainted with Durocher, I had seen a lot of MacPhail. I first met him when I was in Kentucky politics and he was manager of the Cincinnati Reds. Larry occasionally had a little problem of his own—the bottle. As a matter of fact, and a sad one, Larry departed Cincinnati after a little set-to in which MacPhail got skinned knuckles and a city detective sustained a broken jaw.

Several times after I became commissioner he called me while drunk. Despite our close friendship, I didn't have time for drunks. "Call back, Larry, when you are sober." I'd hang up. They say Larry fired Durocher by phone two or three times. I don't know about that. I do know that when MacPhail quit the Dodgers after the 1942 season to become boss of the New York Yankees, Branch Rickey moved in as the squire of Ebbets Field and inherited Leo Durocher as his manager. Rickey had a real handful there, and though I didn't know it until later—so did I.

By the time he arrived in Brooklyn, Rickey had been in baseball thirty years, was just into his sixties, and a pretty wise old bird. Nobody could fool him about the atmosphere around his club. As one baseball historian, Arthur Mann, recounted, Rickey "found a Dodger club and clubhouse torn asunder by gamblers and bookmakers and racing handicappers and ticket scalpers. They had long enjoyed free access to Ebbets Field, and scurried from dugout to locker room like happy, squealing vermin in the rat runs of an aging barn."

Lord have mercy! Imagine a situation that crummy. You can be sure it was a big worry to Branch Rickey, who was aggressive in baseball and a sharp trader, but impeccably honest, God-fearing, and a decent gentleman. But he liked to win baseball games. And he knew well enough that no club in either the National or American Leagues had ever sent nine angels out on the field. He had learned to be tolerant because ballplayers were no different from other men; some of them liked to drink, gamble, and womanize, along with showing off and popping off. Unless things got too out of hand, Rickey tried to look the other way when he could.

But with his team manager, Branch was having a devil of a time looking the other way. Leo was visible, and he was making waves—big ones, nasty ones.

This all began while Commissioner Landis was still in control. I wasn't involved in the controversies at the start; but several books, hundreds of magazine articles, and millions of words of newspaper copy have been written about Durocher's exploits, so I am pretty well up on the whole story.

What chiefly upset Branch Rickey and others who were concerned about the integrity of the game was the crowd Durocher ran around with—chiefly gamblers and gangsters. A few were just pool-hall sharks because Durocher had a passion, they said, for those late-night high-stakes billiards. And he was supposed to be pretty good with a cue stick.

But his chief pals were big-time operators. I'm not sure how he got in with them, but there is no doubt he did. The newspapers said he was close to the slick and notorious Joe Adonis, who was a kingpin in the biggest Brooklyn and national gambling syndicates that financed New York rackets and swank hangouts for the sporting mob. Durocher was directly linked to the high-rolling twosome of "Memphis" Engelberg and Connie Immerman, and admitted they helped him pick horses at the racetrack. And further, beyond any doubt, Durocher was an almost constant off-the-field companion of George Raft, the movie star who became a Hollywood hit playing gangster "heavies." That seemed to be a role that suited George Raft in real life as well. He was on close terms with some of the worst murdering thugs in the rackets and through him Durocher was on some kind of terms with Lucky Luciano and "Bugsy" Siegel. Durocher admitted that he gave George Raft a key to his Manhattan apartment, and the story was widely circulated that the movie star was running a floating crap game there. One victim squawked that Raft cheated him out of $30,000 by making thirteen straight passes with loaded dice.

In the Flatbush ballpark, too, Leo was in first one scrape and then another. Branch Rickey didn't seem to be bothered that Durocher was a skittish manager, switching his players and pitchers every ten minutes. He seemed to be in almost constant rhubarbs with the umpires. Maybe that was all in the game. But Leo's other faults were the ones that kept the Dodger president in a stew.

A young fan in Brooklyn spent a whole game shouting insults to Durocher. That's part of the game; a player or manager has to expect that. But not hot-tempered Durocher. He chased the kid under the stands and caught him. Fists were swinging. The fan got a broken jaw. Durocher said the boy slipped on a wet spot and fell into the water fountain.

Assault charges were filed. They didn't have enough evidence to convict Leo. But he squelched the threat of civil action by paying a settlement to the boy of something like six or seven thousand dollars.

About the time I took over as baseball commissioner, Leo fell in love—again. He already had been married at least twice. His new love turned out to be the young movie star who was a sensational hit in the Dr. Kildare stories, Laraine Day, a slender girl, pretty much a knockout. As I heard the story, somebody introduced them in an airport cafeteria and on a transcontinental flight they fell in love.

However, there was a little problem—Laraine Day was married, and at that time, if I remember correctly, so was Leo.

But love, they say, will find a way. Miss Day took the path leading to the divorce court to shed her husband, who was a clerk or something at an airport in Los Angeles. And Durocher began legal moves to end his marriage. A glitch developed on the movie star's side, however; her husband, a fellow named Ray Hendricks, knew all about California's community property law wherein a spouse may claim half the other's estate. Laraine Day had a woodsy mansion, with a swimming pool, in Santa Monica, and hefty loot from films stashed in her bank. Getting a divorce might make her husband a rich fellow, and the newspapers said she was trying to wiggle out of that.

All kinds of stories started appearing in newspapers about Leo's "fiery romance" with the beautiful heroine of the silver screen. On the sports pages there were colorful features on the "Dodger Don Juan." The baseball writers found that kind of yarn more spicy than their usual hot-stove league stuff. With a wealthy movie star pitted against a relatively "unknown" clerk-type, their divorce struggle occasionally hit the front pages.

Invariably there would appear broad innuendos in the newspapers picturing the sharp-featured Dodger manager, as one account termed him, "a sly and designing homewrecker, invading the privacy of an unsuspecting husband." It was common knowledge that Leo Durocher was spending the off-season months of 1946–47 in Hollywood, where he was frequently seen escorting Laraine Day. Just at that juncture the militant newspaper columnist Westbrook Pegler zeroed on Durocher and his gambling pals. Pegler was read coast-to-coast and once onto a scandal rarely let loose until he had practically gnawed it to death. Pegler was aware that in 1944 Commissioner Landis had called Leo on the carpet and warned him to be careful about associating with unsavory characters. Rickey, too, had tried to give his manager sound fatherly advice on the same subject. To no avail.

An "inside" account of how Rickey struggled to get Durocher on the right track has been provided by Arthur Mann, who covered sports for several of the New York dailies before giving up the newspaper game to become the Dodger president's right-hand executive assistant. Later he wrote a book about the affair. In it he says Pegler telephoned Rickey one night at his Forest Hills home and got right to the point: "When are you going to get rid of Durocher?"

It was not without cause that Branch Rickey was tagged the Mahatma by the sports writers, and you can be sure that he bridled at the effrontery of anyone, even a famous and powerful columnist, trying to tell who was qualified to be manager of his ball club. According to Mann's book, Rickey argued for about an hour with Pegler, pointing out that Durocher was a good manager, a sound strategist and an astute field man. He was going a bit overboard to try to be loyal; for he had secret doubts of his own, of course. Even about The Lip's skill as a manager. Once Rickey was quoted as saying: "Leo has the most fertile talent in the world for making a bad situation infinitely worse."

But now he tried to fend off Pegler's criticism, asserting he had known Leo since he was practically a boy and was working to rehabilitate him. Pegler shot back that Durocher was a "moral delinquent" who would never be any good and who eventually would "drag Rickey and baseball down to his own level of shame." Then the columnist stunned Rickey with a couple more blockbusters. One was that the district attorney investigating an $800,000 check-cashing swindle that involved Hollywood racketeers, a couple of movie people and a casino operator, had discovered Durocher's name on some of the drafts. Moreover, the D.A. had put a tap on the phone in Durocher's Manhattan apartment and had recorded suspicious conversations from Ebbets Field.

"If he is so smart, why is he still living with George Raft?" Pegler demanded.

That was news to Rickey, and it shook him. That seemed to mean that Durocher, now in Hollywood, had moved in with Raft. Pegler said he was getting ready to launch a sports gambling expose in his column that would feature "the Durocher situation."

Confronted with a threat of that magnitude, and a potential scandal, Rickey wisely decided he could use some intervention by the high commissioner of baseball. He immediately sent Arthur Mann to my headquarters in Cincinnati.

We sat in my private office and Mann explained he was on a confidential mission, not to register a formal complaint, but to get some help. "Mr. Rickey has been building his organization toward a postwar peak," Mann explained, "and he doesn't want to encounter unforeseen difficulties that can be avoided by acting now." He paused, and I waited for him to continue. "Somehow Leo Durocher hasn't been sufficiently impressed by the fact that all his difficulties spring directly from his associations off the field." I asked again if there was a specific complaint. Mann said not, and didn't want Leo to know the Dodgers were sticking their oar in, but just wanted me to do something.

"Mr. Rickey is disturbed because Durocher is living under George Raft's roof in Hollywood right now. The actor may be all right, and a good lime-light friend, but Mr. Rickey wants Leo to move, and he feels that your taking a hand will impress him once and for all."

Mann's suggestion seemed reasonable and I immediately put in a call for Durocher at George Raft's house. He wasn't there. He had left for an afternoon rehearsal of the Jack Benny radio show. The call went next to the N.B.C. studio, where a chilly receptionist announced: "*Mister* Durocher is rehearsing and *cannot* be disturbed."

My hackles began to rise. "Tell him Commissioner Chandler is on the phone," I snapped. "That'll disturb him. And tell him to come right out!"

In a minute or two, Durocher was on the phone. We exchanged guarded pleasantries, and then I told him: "Meet me Friday morning, November 22, at the Claremont Country Club, that's between Oakland and Berkeley. That's five days from now. We've got some business to attend to."

On the California end of the line, it sounded like Durocher was choking. "Well, Mister Commissioner," he spluttered, "I can't meet you. I'm due in Texas next Friday—on important personal business."

I brusquely shook off his refusal. "There's nothing more *important* than meeting me, and certainly nothing more *personal*." I gave him a moment for that to sink in. "You'll be there, boy...Claremont Country Club...Friday morning...eleven o'clock...the eighth green! I know you won't disappoint me. Now, go back to your rehearsal and give a good show tonight."

I don't think I caught that Jack Benny broadcast. But Leo

must have been considerably shook up. They tell me his lack-luster performance probably reflected the impact of his unexpected summons, and that it was a wonder he was able to read his lines at all.

But Leo heard his master's voice. Five days later when I came to the green on Number 8 at the Claremont Country Club there stood the dapper Dodger manager, his creases sharp as a razor and his dark hair slicked back. He had an uneasy grin on his face.

I tried to make it as pleasant and businesslike as possible. We didn't spar around. I got straight to our business, and told him there were certain people whose interests were inimical to the integrity of organized baseball. You didn't have to smash Leo with a Louisville Slugger to make him see the light. I reached in my breast pocket and pulled out a little card. It had seven or eight names on it. The top name was George Raft. You can guess the others.

I handed the card to Durocher. "You can't associate with these undesirables, and remain in baseball," I warned. Leo did not argue. He promised to avoid them, and be good.

We didn't have a long conversation, fifteen or twenty minutes. But Laraine Day's name came up. He seemed to want to talk about her. For some reason I don't understand, Leo told me he had just been in her bedroom arguing with her husband about which of them was going to take her. I remember giving him a look and I'll never forget what I said to him.

"You come down to my country," I said, "and do that—well, I'll make a setup for you and I won't have to be bothered with you any more, Durocher."

He looked puzzled. "Why?"

"They'll kill you," I answered. "If you go into some fellow's bedroom and argue with him about who's going to take his wife, they'll kill you. I won't have to be bothered with you any more."

To his credit, Durocher wasted no time in packing up his big wardrobe and moving out of George Raft's sumptuous house. He parked himself in bachelor solitude in the quiet Miramar Hotel at Santa Monica, many miles from glamorous Hollywood and Vine. Of course, the lovesick Durocher was pretty crafty at that; in his new abode, he was much, much closer to Laraine Day's place.

Next time I was in New York I got a squawk from George

Raft. He came to see me at the Sherry-Netherland Hotel. I liked to see his movies; I didn't have anything against him except his gambling and gangland pals.

I didn't want to hear his argument.

"George, do you have a contract in baseball?"

"No," he said.

"Then we haven't got anything to talk about. What you do is not my business. If Durocher plays cards and gambles for money, I have to be concerned with him. But not you. So, please, just go away."

"But," Raft blurted, "I got a bum rap!"

"I didn't give it to you."

From all reports reaching my office, Durocher was avoiding George Raft and that whole sleazy racketeering crowd. He was so wrapped up in his movieland romance, he probably didn't have much free time anyhow. Laraine went ahead and got her divorce on grounds of extreme cruelty. But the judge threw her a curve by decreeing that she could not marry and reside in California as a wedded person within one year. That was all in the papers, along with groans of anguish and frustration from the sweethearts.

Just then came another bombshell in the newspapers—on December 13, 1946. Westbrook Pegler unleashed his syndicated column on the exposé he had warned Branch Rickey was coming. He jumped on Leo Durocher and his "undesirable associates." It was first class muckraking of the old newspaper school. Naturally, Pegler painted the situation far worse than it actually was; you would have thought gamblers and racketeers were secretly pulling strings behind the scenes in every baseball park in the land, pretty much as they had always tried to do in the prizefight game.

Pegler had some solid facts, bringing up that celebrated George Raft dice game in Leo's New York City apartment. And he identified Raft as a pal of the notorious Ownie Madden, king of the mid-twenties rum runners, and with a whole coterie of West Coast racketeers, including "Bugsy" Siegal, who on June 20, 1947, was shot to death by hit men in his mistress's Beverly Hills hideaway. Once off to a good start, the Pegler column kept slinging the tar brush daily.

But Pegler was totally off base when he inferred that I was taking no action, and couldn't see the danger. The sports writers all descended on me with a demand that I do something about "the gambling element in baseball, and particularly about Leo Durocher."

There were two points of rebuttal I wanted to make with the baseball reporters. The first was that the dice game incident which Pegler was disinterring had occurred in March 1944. "Be fair," I told them. "That was when Landis was still high commissioner—I didn't actually become the paid baseball commissioner until a year and a half later. So I can't be held accountable for Leo and George Raft in 1944. But I'll tell you what I have done about Durocher palling around with George Raft and others whom Pegler classifies as undesirables . . . . "

Then I made my second point by revealing the personal warning I had given Durocher in late November on the golf course in California, and his avowal that he would clean up his act. Despite my explanations, many sports pages erupted with claims that I was not taking sufficient action.

I could not correct every distortion. But I tackled some. The *Cincinnati Times-Star*'s Nixson Denton critically accused me of adopting a do-nothing attitude. I reminded him the George Raft dice game occurred before my time, and added:

"I would like, moreover, to find from you what information you have concerning what I might have said to Durocher. You say that 'he hasn't even been questioned,' while no publicity was given to the fact that Durocher has been questioned and at length, although the incident so publicized by Mr. Pegler occurred during the tenure of office of the late Judge Landis. The statement in your column that 'Happy Chandler has done nothing' simply isn't true."

I fired a sharp letter to Red Smith, and in his *New York Herald-Tribune* column he printed this portion of it:

> The Commissioner and members of his staff are doing everything humanly possible to prevent gambling in baseball and it is unnecessary for us to apologize to you or anyone else in our efforts. If you have any evidence of gambling in baseball, it is your duty as a sports writer to furnish it to us. The writing of such pure and unadulterated tripe as appeared in your column is not helpful in any way to baseball or any of its problems.
>
> Yours very truly,
> A. B. CHANDLER

Needless to say, Red Smith didn't come forward with any helpful information, in fact with anything at all.

The Durocher mess just wouldn't go away. Rumors seeped out there was gambling in the Dodger clubhouse. The breaking up of Laraine Day's marriage got Durocher frequently pictured as the other man. They did make their romance legal. Laraine Day slipped over to Mexico, got one of those one-day "quickie" divorces. Then she recrossed the Rio Grande and married Leo in El Paso, Texas on January 21, 1947. Of course their honeymoon put Durocher squarely right back in the page one spotlight, just on the eve of the beginning of Spring training.

Outsiders took notice. Frank Murphy, the Supreme Court justice, wrote me a confidential protest as head of the National Catholic Youth Organization. I had known Frank since his days as governor of Michigan. Murphy was irate over the breaking of the young fan's jaw and, I'm certain, considered the Laraine Day scandal a deplorable example for Catholic youngsters who tended to heroize big leaguers.

He said something like, "I want you to handle this fellow, and you are a man of character. If he is manager we'll tell the kids, the Catholic Youth Organization, not to go to the ball games next year." I've got to pay some attention to a letter like that. If I have a fellow who's so obnoxious he keeps kids out of the stands, I can't let that happen. No sir.

While I was mulling over what course of action to take on Justice Murphy's letter, Fate was cooking up another violent explosion for the Durocher "thing." And, of course, as commissioner I would be right in the big middle of it.

The spark that ignited this newest controversy was struck in early March in Havana. The Brooklyn Club had shifted its 1947 spring training camp to Cuba. These were the fairly peaceful days before Castro came to power. The Cubans have always been nuts about baseball. Havana had a new, gleaming ballpark called Grand Stadium. The Dodgers were quartered at the National Hotel; meaning Rickey, his family, and retinue, and of course Durocher, the coaches, and players. Leo was at the moment a temporary bachelor, his new bride being detained in Hollywood to finish a movie. All sorts of Americans had followed the baseball crowd to Havana. And not just sports writers. . . .

From the Yankee training camp in Florida, Larry MacPhail had brought his New York team over to Havana for a series of exhibition games with Brooklyn. I was not present and did not witness any of this, but I certainly received enough written reports, saw enough evidence, and heard sufficient testimony that I have a complete version of what took place.

Out on the field watching his players warming up, Leo looked around and spotted a couple of very familiar faces in the box seats. They were two of the principal undesirables that I had barred him from associating with—"Memphis" Engelberg, the racetrack handicapper and gambler, and Connie Immerman, the New York gambler who was just then boss of the Havana casino.

The two gamblers were in the section just back of the Yankee dugout, and sitting in seats immediately behind Larry MacPhail. Durocher's hackles went up; he promptly leaped to the conclusion that these undesirable characters were "guests" in the Yankee box section.

And he did not intend to let the episode go unnoticed. Durocher hustled over to Branch Rickey's box and alerted him to the situation. The Dodger president, too, got all worked up. He also jumped to the conclusion that MacPhail had invited the well-known gamblers to sit in his box. He and MacPhail were already pretty much on the outs—and the net of this controversy would mean that they parted enemies. I don't believe they ever spoke to each other again.

But at the moment in Havana they were both talking—to the press, and vigorously. As was Durocher. The Associated Press carried a long piece saying that Rickey specifically charged that MacPhail had the two alleged gamblers as his guests, quoting him further as saying, "If these men were on the other side of the field behind the Brooklyn dugout, Durocher would have been in hot water with A. B. Chandler, Commissioner of Baseball."

Havana was teeming with New York sports writers and they immediately hopped on the quarrel between two titans of the diamond. One reporter quoted Rickey: "If I saw these men in the Brooklyn ballpark, I would have them thrown out. Yet, there they are as guests of the president of the Yankees. Why, my own manager can't even say hello to this actor, George what's-his-name. He won't have anything to do with these gamblers, or any gamblers. But apparently there are rules for Durocher and other rules for the rest of baseball."

Durocher himself was quoted in the *New York Daily News* as asking: "Are there two sets of rules, one applying to managers and the other to club owners? Where does MacPhail come off, flaunting his company with known gamblers right in the players' faces? If I even said 'hello' to one of those guys, I'd be called before Commissioner Chandler and probably barred."

Leo was contributing a daily column called "Durocher Says" to the *Brooklyn Eagle,* which was ghostwritten for him by Harold Parrott, the Dodgers traveling secretary. Parrott wired the paper a long dispatch under Durocher's byline, making the same charges, and whipping the incident up to a fury.

Larry MacPhail reacted with indignation, telling the *Daily News:* "In the first place it is none of Durocher's business who I have in my box. In the second place, if Durocher was quoted correctly, he is a liar. I understand in the box next to me were two gentlemen later identified as alleged gamblers. I had nothing to do with their being there. And you can quote me as saying it's none of Durocher's business."

The upshot was that it all fell in my lap—a real can of worms!

With the spectre of sports gambling still fresh in mind, the baseball writers were not about to let this choice tidbit perish. So they pumped it up with every possible angle they could turn up. Then MacPhail brought the incident to a head officially by lodging a formal complaint with my office requesting a hearing to determine the truth or falsity of the statements published by Branch Rickey and Leo Durocher.

All the parties directly involved were summoned to a hearing at my hotel in Sarasota. The press was excluded. We wound up holding a second session in St. Petersburg. But it was not possible to develop a totally clear picture of what had happened. For one thing the principals could hardly afford to contradict the statements they had made to the newspapermen—if they expected to have man-to-man relations later with the press; regardless how much it sounded like popping off, they were stuck with the printed word. They did wiggle and try to shade it here and there.

Another difficulty was that we could not get to the bottom of the question of how Engelberg and Immerman received their gratis tickets to the seats in the Yankee box. To begin with the Grand Stadium seat distribution was handled by the Brooklyn ball club! The officials in charge of tickets had handled so many passes to the exhibition games they could not be positive how those two seats were assigned.

Even Durocher tried to shade the criticism he had expresed in his *Brooklyn Eagle* column. In the witness chair, Leo shrugged and said: "It seemed just another rhubarb. We went on like that, Mr. MacPhail and I, for years. Why, he fired me many times after such arguments and hired me back. But we always laughed it off."

The Lip turned and faced the Yankee president. "If I've said anything in that article to hurt Larry's feelings, I'm sorry and I apologize."

MacPhail nodded. "That's good enough for me," he said. The two men reached out and shook hands.

Leo got a big smile on his face. I suppose he figured he had slipped out of another nasty situation, and the whole Havana incident was going to be swept under the rug. I asked him to keep his seat because I had a few more questions for him.

For a number of days I had been doing some serious thinking about what it would take to improve the atmosphere of the big leagues, what was really needed to eradicate the odor of sleaziness that had so strongly crept in. I couldn't get Frank Murphy's letter out of my mind. If little kids couldn't go to the ball parks and look up to the players as their heroes and role models . . . ? What was organized baseball coming to?

Durocher sat there, smoothing out the creases of his trousers, waiting for my questions. I fired the first one out like a bullet:

"Have you-all been gambling in the Dodger clubhouse?"

He started, but he didn't hedge.

"Yes," said Durocher.

"For high stakes?"

"Yes."

"With whom?"

"Just one player—Kirby Higbe."

I had heard a lot about Kirby Higbe, a pretty good pitcher,

but so handsome that off the field women chased after him and distracted him.

"I'd take his money in card games," Durocher continued, "and give it back to him for pitching well." Higbe's womanizing was generally known, and Durocher went on to explain what he called a "double purpose" of gambling with Higbe. "That kept Kirby short of cash, which if he didn't have, he couldn't go out and squander. And naturally knowing I'd give it back, he had an incentive to pitch winning ball."

I shifted then over to another matter. MacPhail and Durocher had some conversation about Leo coming over to the Yankees as manager. That talk or talks had apparently occurred while Durocher was still under contract with the Dodgers, a violation of the rules. How that came about was not clear, either. It was, as I said earlier, quite a can of worms. But my job as commissioner meant I had to sort things out and take appropriate action. First, there was no hard evidence that the gamblers were MacPhail's guests. Durocher, of course, admitted he had made such an accusation. Rickey confessed he had echoed Leo's words, but denied telling reporters, "Apparently there are rules for Durocher and other rules for the rest of baseball." Further, MacPhail accepted Rickey's statement that he had not intended to say anything detrimental to Larry's character and integrity, either personally or as a club owner.

Still the rhubarb in Cuba gave baseball another black eye. As I wrote in my findings: "The incident in Havana which brought considerable unfavorable comment to baseball generally was one of a series of publicity-producing affairs in which Manager Durocher has been involved in the last few months."

That was actually the most damaging aspect of the Havana episode. There was nothing I could do except tack that on Durocher's long list of other "sins." It had finally come time to crack down on him.

I announced my decision on April 9 in a press release slapping $2,000 fines on Rickey's Dodger club and MacPhail's Yankees. I stuck Harold Parrott, Leo's ghostwriter, five hundred dollars for sticking his nose in where it didn't belong. (When he came crawling and begging later, I gave it back to him.)

And I suspended Durocher from baseball for one year.

I stated simply that he had been "adjudged guilty of conduct detrimental to the game." I thought everyone would understand precisely what that covered and meant. I didn't list the particulars, and even today some of the sports writers who were always in my corner believe it was a mistake not to list all of Leo's infractions.

Leo's banishment was described on most sports pages as "a stunning surprise." In an editorial titled "The Commissioner Gets Tough," *Sporting News* observed:

> To be sure, the decision was a drastic one in appearance, unduly harsh in complexion, and perhaps even born of animus. However, Durocher had asked for it . . . . He had been warned once . . . twice . . . and told there would be no third "Beware."
>
> Those who regard the suspension as altogether out of proportion to the diamond crimes and public relations infractions committed have failed to comprehend the factors which entered into the commissioner's action. Chandler's 1,000-word decision makes it quite plain that his action was based on a long string of circumstances.
>
> The Ebbets Field slugging case, the dice game in Durocher's apartment while the Brooklyn manager was away, the charges aired by Westbrook Pegler to the tremendous detriment of all baseball and the personal derogation of Leo, the defection of the Catholic Youth Organization from the Ebbets Field Knothole Gang, Durocher's attack on Judge Dockweiler of Los Angeles in the matter of Laraine Day's divorce and Leo's subsequent El Paso marriage with the movie actress, and finally his pieces in the *Brooklyn Eagle* piled up a devastating case against the pilot of the Dodgers.
>
> The public, a large portion of the sports press, even national magazines only vicariously interested in the diamond, had criticized Chandler for being too benevolent a boss. Kicked around unmercifully, maligned, even libeled and slandered, Chandler took stock of himself.
>
> "I have been trying to be a good guy, to run this game on the Golden Rule precept, to be kind to the good and sympathetic toward the transgressor, and they don't seem to like it," Chandler said to himself. "Well, here's where they get a tough commissioner."

> For Organized Baseball, Leo's suspension is a general warning . . . . From now on, men connected with baseball under the jurisdiction of Albert Benjamin Chandler must

exercise a care and circumspection never before demanded of them.

The sum total of all this for the game of baseball is a gorgeous benefice.

A good many New York sports writers, no fans of mine anyhow, jumped to the defense of their fallen hero. Leo and his didoes had always meant good copy for them. *Time* magazine made an accurate summation of that situation, saying: "Commissioner Chandler had done the seemingly impossible; he has made Leo Durocher a sympathetic figure." Well, I'll have to confess, I didn't think anybody could do that.

Even Durocher's ex-wife, Grace Dozier, despite the Laraine Day scandal, came and stood in front of my box at Yankee Stadium and remonstrated with me. She was the prettiest little thing, a dressmaker from St. Louis. She was defending him, although he had divorced her to marry the Hollywood woman.

I listened to her carefully. When she got through, I said: "Grace, I want to tell you how much I admire any woman who defends her husband. That means he's a lucky fellow. But you can't do anything to help Leo. This suspension is not against you, it's against him. And it's going to stick."

A year later I'm at Yankee Stadium at an early season game and Grace Dozier comes up and stands in front of me again. She held out her hand.

"Commissioner," she said, "you knew he was a son of a bitch all the time, didn't you?"

"Grace, I didn't say that. You said that."

What a difference a year makes.

In retrospect I don't know just how much the penalty hurt Durocher. The Dodger organization kept him on the payroll. He probably laughed every time he cashed a salary check. He had more free time, too, for his honeymoon. The newspapers reported from time to time what the newlyweds were up to; once there was a story he was out in Hollywood installing her sprinkling system.

The New York fans, gleefully egged on by my sports page critics, wouldn't let me forget throwing him out.

Ironically, I caught the heaviest flak just at the moment I was trying to drum up some recognition and appreciation for a fading Yankee hero and legend—Babe Ruth.

The Babe was desperately ill. His bacchanalian life had wrecked him. Too much booze and too many women. I went to see him in 1947 when he thought he was going to die. I was the only fellow in baseball who visited him. They had deserted him. Baseball wouldn't even find him a job. They give a lot of people shabby treatment. They ought to be ashamed of themselves, but I don't think they are. Owners can be pretty tough.

When I came into his hospital room, Ruth recognized me. He buried his face in his pillow and just cried like a baby. His huge physique had wasted away. His big home run arms were just shriveled up. Such a sad, sad ending for a memorable life.

But we got him up, and got a job for him with the Ford Motor Company, thanks to Henry Ford II, who remembered the Babe Ruth glory days. People should not be permitted to forget such a baseball legend. We decided to lift Babe Ruth's sagging spirits by paying public tribute to him in ceremonies in all major league parks on Sunday, April 27, 1947. Ruth was well enough to agree to appear at Yankee Stadium, and I was scheduled to speak there.

But it had been less than three weeks since the Durocher suspension. The name Commissioner Chandler was still anathema to New York baseball fans. Friends warned me that I was too unpopular to make a public appearance at the Stadium, where seventy thousand were expected.

"I'll be there, boos or no boos," I said.

But I had not expected such a raspberry as I got when I walked out to the mikes set up at home plate. The whole stadium erupted. Mel Allen, the announcer, tried to quiet the crowd. They kept booing. I just stood there, holding little note cards. I didn't intend to talk long. Just a short tribute to the Babe. He was standing back, in his camel-hair overcoat, wearing a gray slouch hat, frail and tottering, but game and ready to step forward for his introduction.

Suddenly the boos began to die down. I don't know whether the Yankee fans just got tired of bitching, or had second thoughts, or caught sight of Ruth looking bewildered. In any event, their mood abruptly and dramatically reversed itself. The whole stadium broke into cheers. Oh, what a beautiful sound!

I managed to make my short speech. The Babe, leaning pitifully into the mike and in a raspy voice that was barely audible, expressed his appreciation for the fans' tribute. One year later he made another appearance in uniform in Yankee Stadium when the club retired his number. He had to lean on his bat for a crutch; he was fading fast. He died in August 1948, and I helped carry him to the grave.

Never did I have any regrets about the Durocher suspension. One New York writer said, "Durocher ran a red light, and got the electric chair." If I know anything about it, Leo ran a thousand red lights! Branch Rickey restored him as manager one year later. Leo fizzled before the season was over. He bounced around a long time, going club to club, but never achieved what I would consider real greatness. When I collared him, he was at the point where he thought he was beyond the law. Maybe he considered himself bigger than baseball itself.

As a matter of fact, Leo could no more shed his pugnacity than a leopard can change his spots. I had to get him on the carpet again in the spring of 1949. That year Durocher was manager of the New York Giants.

I got a call from Bojangles Robinson, a great friend of mine. "Commissioner, Durocher's done hit a little black boy behind second base at the Polo Grounds." There had been an altercation between a fan who snatched off Leo's cap and ran away with it. I temporarily suspended Durocher while I had my men investigate the incident. Four days later I lifted the suspension; for once, Leo was not considered at fault.

To his credit, he never came crying to me. We didn't see each other for more than a year after I suspended him—not until 1948, when the Dodgers dedicated their new spring training site at Vero Beach, Florida. Branch Rickey guided me over to a batting cage where Durocher was standing and we shook hands. That didn't mean anything to me. "Good luck," I said. "Thank you, Commissioner," Leo responded. That was all.

Next time I saw him was in the late sixties. I was walking with friends down a hotel corridor in San Francisco when we met him. We didn't have a scintillating conversation. "Hello, Commissioner." "Hello, Leo." We shook hands. Later some sports reporters teased Durocher about his performance. "You are always talking," they chided, "about what you're going to do to Chandler. You all but hugged him."

They say Leo replied, "My first impulse when we shook hands was to take my free hand and hit him."

Probably he didn't mean that. But his crack was printed in a lot of newspapers and upset some of my loyal friends, one of whom was a husky construction boss back in Lexington named Frank Hare. I met Frank through my son Ben. They went through the University of Kentucky together. He's gone now. I hated to lose him. He was with me at the time and when he saw Durocher's quote immediately fired off a letter:

> Mr. Durocher, my name is Frank Hare and I live at such and such address, and I was standing behind Governor Chandler when you shook hands with him in San Francisco. I noticed you're quoted as regretting you didn't take your free hand and hit Governor Chandler. If you so desire, I will arrange to have the scene set up again at whatever place and time you choose, because if you are so inclined, I would take great pleasure in knocking your head off.

Neither Frank Hare nor I ever heard any more from Leo.

When I look back on the Durocher suspension, I can see that instead of strengthening my position as commissioner of baseball, it weakened it. At least as far as the owners went. I don't think they minded losing Durocher for a year. No one bitched to me about that.

But that reminded them just one more time that I was determined to be baseball czar, the man in charge, a strong commissioner. They didn't want that. They still wanted to fiddle with this and fiddle with that, and most of all, they wanted a chance to cheat when they felt like it.

So in the end you might say I was the loser and Leo the winner. At least he stayed in baseball. The owners were busy greasing the skids for my exit.

17

Jackie Robinson, and My Downfall

From beneath black beetle brows, the hostile stare of Branch Rickey came boring in on me. We faced each other in my walnut log cabin in my back yard at Versailles. Rickey had been backed into a corner—and came to me seeking a way out. He wanted to do a daring thing—break the color line in the big leagues. The fifteen other major league owners had just voted him down.

"They'll never agree, Branch," I said. "You're all alone on this one."

We sat on opposite sides of the big old desk where I made most of my important decisions, in the cabin's vaulted, book-lined study. In my great stone fireplace, logs blazed and crackled. We needed that fire; it was a cold, raw January day.

The year was 1947, and I will never forget that particular winter afternoon. We talked and talked and talked. What Rickey wanted to do, he could not do without me. If we got together the two of us would be writing an exciting and significant chapter in the history of baseball.

As I listened, it suddenly came to me that I'd personally known this fellow at least thirty years. Born in 1881 in a little town up in central Ohio, Rickey graduated from Ohio Wesleyan and broke into the big leagues as a catcher in 1905 with the St. Louis Browns. He went back to school and got a law degree from the University of Michigan, where he was also baseball coach. In 1914 he went back to the Browns in a front office job, spent World War I in France and came out a major. He became manager of the St. Louis Cardinals in 1919, and was on his way up.

It was just about that year that I first met Rickey. He was scheduled to make a speech at Berea College and they had me, then a student at Transylvania, introduce him. I guess I was selected because I was a player and knew baseball. Many, many years later I also introduced him for a talk at Morehead University.

So I was pretty well up on Branch Rickey. Not everybody in the game was wild about him. He was quick and smart. Proof of that is his invention of the farm system, where big league owners had clubs in the minors where they could try out promising youngsters and develop them and thus escape having to engage in big bidding wars for potential stars. Rickey was aggressive, and imaginative. He picked up the reputation as something of a skinflint because he usually arranged to pocket a percentage of the profits from any club he took over. Thus it would be to his advantage to hold down salaries and other expenses.

"If you trade with Rickey," the word was, "don't drink, and keep your hands in your pockets. He'll hornswaggle you." I thought that was a trifle harsh. But Branch definitely did want to win league pennants and World Series, so tried to find every advantage he could.

That's what had brought him to my cabin. He felt the winds of change stirring in postwar America. There was talk everywhere of the need to lower racial barriers. The major leagues were totally segregated, always had been limited strictly to white players. Rickey began talking seriously about breaking the color line by bringing Negro ballplayers to his Brooklyn Dodgers. Other baseball people, for the most part, were outraged.

Even so, Rickey got a jump on the other clubs by having his scouts search during the World War II years for a black player who had the skill to play big league ball. There had always been great talent in the segregated Negro leagues, known as the American Negro League and the National Negro

League. The blacks played each other on such teams as the Chattanooga Lookouts, Birmingham Black Barons, New Orleans Pelicans, Baltimore Black Sox, Chicago American Giants, the Homestead Grays, the Pittsburgh Crawfords. These Negro ball players led a miserable existence, overworked and underpaid, traveling around in rattletrap buses, with poor accommodations and rundown ballparks—except when their owners rented the major league parks in Chicago, New York, Washington and elsewhere for big games.

But out of the Negro leagues came some of the greatest baseball players in America—Satchel (for "Satchelfoot") Paige, the phenomenal fire-baller, and Josh Gibson, one of the most superb catchers who ever donned a mitt.

The Brooklyn Dodger scouts settled on an infielder named Jackie Robinson, who was born in Georgia and attended U.C.L.A., becoming a standout both in collegiate football and baseball. Rickey's men took him in 1945 off the all-Negro Kansas City Monarchs where he was playing second base. And "took him" is exactly what they did, because the black leagues in their haphazard way of doing business had no legitimate contracts and their players could go wherever they could get the most money.

In the warmth of the log fire, Rickey and I reviewed all of this, and talked about the consequences that might ensue from rupture of segregation in the big leagues.

Whomever would be the first black man to don a major league uniform unquestionably would face extreme difficulties, animosity, prejudice and hatred. It would require stamina and a special tolerance or patience to cope with the insults that were bound to be thrown at him. Rickey said he had the right man.

I had my doubts. I could have seen him reaching out for Satchel Paige or Josh Gibson or some other Negro who had truly demonstrated his greatness on the diamond in their leagues or in competition against the off-season big league white barnstormers. I believe Rickey thought Paige and Gibson were too old. But Robinson, already twenty-six, certainly was no youngster. Besides, he had played only second-string shortstop for the Kansas City Monarchs, was not an outstanding hitter, though one hell of a base runner. It was a question at that time whether he was really major league material.

Rickey, however, signed Jackie Robinson to a contract and sent him to his farm club in the International League, the Montreal Royals, to play short. He could do that because the minors were not under major league control, and hence not necessarily segregated.

The signing of Jackie Robinson for Montreal in 1945 caused a great commotion. That immediately brought to the fore the issue of segregation in organized baseball. Virtually every knowledgeable person in the game expected Rickey to try to bring Robinson into the Dodger club, sundering the color line. It seemed that he was just waiting for what he considered the right time.

There was great fear that would be the wrong thing to do. The other owners were vehemently against desegregation of baseball. To a man, they were at least pocketbook racists; they feared their white patrons would resent bringing in Negro players, would make protests, perhaps stay away from the parks and seriously cut ticket sales. Most of the big leaguer players are called "chicken fried"—that is, products of the small towns below the Mason-Dixon line. I'm a Confederate myself, so I could totally understand the Dixie heritage they grew up with. It was simply that "niggers" were not their equals, and ought to know their place, and keep it. Those old customs of blacks coming to the back door, sitting in the back of the bus, and having their separate drinking fountains, cafes and even churches—those old ways die hard. And they were far from dead among the Southerners in baseball when the Jackie Robinson affair came up. Would the Southern players boycott a team with a black player? That was a big question.

Jackie Robinson had a good year in Montreal, and Branch Rickey decided he might as well make his move. A secret meeting was called by the owners. It was held right after New Year's 1947 in New York at the Waldorf-Astoria hotel. No minutes were taken at that meeting. It was held for the purpose of letting the other owners know what Rickey was planning to do. If I can't remember every word said, I have a clear and vivid memory of the tone of that session. The owners were against Rickey doing this thing, and they implored him to forget the whole idea.

He talked for a long while about how bringing a Negro

player into the game was just the right thing to do and how
Jackie Robinson had earned his chance by the fine year he had
in Montreal and how he was going to bring him up that spring.
There was a resolution of support proposed by Rickey. He
wanted the owners to go on record as saying they endorsed his
plan and would go along with it. I don't think he was looking
for any help, he was just looking to see that his fellow owners
would not get in his way.

After a lot of talk the vote was finally taken and it was 15
to 1 against Rickey. I was at the head of this big table at one of
the large meeting rooms in the hotel. I read the votes one by
one and they were all "no" except that single "yes" vote in Rickey's hand. He was very angry and got up and walked out of the
meeting room.

I came back to Versailles and a few days later I got a call
from Rickey. He said he was very bothered by the vote of his
fellow owners and said he was concerned about the situation
now more than ever. I suggested he come down and we would
talk it all out.

So he climbed aboard the Dodgers' twin-engine Beechcraft
and flew to Kentucky. He came on over to my place alone, and
just the two of us sat out there in the guest cabin to settle it.

Rickey was as emotional as I had ever seen him. He said he
didn't know if he could do this in light of the opposition of his
partners. He said, on the other hand, Negro people expected
Jackie to be brought up.

"If I don't do it," he said with a dark scowl, "there probably
will be riots. You know the Polo Grounds are right in the middle
of Harlem, and if we go there to play the Giants without Robinson, the blacks will have a riot and burn the place down. And
no telling what—fires, too, I suppose—would happen at Ebbets
Field." I remember he sighed very heavily. "Of course, you
heard what my partners said at our last meeting—there'll be riots if we do bring in a Negro."

Rickey rubbed one big hand across his eyes and turned and
stared absently into the fire for a long moment. "Commissioner," he said, "I can't do this without I'm assured of your
complete cooperation."

I nodded. "I know that, Branch. If Judge Landis was still
alive you couldn't even ask him. I've read the minutes of his

meetings. For twenty-four years he had one answer every time the question came up—no!" You could call the old judge a racist, because that's what the owners wanted. They wanted to keep the majors segregated and totally white. I don't want to be too hard on the old man, because he wanted to keep his job, and he kept it. He was doing what the owners wanted him to do.

In 1944 before he died, I remember, someone made a final run at him. Landis said, "Everything has been said that's going to be said. My answer is no!" He was adamant. If you had black skin, that automatically disqualified you from the majors.

"Branch, that fifteen to one turndown your partners gave you at the Waldorf meeting—I think that was supposed to mainly be for my guidance, wouldn't you say?"

He nodded.

"So I know why you are here asking me for help. I am the only person on earth who can approve the transfer of that contract from Montreal to Brooklyn. Nobody else. You still want to go ahead, and go through with it?"

"I'd like to, Commissioner."

"Can Robinson play baseball?"

"No question about that," Rickey said.

"Is he a major leaguer? All I know is what I've read. I have never seen him play."

"Yes, sir."

"I've already done a lot of thinking about this whole racial situation in our country," I told Rickey. "As a member of the Senate Military Affairs Committee I got to know a lot about our casualties during the war. Plenty of Negro boys were willing to go out and fight and die for this country. Is it right when they came back to tell them they can't play the national pastime? You know, Branch, I'm going to have to meet my Maker some day and if He asks me why I didn't let this boy play and I say it's because he's black that might not be a satisfactory answer.

"If the Lord made some people black, and some white, and some red or yellow, he must have had a pretty good reason. It isn't my job to decide which colors can play big league baseball. It is my job to see that the game is fairly played and that everybody has an equal chance. I think if I do that, I can face my Maker with a clear conscience.

"So bring him in. Transfer Robinson. And we'll make the fight. There's going to be trouble."

And there was. Branch Rickey was not largely inspired by altruistic motives, or a liberal-minded desire to tear down the barriers for blacks. I'm sure he had reasonable humanitarian feelings. But he made no bones that he chiefly wanted Robinson to help him win a championship. "I'd play an elephant with pink horns," he was quoted as saying, "if it could win the pennant."

During our hours together out in the cabin I kept getting the impression that Rickey felt he was God Almighty, and that he was somehow the Savior of the black people. He tried his best—and this I know—he and his whole outfit moved in to give him the full credit for breaking the baseball color line. They wanted to keep everybody else, including me, out of it. But of course he couldn't have done it without my approval. When he came down to Versailles, he had two chances: slim and none. But I did it for him, made it possible. I never could understand why he always cut me out of it, every time he mentioned the Jackie Robinson decision. I was surprised, and I suppose somewhat hurt, by his attitude. But I never brought it up to him. I just let that pass.

Even with my green light, Rickey bided his time and didn't make his historic baseball move until April 10, 1947. That, incidentally, was one day after I had suspended Leo Durocher for a year and Rickey had summoned Burt Shotton to be his interim pilot.

In breaking the color line, Rickey expected to stir up resentment. He drew more than he expected—even in his own clubhouse. It was an experience too emotional for the Southern players to handle. I could understand why they were upset. After all, my grandfather was second sergeant in General Morgan's cavalry, and I was brought up in the Confederate heritage. The Dodgers from the Deep South simply didn't want Jackie Robinson in the same locker room, the same shower, the same hotel, the same taxicab, or on the same team.

Dixie Walker led the Dodger revolt. His opinion counted. Brooklyn fans loved him for his magnificent outfielding and his hot bat. They nicknamed him "the People's *Cherce.*" Pee Wee Reese was team captain, but Dixie, born in Georgia and raised in Alabama, was the real leader. He and other southern players began circulating a petition against a Negro joining the team. When Rickey heard about that, he called a team meeting and read his men the riot act. But the resentment was deep.

"I'm not going to play with any nigger," Dixie said. "I think I'll go home and paint my house."

By that time, of course, I was into it.

"Dixie, you may not play," I said. "But he's going to play."

Fortunately, Dixie, a really decent, kind and gentle man, changed his mind. But resentment and near-rebellion flared up on many of the major clubs.

The manager of the Phillies, Ben Chapman, a native of Nashville, was quoted on the sports pages as saying his players would "take care of" Robinson when he got to Philadelphia.

I sent Chapman a telegram. It said: "If you make trouble for Robinson, I'll make trouble for you."

There was no trouble in Philadelphia, but I expected something untoward to happen somewhere. So I gave Robinson a secret shadow. I assigned Frenchy DeMoisey to follow the Dodgers, at home and on the road, and keep an eye on him and try to avert problems. We didn't tell Jackie. He wasn't special; I just wanted him to have the same chance to make good in the big leagues as anybody else.

At times I felt Rickey may have been a little too stringent with Robinson. But he was closer to the situation and the mood of the man than was Frenchy. I told Branch, "Don't bridle him. Don't shackle him. Just tell him to conduct himself properly."

By the end of his first year, Jackie led the National League in stolen bases (39), and was *Sporting News* Rookie of The Year, and eventually went into the Hall of Fame in 1962. But, unfortunately at the start, Jackie made trouble for himself. He definitely had a chip on his shoulder. I guess he couldn't be blamed with all the jeers and insults thrown at him every day. You've got to understand that baseball players have always taunted each other, especially with ridicule about physical characteristics. It was a mean but customary ritual to lampoon your opponents with such endearments as: Fatty, Slim, Slats, Schnoz, Bullet Face, Pock Face, Cue Ball, Skinhead, Ears, Irish, Dago, Dutchman, etc. I remember some fans even jeered Babe Ruth as "nigger lips."

On reflection I believe this stands partially as a tribute to the general insensitivity of mid-twentieth century America. Sports writers, more from misguided mischief than malevolence, hopped on racial stereotypes, and made fun of long ethnic names, Latin accents, and presumed personality attributes of various nationalities. One sports scribe, thinking himself hilarious and not necessarily racist, often quoted a character named "Ku Klux Clancy, the Invisible Umpire."

Jackie Robinson heard plenty of "nigger" from the stands and dugouts. He was called snowflake, Little Black Sambo, watermelon-eater—all of the standard insults. Plus a lot of filthy ones.

Then came a blockbuster—the St. Louis Cardinals were reported ready to strike rather than play against Jackie!

That story broke May 9 in the *New York Herald Tribune* under the byline of sports editor Stanley Woodward. A lot of southerners were on the Cards; the inside scoop was that three of them—Enos Slaughter, Terry Moore and Marty Marion— were the alleged ringleaders. Tip for the story was supposed to have come from an insider, Cardinal physician Dr. Bob Hyland.

Team owner Sam Breadon got wind of the "revolt" and could not authenticate it or identify anyone willing to say they planned to strike. By the time I was notified, the story had fizzled out. In any event, there was no strike in St. Louis.

The whole season was edgy. Robinson was having a so-so year in Dodger uniform. The big league curve ball gave him fits and he fell into a hitting slump. But on the bases he was a terror. Any time he got on first, he'd begin to jump around and taunt the pitcher. "I'm going. . . . I'm going!" he'd yell. And most of the time he would go. He was a hell of a base stealer— even stealing home.

But his mouth made trouble for me. Jackie was too quick to pop off. Sports writers egged him on to make critical remarks, and then played them up. Unfortunately, Jackie interpreted everything bad that happened to him as strictly on account of his color, and not because he had failed to perform correctly as a ballplayer. One New York writer said Jackie always "saw racism and prejudice under the bed." He must have become aware of the situation, because I once saw him confess on one sports page: "When I get hot, I pop off and say a lot of things I shouldn't."

There is no doubt in my mind that as rough as Jackie Robinson's rites of passage were in the big leagues, the situation would have been infinitely worse if we hadn't managed to anticipate and defuse a lot of potential trouble through Frenchy De-Moisey's keen surveillance.

For nearly three years I had very little direct contact with Jackie. His skill as a player won over some of the Southern men. Pee Wee Reese was one of the first Dodgers to go out of his way to sit down on the train beside Jackie, or to eat with him. Even Dixie Walker relented, and volunteered some batting tips, graciously accepted by his black teammate. But after his first few seasons, Jackie, continually on the muscle, got the reputation of "rabble rouser," and lost much of his popularity even with the Negro sports reporters. Robinson himself observed later that after initial sympathetic acceptance as an "underdog," he found that by sounding off he became identified as "a swellhead, wise guy, an 'uppity' nigger."

I had to call him on the carpet at the start of Spring training in 1949. He was particularly mean and aggressive when he showed up at the Dodger training camp at Vero Beach. "They'd better be prepared to be rough this year," he announced, "because I'm going to be rough on them." Ordinarily that might have passed by as just spirited preseason yakking, but some officials saw racial overtones in his comment.

And his racist animosity certainly was apparent a few days later when he tangled with a Dodger rookie, a pitcher named Chris Van Kuyk. The report that reached me described the incident as "a genuinely nasty, name-calling, beanballing spat."

I summoned Jackie to my hotel. I wasn't just whistling "Dixie," and my message was short if not sweet. Certain conduct is required of a professional in the big leagues. No ifs, ands, or buts . . . . Robinson's ears may have been burning a little after our visit, but he had a crystal clear idea of how he must behave in the future.

From the beginning Robinson initiated a simmering feud with umpires. He mouthed around that some of them were "on" him. He frequently taunted them. In the case of Cal Hubbard,

Jackie would glare at the umpire, drag his hand across his own throat, making the "choke up" sign. Cal didn't like that, and I don't blame him.

I always considered my friend Jocko Conlan about as fine and fair an umpire as ever brushed off home plate, but he had a poor opinion of Robinson's attitude. In his autobiography, Jocko wrote: "He was the most difficult ballplayer I had to deal with as an umpire. Jackie was one of those players who could never accept a decision."

It was not until late in his third season that I had to personally get on Robinson's case again—and even then I managed to do it indirectly. The Dodgers were playing the Yankees in the 1949 World Series. In the game that stirred me up, Don Newcombe, the third Negro to be put on the Brooklyn roster, was pitching.

In the eighth inning, Umpire Cal Hubbard, behind the plate, called a strike on the Dodgers' Spider Jorgensen. Brooklyn lost and after the game Jackie Robinson talked to reporters and criticized Hubbard's call. I didn't like that.

I sought out Don Newcombe in the dressing room. "What kind of a game did Hubbard call today?" I asked.

"Fine," said Newcombe. He might have been primed for a few sour grapes, considering the fact that he had just lost the game. In the ninth inning Tommy Heinrich connected for a home run. Newcombe just took one look at that soaring fly ball, jammed his glove in his pocket, and came off the mound.

"How many pitches do you think he missed today?" I persisted.

"Maybe one," said Newcombe. "Maybe two."

"Well, Don, that's good umpiring, isn't it?"

"Yes, Commissioner, I'd say so."

Back at the hotel I called the Brooklyn manager, Burt Shotton. I asked him, "Do you need Robinson to play second base for you tomorrow?"

"Oh, yes, Commissioner. I need him badly. Why do you ask?"

"Well, I want you to give him a message for me. I've got plenty of umpires. I don't need him to umpire. I thought if you didn't need him to play second base, we'd give him the day off."

I knew Shotton as a totally decent fellow. He had been called in again to manage the Dodgers after Leo Durocher jumped over to the Giants. "I'll do that. I need him."

"That's all right," I said. "But if he gives us trouble tomorrow, I'll stop the game—and take him out!"

There was no more trouble in the Series, which the Yankees took four games to one.

So that about covers the Jackie Robinson episode. Curiously, except for Branch Rickey, none of the other owners ever brought up the subject with me. I know for certain, however, as a result of subsequent events, that a majority of them resented me helping break the color line. Robinson developed serious diabetes problems and died in 1972. But he took time back in 1956 to write and acknowledge my role bringing him into the big leagues: "I will never forget your part in the so-called Rickey experiment. . . ."

Not only was I known as a "players' commissioner," I was also called an "umpires' commissioner." I didn't object to that. Umpires have made American baseball the great game it is. There has never been one single case where a major league umpire was charged with doing a dishonorable thing.

I love umpires. That affection goes way back to my youth— all the way to Uncle Charley Moran, who spent his summers umpiring in the big leagues. The year I went home from Harvard I stopped off in Philadelphia where Uncle Charley was officiating. He got me a grandstand ticket and promised to take me to dinner.

In a late inning the Phillies had men on second and third with one out, and the batter hit a line drive down the left field line. We call it a blue darter.

The two base runners rushed in to score, and the crowd cheered. In the excitement nobody seemed to notice that behind third base Uncle Charley had his right arm up pumping the ball foul.

When the Phillies saw that, the whole team rushed out and converged on Moran. There was a hot argument. It was furious. But Uncle Charley stood his ground. The two runners had to go back. The batter then popped out, and the next man struck out, and the Phillies went down to defeat.

That night Uncle Charley was about the most unpopular

fellow you could find in Philadelphia. He didn't mention the call after the game and I tried to kid him about it at dinner.

"There's been a move afoot to take the umpires off the field and put them in the grandstands," I cracked. "They can see better from there."

That didn't get a rise. He sat there chewing his steak.

"Tell me the truth, Unc, what about that ball hit past third base this afternoon?"

He looked up, glaring. "All right, what about it?"

"Was it close?"

"Naw."

"Was it fair or foul?"

"Foul," he grunted. He suddenly looked mean, reached across the table, seized my shoulders and shook me. "I want to tell you something, son, and never forget it. There are no close ones. They are either fair or foul, safe or out."

He shook me again.

"And they ain't nothing 'til I call 'em." He relaxed. "As long as you and I live, that's going to be a foul ball."

Some of my best friends in baseball are umpires—Mr. Jocko Conlan, Mr. E. C. Quigley, Mr. Bill Klem.... Notice I call them *mister*; they deserve it. I never saw such a fine set of men. Add to my list Mr. Larry Goetz, Mr. Al Barlick, Mr. Cal Hubbard, Mr. Bill Summers, Mr. Charlie Berry, Mr. Augie Donatelli, Mr. Ernie Stewart, Mr. Bill Stewart, Mr. Billy Evans, Mr. Beans Reardon....

Despite all my admiration and respect for umpires, I got caught up in a nasty little rhubarb over them and found out that the high commissioner really didn't have much say over them. The umps are under control of the National League and the American League.

It was Ernie Stewart who precipitated the rhubarb. In July 1945 he and his partner ran into me in the clubhouse in Washington after a game. The complained about the bad treatment American League president Will Harridge gave them. He didn't give a damn about them. He was an owners' man, and he demonstrated that all the time he was in office.

Harridge didn't mind mistreating the umpires. After they complained and he found out about it, he fired them. That was a dirty thing. The umpires were not well paid, averaging no more than $7,500 a year. That was shabby treatment and I thought the umpires were too important to the success of the game to be treated second class. I'm very pleased now that their salaries are more fair and adequate, but that was too long coming.

Players these days get fantastic pensions, and they deserve them. Fate thrust me into a major role in setting them up. Remember how saddened I was to see those two greats, Grover Cleveland Alexander and Dazzy Vance, having to make one-night stands to survive? It is fortunate, too, that Larry Mac-Phail saw the need just as I did to provide for retired major leaguers. We began planning and I had some actuaries move in and figure out what we would need for a sound program.

The owners really didn't want to start the pension program, but they agreed to give it a trial, with the option to pull out at the end of five years. Under our scheme, the players contributed thirteen percent and the owners provided the remainder. I don't believe the owners would have continued, except for another stroke of fate.

Television came along. NBC wanted to broadcast the World Series. A fellow named Tom Gallery and I negotiated a six-year contract for several million dollars under sponsorship of the Gillette Razor Company. It was the best World Series contract that had been made up to that time. Of course they are far bigger now.

But the importance of my deal was that I designated that eighty-one percent of the television contract revenue must go into the player pension fund. That assured the solvency and success of the pension scheme. Actually that was owners' money, and after that they couldn't back out of the pension scheme.

One of the great thrills of my life was being able to take my father to the World Series. And, believe me, that was the highlight of his, too. His heroes were Connie Mack, Clark Griffith, Walter Johnson, Muggsy McGraw—the real old-timers.

When I introduced Dad to Clark Griffith, he just beamed and murmured: "The old fox." And when he shook Connie Mack's hand, he just let out a long sigh, such a plaintive, never-to-be-forgotten sound: "Mister Cornelius McGillicuddy." These were people my father had never expected to see in person, much less from the box of the high commissioner of baseball. I had a lot of satisfaction out of that.

I got a dig from sports writers about part of the family—Mama and Mimi. They were photographed at Churchill Downs attending the races. I had been cracking down on gambling and banned baseball players from going to the racetracks. Ah ha! Double standard, jeered the sports writers, if you let your wife and daughter go. I fixed the reporters right quick. "What team do they have a contract with?"

In his twenty-four years Judge Landis had totally ignored the minor leagues. I don't believe he ever set foot in one of their parks. Larry MacPhail pointed that out, and suggested I ought to occasionally go out and visit the minor league teams.

"That's where we get our players," Larry said. "These fellows generally have shoestring operations, and they have a tough time. They don't have much money, but if you went and gave them a special day, it would be a big boost for attendance."

I did that. There were at that time a record number of minors—forty-nine—and I visited practically all of them. I made hundreds of trips, by train or car, naturally, since I won't fly. Typically, I'd leave my office and swing south through Tennessee, Georgia, Alabama. They'd advertise that I was coming and maybe I'd throw out the first ball. In the afternoon I'd usually play golf with the owners. I did more of that than anybody on earth, and there's nobody gonna equal my record in any way. Because nobody does that now.

Hark back to that saying of mine about picked-green ball players. To be successful they had to be mature and smart. Mature they would eventually be, smart maybe never. Perhaps there is some formula as well that applies to high commissioners of baseball.

I've thought of that fellow I sent up for a tryout, the pitcher who turned out to have "a million dollar arm and a ten-cent head." I don't believe I fell into that category. But I smelled trouble. Nobody had to tell me. The owners did not directly complain. There was just an unmistakable feeling. I guess in actuality it had been there from the very first—when I demanded all the powers of czardom.

After three or four years, I began to wonder if my number was up. I couldn't change. I intended to go right on, open, straightforward, honest. If the owners still wanted a stooge, someone who would blink and let them cheat, and get away with foolish things, we would never get along. I really loved being commissioner, and I wanted very much to stay in the job. But I had made enemies—Saigh, Perini, Del Webb, Dan Topping. . . .

I could count noses pretty accurately. The anything-to-make-a-buck corporate raiders and the sneaking cheaters held the balance of power. There were still stand-up grass-roots baseball pioneers in the game. The question was: how many of them?

My seven-year contract as commissioner ran to April, 1952. If there was any question it might not be renewed, I decided I ought to know that in advance, so I could plan for my own future. I was now in my mid-life prime, with plenty of energy and imagination to devote to the law, to politics, or something else.

It would take affirmative votes from twelve of the sixteen owners to renew my contract. "If Jesus Christ were baseball commissioner," I told Mama, "I'm not sure he could carry twelve votes."

But I gave it a try. My request was first taken up in December 1950 at the winter meeting in St. Petersburg, Florida. I felt pretty confident. Joe Williams, the columnist, had taken an informal poll of owners. "You'll be given a new contract," Joe told me, pleased.

But Del Webb and his crowd had spread plenty of poison. They were leading a behind-the-scenes palace revolt. They didn't have to win over the majority to scuttle Happy Chandler. All they needed was to guarantee five negative votes.

Their arm-twisting garnered more than that. The tally was nine votes for me, seven against. Three votes short of the necessary three-fourths majority!

That was hurtful. I was disappointed that my fair-minded friends among the owners had not made a stronger fight to keep in office a commissioner who refused to be a stooge for the cheaters.

The news went out on the wires that I had lost and the owners were now looking for a new commissioner. That night I got a call from Clark Griffith of the Washington Senators. He had not come to the meeting.

"What's going on down there?" he asked.

I told him.

"They can't do that," he said. "Just hang tight. You're the commissioner and you're going to stay commissioner."

Griffith immediately began stirring things up to put my contract to another vote. I had a lot of friends who started lobbying the doubtful owners to keep me in office. I just went about my duties as before. My contract still had nearly a year and a half to run.

But my future in baseball was clearly up in the air. I considered the outlook gloomy. Clark Griffith kept reassuring me that he and others were confident they could muster a three-fourths majority.

It came to a head again on March 12, 1951, at the owners Spring meeting in Miami Beach. I was excused from the conference room in the Shoremede Hotel while the sixteen of them took another vote.

John Galbreath summoned me to come back and hear the result.

The vote was nine to seven. No change. I had lost again. I sat at the head of the long conference table and searched their faces. My pride was stung. I'd done them a good job. And they didn't appreciate it. They didn't cite any reasons or give any excuses. They didn't need any. All they needed was to hang on to control of five negative votes. And they clearly understood that.

There was a lot of uneasy silence in that hotel room. I could not leave there without having my say, getting a few things off my chest. I told them I had not sought the job of commissioner of baseball, and that I would not seek to retain it against their wishes.

"The record will show," I said, "that we have made substantial progress in the last six years. I am certain I have not done one thing to lessen the respect people have for baseball."

I paused and looked up and down the table. The owners just sat there like a bunch of mummies. My emotions were getting the better of me. I was turning a little angry. "It's a dangerous thing," I said, "to let a minority control a sport. That's what you are doing here today. I never expected to be able to please you all. But I did believe I could earn your respect. What puzzles me most is that I have not determined in what way I have failed, if, in fact, I have." Again I searched their faces. "None of you has pointed out a failure."

So I dared them. It was more than a challenge. It was a straight-out dare. "If any of you fellows know of anything I've done that reflected adversely on the integrity of the sport, I challenge you to speak up—here and now."

Nobody said anything. So I started going around the table, calling them by name, one at a time. It was futile. Still nobody said a word.

I arose and got my hat. "Thank you, gentlemen," I said. I went around and shook hands with Clark Griffith and some of the others who had been friendly. My enemies I ignored.

Webb, suddenly very solicitous, came up to me with Phil Wrigley. "Let us get you a Coca-Cola and a sandwich," one of them said.

I gave them an indifferent look. "Thank you. I'm not hungry," I said, and left the room.

I was surprised that I didn't choke up. It was a deeply emotional scene, one of the worst I have ever gone through.

As I walked down the steps to the lobby I came face to face with Jocko Conlan, my umpire friend. In the baseball world news travels fast and he already knew. Tears were running down his cheeks. That hurt.

The night of my downfall Gabe Paul walked with me for a long time on the dark streets of St. Petersburg, offering the best consolation and counsel a loyal friend could muster. Then when it came time to start back to Kentucky, my West Coast buddy, "Torchy" Torrence, general manager of the Seattle Rainers, insisted on driving me. We stopped over a few days in North Carolina to visit my daughter Marcella and her family. When we got to Versailles, "Torchy" stayed with Mama and me for several days, wanting to make absolutely sure that anything I needed he would try to do. Anybody's lucky to have friends like that.

There was no point in continuing as a lame-duck commissioner. My effectiveness was beyond repair. So I worked out an arrangement to terminate my contract in ninety days. It was all over—and I didn't feel too bad. Clark Griffith, in a letter that I proudly keep, summed it up succinctly: "Happy, I was raised in the West and have seen many games played with stacked decks. This was one.... It was clear to everybody there that when the meeting was over you were the biggest man in the room."

Branch Rickey wrote me: "It is my firm belief that throughout the country you have greater popular support now than you had when you became commissioner, and if I know you at all, you will continue to grow both in personal friendships and public service."

I must say that I look back on my term as baseball commissioner with pride and pleasure. I am not alone in thinking I served the game well. Not long ago a distinguished baseball historian made this assessment:

> As commissioner, A. B. Chandler was neither a visionary nor a crusading reformer. He was at heart a baseball fan, a man who wanted to take the commissioner's position off its pedestal, to humanize it, and to share himself and the game with its followers. In this he succeeded admirably....
>
> To his credit, Chandler left the game in a stronger position than he found it: sound and vibrant, ready to face the changing technologies, the increased popularity of other professional sports, and a public with increasing leisure time and mobility.
>
> At the very least, he should be remembered as a good commissioner, a man who used his abilities to the utmost to imbue the game he loved with fairness and stability.

There had to be a new commissioner. The owners made overtures to J. Edgar Hoover. The FBI chief said no. He rejected the job, saying, "After the way you treated Governor Chandler, I wouldn't touch it with a ten foot pole."

For a while it seemed they couldn't find a successor. And then they turned to the man his fellow sports writers had always boosted, Ford Frick.

What I said about that was, the owners had a vacancy and they decided to continue with it!

So I reached the end of the road as baseball commissioner. I looked out my office window toward the promised land. I was ready and pleased to be going back home—to Kentucky.

My last official act as the high commissioner was to dedicate a new stadium at Reading, Pennsylvania, on June 15, 1951.

There was a crowd of five thousand people. To wind up the ceremony I sang a song—"My Old Kentucky Home."

That was about as fitting a swan song as I could think of.

Believe me, there wasn't a dry eye in the stands.

18

"Wipe Your Shoes On a $20,000 Rug!"

"Boys," I said from the speaking platform in Lexington, "I want you to bring Mrs. Jenkins up here. She's an old friend of mine."

Out of the crowd of about five thousand came a plain, modestly-dressed mountain woman. She stood beside me at the mike and I put my arm around her. "I want you people to know that you are looking at the mother of a real hero. This is the mother of Captain John Jenkins who was shot down in North Africa in defense of his country."

It became so quiet you could hear a pin drop.

"On my trip to the warfronts for the Senate Military Affairs Committee I visited Captain Jenkins in the hospital. I perceived he was not far from that land from whence no traveler has returned."

Mrs. Jenkins began crying softly.

"I went back the next day and Captain Jenkins had crossed over. I cabled you, didn't I?"

Mrs. Jenkins lifted her bowed head. "Yes," she said.

"Every night," I told the audience, "she has said a prayer for me. Haven't you?"

"Yes."

"You keep saying your prayers, my dear, and we'll let Clementine and Wetherbine and all the rest of them do just anything they want to do. . . ."

My campaign manager, lawyer Joe Leary, was in the crowd standing with Allan Trout of the *Courier-Journal.* All around them people were openly sobbing. Trout turned to Leary, who was crying, too. "Hell, I'm getting out of here. Nobody can beat that guy!"

This scene took place in February 1955. I had come back to Kentucky politics. Once again I was on the campaign trail to try to capture the best job I ever had—governor of Kentucky. I was at that time three years shy of sixty, but I still had desire, ideas and energy. My memory for names and faces was undimmed. I still bear-hugged and shook hands with a vise-grip. My main message followed a familiar line that people recognized.

"Do you want four more years of the tax-crazy, spend-crazy, and waste-crazy dictators, or do you want an administration that knows the value of a dollar? There must be a halting place some time. The people are taxed to the limit. I intend to give you some relief.

"Look at me! I'm the only man in the history of Kentucky that ever cut your taxes!"

And I made a brand-new pledge. If elected, I would build a new medical school at the University of Kentucky. There was only one in the state, at the University of Louisville. Not adequate! A hundred years ago we had a medical school at Transylvania University in Lexington, but it had closed in 1860 for lack of support. A desperate need had developed—especially in eastern Kentucky—for more physicians. In 1949 five thousand babies were born in our state with no doctor in attendance at the time of the child's birth. We lost many babies, and we lost too many mothers. In sixteen counties of Kentucky in 1949 there wasn't a single dentist!

We could not afford in this modern world to keep being that backward. My promise was a sacred oath.

My transition from high commissioner of baseball back to the hustings of my home state did not, of course, come overnight. There are two reasons why there was an interim that covered more than three years. Number One: I was still obligated by commitments to the world of baseball that I felt I must honor. And Number Two: The Kentucky political scene had undergone sharp and drastic changes that required me to reestablish my old network of political loyalists throughout the commonwealth.

I did both.

The players in the major leagues were in my corner all the way in my confrontation with the owners. Their leaders pleaded with the owners to renew my contract. If they had a vote, I would still be commissioner. But they didn't.

Still the players wanted to demonstrate their high regard for me. Four players were appointed to represent the two leagues—Freddie Hutchinson, Danny Litwhiler, Allie Reynolds and Ralph Kiner. They met and finally decided to create a silver tray for me. It is a beautiful and priceless treasure. At each end is a baseball bat, glove and ball. The names of all sixteen teams are engraved on it. And the inscription says it was presented to me "for valuable services rendered to the players of the major leagues."

Then they broke the mold. They never gave any other commissioner such an honor, and they said they intended this to be a once in a lifetime award. I wouldn't take anything for that tray, and I'm always proud to take it out of its hiding place and show it to visitors.

Right after the owners fired me, some of my Hollywood friends decided to give me an appreciation or testimonial dinner. It was held in Chasens, one of the favorite movieland restaurants. Several hundred friends turned out. Bob Hope, who was master of ceremonies, cracked: "This is the biggest crowd I've ever seen come out to honor a fellow who's just been fired!"

My biggest post-commissioner assignment was to escort a U.S. Army baseball team to Japan for a series of exhibition games. I appreciated the honor, but I certainly did not look forward to crossing the Pacific by air. I have been averse to flying since my close call in that bomber over the Aleutian Islands. We were scheduled to go to the Orient—Mama was going, too—on a Pan American Flying Clipper.

All I could do was bow to fatalism and accept the necessity of flying to Japan. My son Dan, who was nineteen at the time, told later of overhearing my pillow-talk with Mama the night before we departed Versailles.

"Well, Mama, at least we've had a good life."

"Hush, Happy. Don't talk like that! Nothing's going to happen."

And nothing bad did. The trip was wonderful. The Japanese are crazy about baseball. They made us feel honored and welcome—even though this was just seven years after we dropped the atomic bomb on Hiroshima.

The Japs were no match for our American team. Of the seven exhibition games we played, our boys lost only one.

Mama turned out to be almost as big a celebrity on the social circuit as our players were on the field. We rode the bullet train to Osaka, and there was party after party. I felt awkward squirming around shoeless to sit on the floor for these festivities. But Mama adapted easily and played her guitar and sang many songs, as I did also. When she learned to down the Japanese beer, which she said was excellent, and give their word for bottoms-up, which was something like "kumbi," they applauded her with great enthusiasm.

When awards were passed out at the final appreciation banquet, I felt sad about the little manager of the Japanese team. His men had tried so hard and come up so empty. In size and ability they were not up to American big leaguers. Watching the little Japanese manager smiling graciously, I suddenly remembered how it felt to be a loser. I had been there.

On impulse, I summoned him to the front. From my finger I pulled off a ring—my handsome World Series ring with a one carat diamond.

"I present you this," I said, "in the spirit of friendship between our two countries and as appreciation for the efforts of you and your players."

The little man was startled. I slipped the ring on his delicate finger. It looked practically ten sizes too big. He was overcome. He bowed and bowed and thanked me—and bowed some more. After that he followed me around everywhere we went. Later, coming to this country as president of a Nippon export firm, he always made a point of stopping in Versailles to see Mama and me. He never showed up without his hand-me-down World Series ring, which he had had cut down for a comfortable fit.

My friendships brought many major leaguers on visits to 191 Elm Street. Ty Cobb came several times from 1950 to 1952. He found our log cabin guest house comfortable, and would walk with me around town, meeting people, and taking time to give our Versailles youngsters batting tips.

Ty Cobb was just about the best baseball player that ever was. He hit .367 over twenty-four years and stole 892 bases. They say Pete Rose beat his hitting record—4,191—but that doesn't really count. Pete had 2,345 more times at bat than did Ty. If Ty Cobb had gone to the plate as many times as Pete did, he'd have had 6,000 hits. I don't want to take anything away from Pete because he's a hustler. But it's not fair to say he broke Ty Cobb's record.

Ty Cobb lost a young son, a doctor, suddenly and as a memorial he built a hospital in his hometown of Royston, Georgia. And financed it completely. I was serving as one of his three trustees at the time of his death on July 17, 1961, at age seventy-five.

Baseball fired me in the spring of 1951. That meant the timing would have been just right for me to immediately jump into the race for governor. But I counseled with Joe Leary, who had started with me as the rather remarkable *sixth* assistant attorney general.

"I don't think you ought to run this time," Joe said. "This is not your year. Wait until 1955—and you can win! I'll manage your campaign."

That advice grated on me harshly, and was hard to swallow. I was eager to leap right into the 1951 race. But I thought it over and finally took Joe Leary's advice—and his offer to manage my 1955 campaign. He had the reputation of being one of the sharpest political strategists in the commonwealth. I knew I would be fortunate to have him for my manager.

Since the day I left the governor's office to go to the United States Senate, Kentucky had had three governors—Keen Johnson, Simeon Willis (a Republican), and Earle Clements. I grew up with "Fats" Clements out in western Kentucky and knew him well. We were the same age—but had wound up in different factions in the Democratic party. Except for poor timing, and lack of communication, we could have been political partners as far back as 1935. And though we became arch rivals, I was able late in Clements's life to keep him from going behind prison bars. More about that later.

Elected governor in 1947, Clements had resigned in 1950 to succeed Alben Barkley as the senior United States Senator from Kentucky when Barkley was elected vice president on the Truman ticket. That elevated Lieutenant Governor Lawrence Wetherby into the governor's chair on November 27, 1950. Now in 1951 Wetherby was making a run to win the office on his own.

At the moment, Senator Clements and Governor Wetherby, who had been Louisville juvenile court judge, controlled the faction that dominated the state Democratic party organization. It would take time to rebuild my strength, as Joe Leary argued. So I set out to do that.

And in 1955 when I announced my race for governor, I was thrown headlong into battle against, not any rivals for the nomination, but the powerful forces of Clements and Wetherby. It took several weeks for them to find someone to put up against me. Their choice was a shy, mousey, little-known judge from the appellate court, Bert T. Combs.

I began my campaign vigorously, coming out swinging not at Bert Combs but at the all-powerful "Clementine and Wetherbine." Reporters have always credited me with being a master of political wit, sarcasm and ridicule. They may be right. I didn't dignify Bert Combs by mentioning his name. I casually brushed him aside as "that little judge." Personally, I felt that Combs was the last of pea time.

Joe Leary was writing my campaign speeches, and sending them out to me from our headquarters in Louisville. I wasn't much for following a script. I'd stand up, look around to read the mood of the kind of crowd I had drawn, and then pretty much react to it. Usually I was good at that.

Political reporters jumped on Leary. "Lookie, here," they fumed. "You gave us this advance text of what Chandler was going to say today in Glasgow. He didn't mention a single word that was in your handout."

Leary got me on the phone. He was upset. He demanded I use the script he'd written. "At least," he said, "one certain paragraph. I'll mark it in red. I'll give that quote to the reporters."

Joe Leary will go down in Kentucky political history as the author of a whole lot of speeches his candidate never delivered. But I did get him off the hook with the press. Every day on the stump I managed to utter the paragraph he'd underlined in red—to keep the reporters' stories honest. But I made it quick—barking out the words like a tobacco auctioneer.

Fortunately, from February to November, my voice never once failed me. That was an ordeal. That campaign should have killed me.

Politicking in Kentucky is controlled by certain time-honored customs. Joe Leary forgot one by scheduling me to speak at the courthouse in Sandy Hook at ten in the morning. Nobody showed up.

I made inquiries and found out that the local custom was to hold political speeches at 2 o'clock. I went back in the afternoon and found a huge crowd. Sandy Hook, incidentally, is an excellent barometer of how any campaign is going. Everybody for one candidate stands on one side, and the rival forces on the other. I noted happily that day my side was far the larger.

Likewise it was a custom to not make political speeches on Sunday. But Joe Leary was getting bad reports from Warren County. His county manager told him: "Have your man at Beech Bend Boat Dock this Sunday and you'll carry Warren county by two thousand." Leary relayed the word to me. The weather was hot and I was about run ragged, and needed that one day's rest.

"You don't want a governor," I yelped to Leary, "you want a dead man."

But I made the Sunday speech at the boat dock. The county manager turned out to be right on target. We carried Warren county by 1,976.

I was making a speech at Frenchburg in Menifee County when a big fellow in the back shouted, "You're a liar!" Three or four men grabbed the guy and started pounding him.

"Wait a minute!" I shouted. "Bring him up here. Let's see what he's talking about." They brought him up. "What do you mean, I'm a liar?"

"Well," he growled, "you damn near got me drowned. I was in the penitentiary in Frankfort when you had that flood. The water come up and damn near got me!"

Everybody just roared.

The black vote is important in a Kentucky campaign and I got nearly all of it. Jackie Robinson, remembering my role in opening up baseball to his race, wrote, "Let me know if I can help...." Joe Leary had copies of that letter spread in every black community. I was acquainted with practically every Negro preacher in Kentucky. One day I was about to make a campaign appearance in Litchfield when I got a long distance call from one of my preacher friends.

"Mister Happy," he said, "Auntie Bates has done crossed over. An' her last request was for you to come sing 'Swing Low, Sweet Chariot' at her funeral tomorrow." I went.

The meat and potatoes issue of my 1955 race against Combs was my attack on the lavish spending of Governor Wetherby. He had chosen a bad time to panel rooms in the governor's capitol suite with African mahogany, and to install air conditioning and new carpeting.

I got some copies of invoices and I waved them at my audiences.

"Our little governor," I shouted, "has sent all the way to Africa to get fancy wood for his office. He's spent $20,000 for a rug. He's paid thousands for unnecessary air conditioning. Listen, when I go back in as governor we'll open all the windows and let in that sweet Kentucky air. And you'll all be welcome to come and wipe your shoes on that $20,000 rug. You paid for it!"

Of course, singing was one staple of my campaign. I sang the old favorites, "Sonny Boy," "There's a Gold Mine in the Sky," "Happy Days Are Here Again," and naturally "My Old Kentucky Home."

I won the nomination by better than 18,000. And the general election by a record majority of 128,000.

Once again I got ready for the big swearing-in ceremony on the capitol steps—as Kentucky's forty-ninth governor. As before, I would ride in the parade behind horses, and my father would stand with me on the platform. It would be the first time in Kentucky history that a father had twice been privileged to witness his son's swearing-in. By tradition the ceremony would take place at noon—this time on December 13, 1955.

"Listen," I told Joe Leary, "I've got a feeling. I don't want to wait till noon. I want to be sworn in just as soon as legally possible—one minute after midnight."

My campaign manager gave me a long, thoughtful look. He began drumming his fingers on his desk. I knew what was going on in his mind.

The feeling that I was somehow mystically touched by a "divine spark" was not new to Leary. He had often talked about it. Joe was more than convinced; to him I was an actual child of destiny. He detected a sign of that in a remarkable incident involving my first lieutenant governor, Keen Johnson.

When Johnson got ready to announce he was running to succeed me, we all crowded onto the balcony of the old state fairgrounds at Shelbyville. Suddenly I turned to Joe Leary. "I'm getting off of here. This balcony is going to fall!"

Leary raised his eyebrows and sniffed. But I left the balcony. When Johnson finished his speech, those on the balcony rushed forward to pat him on the back and shake hands. With the shriek of splintering wood, the balcony collapsed, throwing men and women to the ground. Several were cut and bruised, though luckily none seriously.

Leary picked himself up and sought me out. "You knew something, didn't you?"

I don't know why—exactly—I had this premonition about not waiting to be publicly sworn in as governor. Assassins gunned down one governor—Goebel—on his way to inauguration. There were still violent men in Kentucky politics. I don't know. . . . I couldn't put my finger on anything. . . .

So at midnight we gathered in the parlor of the genteel country home of Judge William B. Ardery at Paris, an hour's drive east of the state capital. Judge Ardery, my long-time friend, administered the oath. Then we all knelt and his wife, Julia, a gracious Southern lady, said a simple prayer.

As I stood up, I felt strangely that some great ominous threat or burden had been lifted. Joe Leary came over. He didn't say anything. He just slid his arm around me and gave a gentle hug. In his eyes I saw the glint of happy tears.

Mama checked out the Executive Mansion before we moved in for our second four-year residency.

"Those dining room chairs," she complained to me, "are falling apart. And the guest bedroom doesn't have any rug."

I answered her sharply. "Hey! I ran on that $20,000 rug. You're not gonna spend a nickel on rugs! Forget those dining room chairs. Make do, woman, make do."

She didn't give me back any sass. She just hopped in her car and whipped over to Versailles. She came back with the rug off our bedroom floor. She also brought her silver and six dining room chairs. She always has been pretty good at making do.

At once she had her hands full with a series of special parties at the Mansion. I was dead level serious about keeping my promise to build a new medical school. I ran up against stiff opposition—the University of Louisville physician clique. In an effort to overcome these critics, we held a series of dinners at the Mansion. I invited in batches of leaders of the medical fraternity from all over Kentucky, and brought in distinguished outside experts to help argue my case.

I argued about how our modern society still negligently relegated the rustic hill folk of eastern Kentucky to horse-and-buggy era medical practice. Likewise I could speak firsthand of not one but two medical tragedies in my father's house. The first was, of course, the tragic death of my little brother Robert, whose life certainly could have been spared by the kind of medical attention we know today.

And I also lost a half-brother. Of my father's second marriage, a son and daughter were born. My half-sister is Katie Bolin, a stockbroker in Lexington, a lovely and distinguished woman. My half-brother, Joseph S. Chandler Jr., also had bright prospects. He studied medicine and was interning at Ball State Hospital in Muncie, Indiana when tragedy overtook him.

At age twenty-seven, Joseph Jr. underwent a routine tonsil operation at his own hospital. His surgeon gave him a shot of pontocaine. Nobody realized he was violently allergic to that particular anesthesia. Within three minutes Joe Jr. was dead. My daddy never got over that.

I struggled to circumvent the united front the Louisville clique set up against a second medical school. Chief leader of the anti force was old Doc Howard, who ran a clinic down in Glasgow. As a physician, he was a saint. But he would brook no competition to the Louisville med school. He showed up one morning in Frankfort and planted himself in front of my desk.

"Boy," he said, "how serious are you about this medical school?" The old-timers still looked on me as the boy-governor.

"Dr. Howard, you know me well. You know I don't tilt at

windmills. And what I think I ought to do, I'm prepared to do, and willing to take the consequences."

"You know the *Courier-Journal's* against you. So are a lot of doctors. Your idea is impractical, not financially feasible, can't be done, and won't succeed."

"I'm dead level serious," I said. "I'm going to build this medical school. I can get the money from the legislature. Five million to start. One idea is to set aside some money to educate these young doctors with the proviso they will go back to their home country to practice."

The doctor from Glasgow tilted his gray head and thought on that idea. I noticed his hostile demeanor begin to soften. Then he smiled.

"All right, boy, then I'm not going to fight you any more."

That was the break I needed. The legislature went along with me. But I still had a couple of hurdles to leap. I needed someone to build the school. I asked Dean Vernon Lippard of Yale Medical School for recommendations. He named five people, with Dean William R. Willard of the medical school at Syracuse University at the top.

"If you can't get him, tear up the list and start over. He's the best in the country."

I phoned Dean Willard and he wasn't interested. But I prevailed on him to come see me. I told him I would pay him $22,000 a year. Then he was interested. I chuckled to myself that it was a repeat of my difficulty in getting a top-flight highway engineer.

There was yet another obstacle. The president of the University of Kentucky, Dr. Frank Dickey, was getting $12,000. I was explaining the plan at a meeting of the university board, of which, as governor, I was chairman.

I got out of my chair and beckoned Dickey to follow me out. I took him into the men's room. "Frank, I have a strong feeling that the main man ought to get the most money. You're the main man, and I'm going to give you $22,500."

He shook his head. "I don't know whether I can do that or not."

I could see he feared criticism for accepting such a big pay raise. "If you don't," I said, "I'll get somebody who will. I'm going to give Willard $22,000."

Dickey gave a big sigh. "All right, I'll do it then."

I went back and told the board. "Dickey thought he'd be criticized," I explained, "for taking too much money. But I have to do this, and I know what I'm doing. We've just settled this in a privy conference."

Then I got Dr. Willard. "Dean Lippard," I said, "tells me you know how to build a medical center. I want you to come here and build this one. And first I want to tell you that I'll not interfere with you and I'll not let anyone else. I'll furnish the money and you can build and staff the center."

I never asked him for a position, wouldn't let anyone else. Let him alone. Let him build. And by God he got some of the top fellows in the country to agree to come there and help him.

Years later he was brought back to the university for a testimonial dinner. "Except for the promises made to me by Governor Chandler," he recalled, "all of which he kept better than he said, I wouldn't have come to Kentucky. I came because I had confidence in what he told me and everything he said turned out just the way he said."

It took a couple of years to build the medical center. The university board decided to call it the Albert B. Chandler Medical Center. I resisted that at first. Then I came to the conclusion that if my name was to be associated with anything except my family, to be connected with the health and welfare and education of your people was about the top thing that could come to you.

Frank Peterson, the university comptroller, said, "If it wasn't for you, this medical school wouldn't exist at all. Your name ought to be on it."

I think now everyone agrees the medical center has filled a vital need for the people of our commonwealth. I am proud it bears my name. Rasty Wright, who went with me to play baseball in North Dakota and came back home to make a fortune as a tobacco warehouseman, left a six million dollar bequest to the Chandler Medical Center. That proves something.

As in my first administration, anyone could get an audience with the governor. That led, of course, to some peculiar episodes. One fellow down in Nicholas county never missed one of my stump speeches. He went nuts over those white suits I wore, and got up nerve enough to ask for one. I sent one down to him. Another man wrote that he was hard up and needed a hat. "Nine and one-half," he wrote. "And brown." He got it.

Into my office one morning came a fellow from Hopkins County called "Walking Munn" Wilson. His nickname derived from making a campaign for the legislature in which he totally ignored the customary horse and buggy or flivver and covered his entire district by ankle express. He was elected for one term. He liked Frankfort and hung around as sort of a permanent fixture.

"Governor, I want to get some breakfast."

"Okay, Munn. Go over to the Mansion. The cook will take care of you."

At the Mansion he sat down in the kitchen and Mary Alice asked what he wanted to eat.

"What did the Governor eat this morning?" he inquired.

"Bacon and eggs."

"Suit me just fine."

When he cleaned his plate, "Walking Munn" suddenly allowed as how he needed new shoes. "The Governor said you'd take care of me."

Mary Alice went upstairs and brought back a pair from my closet.

A little later he was back over at the Capitol, dancing around on the marble floor. Someone asked where he got his new shoes.

"From Governor Chandler. He gave 'em to me. Ain't that nice!"

Glad he got 'em, because that may have been one of the happiest days of "Walking Munn's" life.

Mama had a few trials being First Lady and hostess. One episode involved the Dominican dictator Rafael Trujillo, who came to Kentucky seeking prancing saddle horses for his personal cavalry. The State Department asked Mama to take him on a tour of the horse farms, since I was away in Washington. She put Trujillo in my bedroom. One of our convict servants, as she told me later, carried fresh towels up to the suite and came rushing back with his eyes just rolling, gasping that the Governor's bedroom was full of guns and bodyguards.

In the middle of the night, wild horn-honking erupted across the street at the Capitol. Mama slipped on her robe, took our night-duty trooper by the ear and marched over to quiet the noise before it awakened our Dominican guest. A youngster, son-in-law of the night Capitol guard, was causing the disturbance. He was drunk. Police came and collared him, but he broke and ran. They pulled their guns and fired over his head. The boy leaped over a high wall back of the Mansion and escaped.

Next morning at breakfast, Mama asked the Dominican dictator if he heard the midnight gunfire.

"Yes, I did."

"Just trying to make you feel at home," Mama joked.

Trujillo laughed, but a trifle grimly. "If I had been at home, he wouldn't have gotten away!"

By golly, he wouldn't have, either. But the generalissimo's own days were even then already numbered. Assassins burst into his home on May 30, 1960, and riddled the seventy-year-old dictator with bullets.

Speaking of military confrontation, as governor I twice had to call out troops to put down the threat of civil disobedience.

One occasion was a new eruption of violence in the eastern Kentucky coalfields where John L. Lewis waged long and relentless battle to unionize the mines.

Those mountaineers are rugged people anyway, and clashes became rather frequent along the strikers' picket lines. Several people were hurt, and one man was killed. Local authorities seemed unable to handle the trouble. I sent in three thousand National Guardsmen to preserve order.

One aspect that greatly disturbed me was placing women on the picket lines. If you got a grandma out in front, Lord a mercy, anything can happen! I shuddered to think of one of them getting shot.

I stood up to both sides. I told the folks down there they could join anything they wanted to, pay dues to it long as they wanted to, and quit when they got ready. Nobody could be forced to join. That oughtn't to be a prerequisite to getting a job, to have to join something.

It was quite a storm. But I weathered it.

Out in western Kentucky the crisis came as a result of Brown vs. Topeka Board of Education, the landmark Supreme Court decision that ordered integration of public schools.

The mayor of Clay dug in his heels and vowed that law of the land or not, blacks and whites would not sit in the same classroom in his little town. Clay is in Webster County, hardly thirty miles from my hometown of Corydon where I grew up as a boy with the fellow who was mayor.

"Albert," he told me on the phone, "ain't no nigger going to school down here."

"Herman," I replied, "I don't know whether they are or not, but if they show up they are! You own that town and you are the mayor and you got certain powers that you can exercise, but I'm going to take charge."

I did. I moved in a company of guardsmen. People were startled to see a National Guard tank clank down Main Street and pull up, with it cannon tilted, in front of the Clay school. The town had always been segregated, and the folks out there simply found it hard to make adjustment to the tide of racial change sweeping the country.

In the town, and elsewhere, certain diehards condemned me for sending in a tank. But I knew what I was doing. I wanted to make it clear there could be no backdown on the part of law and order.

My instructions were that the troops were not to put anybody in school, but they were not to let anybody stop anybody who wanted to go to school. We were keeping it open for whites. We kept it open for blacks.

For one day two young blacks had the whole school. Everybody else left. The tank had to sit in Clay for a while. But finally the situation simmered down, and I was able to withdraw the troops.

I was proud that I didn't react to desegregation in the same way Governor Orval Faubus did down in Arkansas. In Little Rock he called out the troops to keep blacks out of school. But we called out the guard to make sure they could get in.

19

Another Run at the White House

My long-cherished dream that destiny would somehow vault me into the White House was ignited again by political developments in 1956.

The popular Ike was a cinch to be renominated by the Republicans. Adlai Stevenson had taken a hard drubbing in 1952, but the Democrats were talking about going to Chicago in the summer and handing him the banner for a second run at the presidency.

If I ever had a chance to be nominated, my strategists counseled, this was the time. Take it away from Adlai.

We started thinking about a bandwagon and the Chicago convention. First I'd have to go there as Kentucky's "favorite son." Traditionally the governor controls the Democratic party organization in Kentucky and dominates the state convention where delegates are chosen.

But Fate stepped in and muddled the normal situation.

The trigger was the unexpected death of my old nemesis Alben Barkley on April 30, 1956, while serving in the unaccustomed role as Kentucky's junior United States Senator. He was making a keynote speech at a mock convention of students at Washington and Lee University. He concluded: "And I am willing to be a junior. I'm glad to sit in the back row, for I would rather be a servant in the house of the Lord than sit in the seats of the mighty."

Barkley stepped back, and fell over dead of a heart attack. He was seventy-eight.

The story circulated that they found fifteen one-thousand-dollar bills in his inside coat pocket. He'd always been in trouble about his income taxes. They say the IRS had been afraid to tackle such a powerful man, but now quickly stepped in and stripped his estate to the bone.

I told Mama, "If I go, don't waste time looking in my pockets. They'll be clean."

Earle Clements was teaming up with Bert Combs and Lawrence Wetherby to try to make trouble for me. Barkley's death gave them a chance to undercut me. There wasn't time to get a candidate to succeed him on the May primary ballot. Clements and his cronies got the Democrats to pick Wetherby as the Senate nominee in the fall general election.

I should have been consulted as nominal titular head of the Kentucky Democrats. I wasn't. Clements was making war on me. I fought him back. I supported a fellow, Joe Bates, against him in the primary for his Senate seat. Clements won. Then they teamed up again to try to grab control of the state Democratic convention to deliberately knock me out of any chance to go to Chicago as a favorite son candidate in the presidential scramble.

It was a hot summer and a hot fight, a real knock-down, drag-out brawl. My strategy was to get my good friend Robert Humphrey, a Frankfort druggist and party wheelhorse, named chairman. We did that. Then Bob Humphrey challenged enough Clements delegates to enable us to select the new Democratic state executive committee.

That triumph assured my going to the Windy City as Kentucky's favorite son. But I let myself in for some opposition by deciding to bolt the party's nominees for the Senate—Clements and Wetherby. I backed the two Republicans, Thurston Morton of Louisville and my old companion, John Sherman Cooper. And they went on to win in the fall general election.

I went to Chicago with mixed feelings. Joe Leary would make the speech nominating me. The Kentucky delegates staged the usual hoopla—parades, bands, and the like. There were banners like "Mamie Move Out, Mama's Coming." I really never saw more than an outside chance. I estimated the possibilities and the probabilities. I was practical about it, and when the reporters asked me in Chicago if I was going to get the nomination I gave them an honest answer.

Joe Leary always thought I'd make a good president. This was an abortive thing. But I had to try. That opportunity just came along, just kept coming along. You wonder why everybody doesn't have that opportunity. It turned out to be an idea whose time had not come, but I still had to entertain it.

My bandwagon ran into a stonewall in Chicago. I have the consolation of knowing that my nomination drew votes from eight states.

I don't believe any Democrat could have beaten Eisenhower that year. If I had been nominated I would not have won, not that year. Stevenson was real smart. He was not an ordinary human being. He walked off the ground. Yet Ike beat him badly.

In the years since then I've thought it over, the enormity of the office, what a tremendous responsibility it is. I've not felt entirely adequate about it, as I once did. You know I got a new estimate of it as I've gotten closer to it; I could have done it better than Lyndon Johnson, better than Harry Truman, I think as well as Roosevelt. Those fellows never convinced me they were interested in the public welfare. None of those fellows.

You can't tell me much about Truman I don't already know. His private secretary and some close cronies went to prison. The Pendergast machine loaned him money on his farm and he never paid it back, so I'm told.

We had a bad experience with that Pendergast crowd. A fellow came down here from Kansas City to bid on a highway job. He was low and we had to give it to him. Bob Humphrey, then highway commissioner, asked just one thing. "Buy the cement in Kentucky," he requested. "The price is the same all over." The contractor agreed to do that.

Then he shipped in the cement from Kansas City. Bob Humphrey jumped him. "You lied to us."

"Yeah," the contractor said, smugly. "If I hadn't you wouldn't have given us the contract." He was part of the Pendergast crowd.

The idea of our taking a European vacation surfaced in 1957. Mama had taken the two boys to London, Paris and

Rome in 1954 for a couple of months. She liked vacationing
with her sons. Just before Ben volunteered for the Korean war,
the three of them took a quick swing by car through the West,
hitting twenty-eight states in twenty-two days. Ben came out of
the Orient with a case of nerves, and Mama hit on taking a European tour to help him calm down. It worked.

Colonel Gottlieb and his wife escorted Mama and me on
our European excursion. I wasn't about to fly, of course, so we
went over on the liner *United States* and returned on the *Li-
berte*. We traveled Europe for two months. In the new state of
Israel we were received by Prime Minister David Ben-Gurion.
He presented me with a Bible, a valuable antique, which remains one of my treasures. Moshe Dayan was our guide. I was
impressed that the Jews were taking scorpion country and
turning it into an oasis and garden for their homeland.

Pope Pius XII received us at his summer residence, Castel
Gondolfo. I gave him greetings from the Bishop of Covington,
my good friend Billy Molloy. The pontiff gave us his blessing.
In Paris, with approval of the French government, I laid a
wreath on the grave of the unknown soldier at the Arch de
Triumphe. I looked up at the arch and marveled that Rasty
Wright had been able to fly through the opening in his little
Jenny to celebrate the end of World War I.

In my absence Lieutenant Governor Harry Lee Waterfield
was acting governor. I'd known Harry Lee for 25 years and figured he had a lot of savvy. I was going to support him in the
1959 race to succeed me. I gave him every bit of help I could. I
wanted him to be successful, but I think he went a little too
fast.

He got mad at the highway comissioner, Tom Moberly of
Bowling Green, and fired him. Some of my friends pleaded with
Harry Lee not to do it, but he told them to go mind their business. He was a bit headstrong in making decisions. He never
mentioned it to me, though we talked on the telephone several
times while I was in Europe. He assumed he was acting governor and he had the right to do it. He shouldn't have. It was my
appointment. Under the same circumstances I wouldn't have
done it.

On my return I tried to counsel with Harry Lee. "I think
you are going to be able to make a better political organization

than we've got here," I told him, "but you won't do it this year. I think I'd plan to do it, but give yourself more time."

He didn't listen. He went a little too fast and made some moves that might have cost him his race for governor. Sadly, we lost Harry Lee in August, 1988—much too young at only seventy-seven.

Of all the steadfast men I ever knew I'm sure my daddy led the list. He stayed the course. He looked on the bright side. He was a happy and optimistic fellow.

Even when he was up in his eighties, Joseph Chandler was able to give me a powerful lesson in optimism.

I got a call at the governor's office. My daddy had been hurt. I called for my car and took off with a trooper for Corydon.

Ever since I can remember, dad had been cutting the grass around our little Campbellite church and in the Corydon graveyard. He felt somehow it was his obligation, and he never shirked. Of course he started out with a hand scythe, but finally graduated to a rotary power motor.

While he was mowing the cemetery a stick got caught in the machine. He reached under the mower to dislodge the stick and the blade severed three of his fingers and half of a fourth.

On the drive up to Corydon I tried to frame in my mind some words of commiseration. When I entered his hospital room and saw my father I knew immediately I need not have worried. He held up his bandaged hand, wiggled his thumb, and shouted: "Look, son, how much I've got left!"

No wonder I've always had a bright outlook on life; I inherited it from my old man.

In most of the years while our children were growing up, we lived in that huge old three-story house in Versailles. Running up and down all those stairs, I was afraid was going to kill Mama. So I decided to build us a new house—everything on one floor, with a full basement for storage.

I started working on the design the last two years of my second term so it would be ready for us when we left the Governor's Mansion and came back to Versailles. In Louisville and Frankfort, I had seen a particular style of brick residence that appealed to me. I sent an architect to look them over, and then laid out the plan I wanted—our bedrooms, dressing rooms, baths, guest room, a big dining room, and my corner study with a rocking chair and fireplace. This room I had paneled in butternut wood—that's white walnut. It ages well, with no stain, just varnish or tung oil. You can't seem to get that wood any more. I had an expert carpenter come in and cut all the moldings, the fireplace mantles, and ceiling beams out in the garage and fit them in right here.

I thought I was going to spend $50,000. Lordy, it cost twice that. But this house had a natural stone foundation and basement like they don't build any more. It'll be here a long, long time.

We built a new foundation on the opposite side of Elm Street on a fifteen-acre farm I own over there. Then we called in the movers. They came one morning and jacked up the old house and put it on rollers. Looked to me like they had the biggest aspidistra in the world. I watched 'em move the house. It was here in the morning and over there on the new foundation in the afternoon. You could put a glass of water on the mantle and it wouldn't have spilled a drop. That smooth! I never saw anything like it. It wasn't cheap—three thousand dollars.

Later I traded that house to my son Dan. He ran into tough times, needed money and sold it for $40,000. I wouldn't have had that happen for anything. I don't believe I would have taken a million dollars cash for that old house. It was so full of fond family memories. But you have to forgive and let life go on . . . .

I learned one curious thing over at Frankfort in my second term. French poodles are smarter than people!

I've always loved dogs. Had a few as a kid. But the first dog I had as a grown-up was a Dalmatian. We called him Champ. He was a good one. Then my public relations man gave us a high-bred French poodle. He was a kennel pup with some high-flown pedigreed name like Winelist Valpennas, son of Champion Spidela of Piperscroft.

I named him Wyatt Earp.

Those poodles are just great. They're just as smart as can be. They behaved well. Courageous. They loved to be loved. They'll pay you back. They're affectionate.

Wyatt Earp had a son and I named him Doc Holiday. Then we got one named Shawnee. We brought the four of them home from the Mansion—Champ, Wyatt Earp, Doc Holiday and

Shawnee. We had tough luck with Shawnee. He went blind and the last two years of his life I had to carry him in and out of the house. He was in pain and the vet finally persuaded me to let him put Shawnee to sleep.

We had another poodle—Nicky, who got run over out in the street. I wasn't sure I wanted any more dogs after that. But we. bought a Scotch terrier we called Hager because we got him up in Hagerstown, Maryland. He got ahold of something and died at twelve—that would have made him eighty-four by man's age. I hated to see him die and after that I told Mama I didn't want any more dogs.

This little fella named Peppo lives down the street. But he comes up here every day. He stays until they come get him at night. Some mornings when I let him in he jumps up in bed with me and takes a little snooze. I worry about him, and these cars running up and down Elm Street . . . .

Trouble flared up every now and then in the final days of my second stint as governor. In one fuss I had to take on the entire Court of Appeals. And it became a dog fight. Charlie O'Connell, the veteran clerk of the court, died and the court gave his deputy, Doris Owens, the job. I protested that the constitution gives the governor the right to fill all vacancies in statewide offices. I appointed Walter Ferguson, a Boone County farmer.

It got nasty. They claimed omnipotent power, wouldn't let us appeal the case—they had the last word. They beat me at every turn, and Doris Owens kept the job, even though she had to run in a special election. The fight got so hot that I lost the friendship of Appellate Judge Jim Milliken. I thought I was one of the best friends he had. And he was the one who said the court had sovereign immunity. You couldn't challenge them. He was high-handed and arrogant.

The word was that he was writing a letter demanding satisfaction, challenging me to a duel. Now wouldn't that have been something! I haven't seen him since. Have no desire to. It's been thirty years.

My political enemies attempted a put-up job on me by spreading the story that I went hunting and bagged a crippled goose, or shot it after dark or out of season. It was a lowdown smear, and a lie!

I had been hunting and fishing at the Ballard Wildlife Con-

servation area. I was the guest of the state commissioner of
fish and wildlife. Naturally he would not have condoned any tri-
fling with hunting regulations.

Still the political skunks kept up their malicious gossip. It
was bandied about that I had been indicted in Ballard County
for some offense. My people urged me to just ignore the rumors.

"Oh no," I said. "I meet this one head-on."

I summoned my car, had a trooper drive me to Ballard
County and went straight into the courthouse where the judge
was presiding.

"Your Honor, I'm Albert Benjamin Chandler, governor of
Kentucky. Have you got a warrant for me?"

"No, sir," he said. "Governor, there's been some mistake."

I said, "Judge, if you want me here, I have to be amenable
to the jurisdiction of your court. I had to come here. You can't
come get me. But I can come here. I am here now. Do you want
me?"

"I'm sorry if we made any trouble for you," the judge said.

"That's all right, Your Honor. Thank you."

I turned around and walked out.

It was all a put-up job.

Sadly, I had a repeat of treachery in my office—a stab in
the back from my executive secretary. His name was Harry
Davis and he came with first-class recommendations. He was
smart as the devil; actually too smart. This fellow would work
to keep people away from me, on the theory there wasn't any
use seeing the governor—he could handle it.

I can't figure out a fellow that's disloyal to somebody who's
given him a good chance to improve his life. Mama caught up
with Davis and tried to warn me. I was too trusting. I've got a
fierce loyalty to the people I'm fond of, and the people I think
are helping me. And I go if they send for me. And if I hear they
need me, I go.

And those fellows who were abusing my trust . . . and I
didn't discover it until after it was over . . . . What are you going
to do about it? I just walked away. You build up bitterness in
your heart if you brood. That destroys people. Why, Jesus, it
eats you. I've seen fellows sit around concerned about being
misused and mistreated. I never did that.

Frenchy Demoisey wanted permission to kill Harry Davis, too. I'm not bitter about anyone. I have never seen Harry Davis except maybe once by accident. If somebody asks me about him, I don't talk, I just say I don't know.

Harry Lee Waterfield had to run a long and grueling campaign for the Democratic nomination for governor in 1959. Bert Combs, whom I had vanquished, was running again. No longer was he the shy, mousey little candidate. He had been eating red meat, and he was dangerous.

For his running mate he picked up the former mayor of Louisville, Wilson Wyatt, such an urbane fellow that I understood he wore spats.

He was my new target for ridicule, the kind that would alert the country folks to the peril such a dandy and citified candidate would bring to Frankfort.

I started lampooning him as "Ankle Blankets." My audiences laughed, and the name stuck. Old "Ankle Blankets" became a regular staple in the campaign rhetoric. I wondered aloud how he'd get by on plowed ground. I continued to dismiss Combs as "the little judge."

But a different tide was running this time. I couldn't do it all by myself.

In the May primary, Waterfield lost to Combs by 31,000— and eighty percent of those votes came from Louisville and Jefferson County. So the jibes at "Ankle Blankets" had not helped a great deal.

Combs and Wyatt went on to victory in the November general election. I was on the platform as outgoing governor when they were sworn in in December. And I had to admire Wyatt's sportsmanship and good humor. In making his remarks, he turned to flash me a smile and then tell the crowd, "Happy, this is a report from Ankle Blankets on the condition of the plowed ground."

The crowd roared, and I had to laugh too at the good-natured ribbing.

This day was the end of my second term as governor. I still resented the lies Bert Combs had used against me in the campaign. I expected him to apologize, but he never did.

As I sat on the platform while the events of this inauguration swirled around me, I was thinking hard on the future.

This is not the end, I fervently and secretly vowed, of Happy Chandler on the Kentucky political scene. The next race for governor would be coming up in 1963. I then would be only sixty-five—and, hopefully, still strong and healthy.

In 1963 my personal political ambition surged again and I decided to go after my third term as governor.

The winds of change were blowing and, as usual, there were ruptures in the old Democratic factions, new alignments and fresh opportunities.

Anybody who shook hands with me still might wince a bit. I was fit, and I was ready. Most of my people were still loyal. The strongest opposition the Combs crowd could find was a forty-three-year-old Hopkinsville lawyer named Ned Breathitt. I didn't expect much fight from him—but I underestimated the dirty trick tactics to which his crowd would descend.

Bert Combs had spent fifty thousand dollars putting in what he called a floral clock back of the Capitol building. I hoorawhed that. Looking at my watch, I'd tell the crowd, "Must be two petunias past the Jimson weed." They'd whoop and holler.

One of the people pushing Breathitt's candidacy was Edward F. Prichard Jr., a Harvard law graduate, a so-called political whiz kid who had served as Justice Felix Frankfurter's clerk and came back to Kentucky and got imprisoned for what amounted to stuffing a ballot box.

There's no doubt Prich had an inventive mind, but after he got out of prison he was a very strange character. He lived in Versailles and I knew all about him. I gave him one of his first jobs in Kentucky, but he became my enemy.

He was counseling with some politicos and they engineered one of the dirtiest deals ever pulled on me.

They sent some people over to my home who pretended to be doing a documentary, and asked if they could get some old informal photos that had been taken of me. Trying to be helpful, Mama led them down into the basement where there were boxes of letters and photos. "We don't want anything posed," they said. "We want candid shots."

They selected a number of photographs and it wasn't until they had gone that Mama realized they had picked out only the most unflattering. "Some of them were just horrible," Mama told me. "Your face was all contorted. . . . You looked like the old devil himself."

"Too late now," I told her.

And it was too late. The so-called documentary turned out to be a vicious smear brochure. They circulated that all over the state and put it on TV.

Dirty tricks were never part of my make-up. I don't know of a time I ever lied on anyone, or accused them of something I couldn't prove. As I have said repeatedly, I wouldn't change a jot or tittle of my public record. I was sober and I meant to do everything I did.

Mama would get upset, but it was pointless to try to answer newspaper attacks. There's no way in the wide world that you can win against them. The less you have to say, the better off you are. I'm not bragging, but looking back on it nobody handled the *Courier-Journal* better than I did. I never remonstrated with them. I never answered. I never sat around and brooded about it. I never wrote them a letter—except once.

A fellow here had been my business associate for thirty-five years. They said I gave him a contract without a bid. And, of course, that was not true. I never gave anybody a contract without a bid. I wrote to the editor of the *Courier-Journal* and said that's a reflection on my honesty and my integrity and I want you to take it back. They took it back the next day.

I think that "documentary" hurt me a lot. It was so vicious and unfair. Still the polls right up to the last showed I was seventy-nine percent ahead against Breathitt.

But that's one primary I can never feel comfortable about. I think I won that race. I didn't get it. But I think I won it. We think it was stolen. That's an educated guess, too. I don't know how they did it. I wish I knew. I'd put 'em in jail if I knew that. Breathitt didn't have any more chance to be governor than my grandson.

The Democrats punished me more than anybody else. Republicans voted for me every time they had a chance. And I had the satisfaction of winning the election every time the Democrats gave me the nomination. But the so-called leaders of the Democrat party were never enthusiastic about me. Most of the things they want done, you oughten to do.

I don't think anybody in this lifetime has had more loyal

friends than I. We've had some right sorry governors in my time. I can't explain it. I don't know why they don't have the determination to do for the public. It is a simple proposition; they are entitled to govern the people according to their wishes and needs and the constitution. But some of those fellows just want to be *governor*—they just want the trimmings.

The worst governor we'd had of all was John Y. Brown Jr. He didn't give a damn, either. His daddy didn't approve of the way he governed. His daddy could have helped him. But he wouldn't let him.

There must be something similar in the blood of old fire horses and political animals. They have to answer the bell!

In 1967 I again jumped into the Democratic primary for governor. The Combs and Breathitt wing found a fellow from Paducah to run against me, Henry Ward. Once a crusading newspaper reporter, Ward had served both as state parks commissioner and highway commissioner.

Once more I waged a vigorous campaign. But it was not successful. Henry Ward won the Democratic nomination. In the general election that fall I switched my support to the Republican nominee, Louie Nunn. I felt he was the better man. Louie Nunn made all sorts of promises to me about what he was going to do to help the people of Kentucky, and I'm sorry to say he reneged on just about all of them.

From time to time overtures were made to bring me back into national politics. In 1968, Governor George Wallace of Alabama asked me to run as his candidate for vice president on the American Party ticket. We had practically agreed on that—but it didn't happen. There were two reasons. Wallace badly needed campaign funds. Somebody offered him a pile of money if he would put General Curtis LeMay on the ticket for vice president. That might have been reason enough, but it also dawned on Wallace that his views and mine on segregation were not at all compatible, were in fact poles apart. I had a public record showing I stood squarely behind legal integration.

Sometime during this period Earle Clements got into trouble on his federal income taxes. Just like Breathitt, Clements got an outstanding corporate job. You don't get those by accident. You often get those by doing favors for fellows that you ought not to do. Clements belonged to the tobacco people.

Clements was afraid he was going to prison.

Some of his friends asked me to intercede. They knew I had been one of President John F. Kennedy's first supporters and was on good terms with his brother, Attorney General Robert F. Kennedy. We had a very close friendship.

I went to Washington and had a meeting with Bob Kennedy in his office at the Justice Department. I told him what I wanted. He summoned his lawyers who were handling the case against Clements.

He said, "Governor Chandler is here to intercede for Earle Clements, and he doesn't want to send him to the penitentiary. Do we have to send him to the penitentiary?"

One of the assistants answered, "We don't, General, unless you say so."

Bobby Kennedy said, "Make arrangements."

That was all.

The day Clements was going to have to show up before a magistrate he gave me an early morning phone call at Versailles. He expected to be indicted, and he felt certain they had him hung up.

"Earle," I said, "go on down there. They're going to try to collect the money they claim you owe them, but they're not going to send you to the penitentiary."

"Governor," he said, "I sure am appreciative."

We never talked about it again.

That event transpired not long before RFK was assassinated on June 5, 1968, in Los Angeles.

At age seventy-three, I still had the desire and energy to make one more race—my fifth!—for governor. I ran in 1971 as an independent candidate, but was not successful. That was the last time I carried a personal banner as a candidate, but I never retired from politics. My advice and help have been sought by a number of office-seekers, and the people of Kentucky still love me. I don't know how big a following I still have, but it's not small. They say, and I believe it, that I could get five thousand votes for Grandma Moses.

20

The Thirty-One-Year Wait

One of my grandsons at age four was doing his nightly chore, standing on his little box at the kitchen sink washing dishes. Half-crying, he turned and told his mother, "Bet you're glad you're not a housewife!"

In our family, the work ethic was Lesson One. Soon as the girls could lift an iron, Mama put them pressing their own dresses. For the boys getting out of bed meant starting chores. Not that there wasn't time for play. Having fun and knowing warm parental love went hand in glove with learning to become disciplined, courteous, and ambitious.

The record will show that our four children didn't turn out too bad. Not perfect—still not too bad. There's certainly been time enough to tell; they've all now hit middle-age. They've given us twelve grandchildren and nine great-grandchildren. And that bunch, too, is mainly pretty decent.

Ben and Mimi remained in Versailles. Marcella is down in Wilson, North Carolina, married to Thomas Davis Miller, who owned a tobacco company. He's a good man and well off. Marcella doesn't need anything so I've taken her out of my will and put in her two daughters from her first marriage. We're real proud of Marcella. She's given us four of our grandchildren and seven of our great-grandkids.

Mimi, our little one-time movie starlet, used to sing and

play records on the radio station I had for a while out here between Lexington and Versailles. One of her favorite songs—and mine, too—was "On the Sunny Side of the Street." I had great hopes for that radio station, thought that went hand-in-hand with owning the local newspaper. But I had some Versailles men in with me as partners. Nobody could seem to manage the thing, and they got scared and wanted to sell. Garvice Kinkaid of Lexington bought the station and made it successful. If my fellows hadn't been such cowards, we'd still be in the broadcasting business.

Cheerful and outgoing, Mimi has always been a sunny and busy individual. She was married a second time, for twenty years, to Jimmy Jack Lewis, but that ended in divorce. For a period of time she was down in Texas with a friend in the dress manufacturing business.

The last ten years she has been Commissioner of Tourism for the state of Kentucky. That's an important position and from all I hear she has performed brilliantly. She commutes every day to her office in Frankfort, just about a twenty-minute drive. She lives right down Elm Street from us in a $100,000 house we bought for her.

Mimi has given us three of our grandchildren and one great-grandson. One of her boys is getting a doctorate at the University of Belgium and the other is a professional musician, and a good one. Her daughter is married to an architect in Phoenix, Arizona. They own our other great-grandson, and from the way the mother writes that must be the most wonderful baby ever born. She just adores him, and his every little burp and fart. Power to her, and to him.

Ben, of course, is the favorite. Every time Mama hollers, he shows up. They get along so well together. Ben loves that paper and Mama has been writing a column in the *Woodford Sun* for thirty years. She's a thinker and a writer and her column is damn good. I don't agree with her views on some things, for instance abortion, but usually she's right on target.

As a boy Ben picked the prep school he and Dan attended, Darlington at Rome, Georgia. I asked him why. His answer made sense: "Must be pretty good. That's where the college presidents send their kids." Ben is quiet, studious, doesn't like crowds, could never have survived the back-slapping hurly-burly of political campaigning. He's a good athlete, crackerjack golfer, and could have been, I think, a major league outfielder if he hadn't lost time in the Army. One baseball scout told me Ben had the best arm he'd ever seen on an outfielder.

Ben jumped into newspapering a neophyte but he has turned himself into a million-dollar publisher. On top of that he's a great writer, and a fine historian. He married Tossie Dunlap, the only daughter of a long-time Scotch friend of mine from out in the country at Pisgah. She's an artist and a love. She'll call up on the phone and I'll say, "Have I told you lately that I love you?" and she'll answer, "No. Tell me." My son Dan says Ben knows the value of a penny, but Tossie is Scotch enough to know the value of a mill!

It was her little boy who was doing dishes at four. Her children—they had three boys—knew if they didn't get their beds made, they'd just be late to school. She's a confirmed feminist. I never was for ERA. I said I thought the women were trying to exchange superiority for equality.

I phoned Tossie once when I was all alone without even a cook to come over and section a grapefruit for me. She wouldn't come, but she obliged by giving directions. Later she went on a trip and there was no one to open the cans and feed her cats. She knows how I hate cats, but she asked and I did it. About a year later I again needed a grapefruit sectioned. I called her. No, no. "Remember who fed your cats," I said. In a few minutes she was in my kitchen, sectioning the grapefruit.

There's no argument that Dan turned out to be our most unusual offspring. Certainly the most peripatetic, and he's every bit as gregarious as I am. He attended the University of Kentucky and played basketball on Rupp's team that had five All-Americans. He became a stockbroker in Lexington and married a girl he knew at the university. They had a boy and a girl. They are now divorced. It's terribly ironic that part of my main duty as baseball commissioner was to protect the major leagues from gamblers and now my youngest son is a well-known executive in casino operations. While working at the Jockey Club in Miami he met Cliff Perlman, the majority owner of Caesar's in Las Vegas. They hit it off and under Perlman's tutelage Dan became a vice president in his organization. Just recently he signed a new contract with Caesar's so I suppose he'll remain in Las Vegas, but I always hoped he'd come back to Kentucky. I'd like to see him here on Elm Street again.

This is a too-brief history of our immediate family. Each one of their lives would make a book, and maybe they'll write 'em some day. Of us all, Mama is the most charming storyteller and writer, and if she ever had time to turn out a book it would be a guaranteed best-seller. I kid you not.

Fortunately I have been blessed my whole life with excellent general health. My eye doctor tells me, "If everybody had eyes like you, I'd go broke." The only time I wear glasses is to read.

The Chandlers have good genes. My grandfather Dan, the old second sergeant in Morgan's cavalry, lived to be ninety, despite trying to drink up half the whiskey in Henderson county. My own daddy would have been ninety if he had lived just a few weeks longer. He was never really sick, just sort of began wearing out and died in May, 1959, and is buried in that little cemetery he loved so at Corydon.

I try to stay away from hospitals, but as the years passed I've had a transurethral resection, a bit of spinal surgery, a rather memorable operation for appendicitis, and something I think belongs in a house of horrors—a wisdom tooth extraction. But it was my own blunder that made it bad.

When I had to have the emergency appendectomy in Lexington I insisted that it be done by my friend Dr. Rankin. "He's a cancer specialist, he can't do this," they told me. "Yes, he can," I said. "He's a surgeon, isn't he?" I said.

In the operating room, Dr. Rankin made an incision. Some of the other doctors there told me about it later. "Aw, that's not right," Dr. Rankin said, stepping back and studying his handiwork. "Well, I'll change it. I'll make it this way." And he made a second incision.

That's why I have a "Y" scar on my belly. But I sure as hell don't have an appendix any more.

When my wisdom tooth began bothering me I went over to the Chandler Medical Center. They put me in the hands of a bright young dental surgeon. He determined that the tooth had to come out.

"What do you want me to give you?" he asked.

I gave him a hard look. "Do I look like a sissy?"

"No, sir."

"Then just pull the damn thing!"

When he started with his forceps I felt pain all the way down to my toes! I thought I was going to die. Then I was afraid I wouldn't. And then it just didn't matter. I never went through anything like that in my life.

Later I had to go back to have another wisdom tooth extracted.

"What do you want me to give you?" the dentist asked.

"Everything you've got in the house!" I said.

My weight has rarely been a problem. Mama thinks I don't eat enough, just tea and toast usually for breakfast, a good old country lunch, usually fried chicken, biscuits and gravy, and generally a snack for supper.

One thing that has helped keep me active and alert is golf. I have been playing since 1932 and I have played all over the United States and with some of the best in the business. Walter Hagen was originally my ideal. In 1932 I was in match play at the Frankfort Country Club with Walter Hagen, Joe Kirkwood and my pal Major Burman. I was a pretty fair golfer for someone who had a baseball swing.

On the first two holes I make pars. One of them is 500 yards and the other 490. I had two pars and I'm five strokes down. Kirkwood had a three and a two. Hagen had two fours and Major Burman had a four and a five. What do you think of that? I played over at the old Lexington Country Club twenty-five or thirty years. I once shot a sixty-seven. I should have quit then.

I was a pretty good putter. I used to laugh and tell them I was president of the Chandler School of Putting. And then for twenty-five years I was "assistant pro" at Bright Leaf over in Mercer County. My Scotch friend over there, Bucky Blankenship, owns that course. So he put my picture up in the clubhouse and said I was assistant pro. I used to help him give lessons occasionally.

I thought I knew the proper way to approach the ball. You hold your left hand tight, and let the right hand sort of go. My legs have been bothering me so last year in the Sheriffs Tournament for their home for boys I couldn't make the rounds, but I putted for my team. I made a 25-footer and a 45-footer. I use my favorite putter, one I've had since grandma fell in the well. I've got the best set of golf clubs in the country. Bucky got them for me.

For years Bucky Blankenship and I had a regular foursome with two of my favorite officers from the Kentucky State Police—Colonel Lloyd Alexander and Roger Wilhoit. What many, many wonderful rounds we played.

I knew Bobby Jones and watched him play, but never played with him. I played with Gene Sarazen, Horton Smith, Lawson Little, Sammy Byrd—he was a New York Yankee outfielder. I began playing with Sam Sneed when he was a caddy house boy at White Sulphur Springs. That's when I was a lawyer for the Chesapeake and Ohio Railroad and Mama and I would go there on my pass a couple of times a year.

One of my most enjoyable business associations was with Claude Poindexter and his Coastal States Life Insurance Company of Atlanta. I was on his board thirty-four years. He never asked me to do anything I didn't do. I never asked him to do anything he didn't do. He was one of the most delightful fellows I've met in my whole lifetime. He was correct.

Take it back—I did turn down one request. After one board meeting while we were milling around, he told me, "Go around there and sit in that chair." It was the main chair. I looked at him; I knew what he meant.

"Do I have to come to Atlanta?"

"Yeah," he said.

I got out of his chair. "I can't do it. My roots are too deep in Kentucky." He wanted me to succeed him as president. Ellis Arnall, the former governor of Georgia and a good friend of mine, was chairman.

Claude Poindexter organized that company with only seven hundred dollars. After his death they sold it to Sun Life of Baltimore. They got it mixed with some housing development out in California and I resigned from the board. They weren't first class.

Most of my life I've been able to keep my cool in confrontations. I was not so lucky in 1970 when trouble erupted at the University of Kentucky over the student newspaper, the *Kernel.* It was a stinking paper; it abused people without justification or excuse. They said they wanted to be independent. I said let's get you off campus, and you'll be wholly independent. I have no objection to that.

I went over to Lexington to attend a meeting of the trustees. There were several young people in the hallway. I passed by and didn't even look at them. One fellow reached out, grabbed my tie, and pulled me around to face him.

He was long-haired, barefooted, and wearing dirty clothes—a typical hippie.

I swung from centerfield and hit him in the nose, and he said, "Ohhh . . ."

The fellow standing next to him said, "You hit him!"

I said, "Yeah. You're next."

J. Edgar Hoover wrote me later about that. He said everybody ought to hit one and we'd straighten them out. I was ashamed of myself. I don't go around hitting students, but it just flew all over me when he grabbed my necktie. It reminded me of the time Uncle Charley Moran the umpire got slugged by a player at home plate. Uncle Charley took off his mask and raked it across the guy's face and they put him in the hospital.

The president of the National League asked for an explanation and Uncle Charley said: "Tell 'em to keep their hands off me and I won't hit 'em."

That hippie student just got a smashed nose. He said, "That old fellow like to knocked my head off!"

A couple days later I apologized. That was not like me. I just didn't want anybody to be grabbing me, that's all.

Over my long lifetime I have been fortunate enough to receive recognition and tributes to satisfy a dozen men. But there was one honor that I thought my due that was very elusive, and I feared would not come in my lifetime, and perhaps never.

That was to be inducted into Baseball's Hall of Fame.

That gallery was started in 1936 at Cooperstown, New York, the legendary birthplace of the game. The first five inductees were all immortals—Babe Ruth, Ty Cobb, Honus Wagner, Christy Mathewson, and Walter "Big Train" Johnson.

The moguls in organized baseball undertook a virtual conspiracy when they fired me to literally erase the name of Happy Chandler from the history of the sport. I am sad to say that they were pretty successful in doing so.

Of course, Ford Frick, with whom I shared mutual hate, did

everything possible to denigrate me and my record. He succeeded me as baseball commissioner in 1951 and remained until 1965. Practically the day after he stepped out of office Ford Frick was voted into the Hall of Fame. I was not alone in thinking that grossly unfair. He never made any contribution greater than warming the seat of his office chair, and a bar stool at Toots Shor's.

Even Commissioner Landis had been voted into the Hall of Fame in 1944. But Commissioner Chandler remained the forgotten man in baseball.

I admit that hurt. I felt I had made major contributions to the game. It was only just and right that I get my niche at Cooperstown.

Still the years passed and nothing happened.

Longtime friends were working behind the scenes. Gabe Paul of the Cleveland Indians and Joe Cronin, who married Clark Griffith's daughter, were pushing my name. "Clark Griffith and Connie Mack would be so pleased," Joe observed.

The great third baseman from the Cincinnati Reds' championship years, Bill Werber, must have written a million letters saying I deserved to be in the Hall of Fame. Two fine gentlemen from California also were championing me: Claire Goodwin, whom I'd met when he headed the Pacific Coast League, and "Brick" Laws, who owned the Oakland minor league team.

Joe Reichler, the veteran sports writer and a member of the Veterans Committee, kept proposing me for membership. I remembered Joe well. Down in Florida one spring when he was covering training camp games, Joe got in a little scrape that didn't amount to much, but they threw him in jail. Joe knew where I was staying and got me on the phone and asked for help. I got him out right away. Joe never forgot.

Bowie Kuhn, the commissioner, was on my side, too. He thought I had been given shabby treatment. They had taken away my World Series box and handed me other little humiliations. Bowie, a fine gentleman, invited me to every World Series and All-Star game.

My true role in the Jackie Robinson story had more or less faded from sight. Most of the public credit for breaking the color line went to Branch Rickey. But the black baseball players, if no one else, knew who had made it possible.

One event that helped tip the scales to get me in the Hall of Fame was a story in the *New York Times* by John Holoway, author of a book on black baseball players, reciting just how the Jackie Robinson episode transpired.

I had been relegated to the shelf by the Baseball Writers Association of America, who largely decide which players get into the Hall of Fame. My name was brought before the Committee of Veterans, whose job it is to consider those who have been passed over by the sports writers.

Baseball does have a conscience—and it was working in my behalf.

In mid-February 1982 I was called to the telephone just as I sat down to lunch with Mama and my son Ben and his family. Bowie Kuhn's executive secretary was calling from Florida.

"Mr. Commissioner, are you sitting down?" he asked.

"Yes."

Bowie got on the phone.

"Mr. Commissioner," he said, "you know how pleased I am that I can tell you that you have just been elected to the Hall of Fame."

It took a moment to get my breath. "I know that you are pleased, Mr. Commissioner," I replied. "And I know except for your support and good will and good wishes it wouldn't have happened."

He said the induction would take place at Cooperstown in August. He said later I cried and he cried, too.

I hung up the phone and walked into the dining room.

"Mama," I said, "your humble servant has been elected to the Baseball Hall of Fame."

They all just exploded.

I sat down and started to finish my lunch. Everybody around the table was all talking at once. They literally bubbled with excitement, gaiety, happiness. . . . It was emotional for me, too emotional. This was a call I had been afraid would never come in my lifetime, something I had wanted, wanted mightily, but just had to wait and hope for.

Now at last it had happened. After thirty-one years. I looked around the table at my loved ones. Then I put my face in my hands and let the tears come.

21

Updating My All-Time All-Star Team

I find a big problem in trying to wind up this memoir. There's too much to say—considering the fact that I have been busy and active for just ten years shy of one century! It becomes quite a chore to shoehorn even the highlights into one hundred thousand words.

There isn't space enough to even mention hundreds of stellar episodes. Of course they are only excruciatingly humorous, monumentally sad, or merely dramatic once-in-a-lifetime cliffhangers.

Hundreds of people who have touched my life ought to appear on these pages, and won't be mentioned. My friends will forgive me, and my enemies—well, those whom I ignore are pretty lucky to escape my literary fist. Readers who know certain facts of sports or politics may conclude your humble servant is dodging unflattering or bad moments. Not so. I'd willingly take the heat, except that space doesn't permit giving a balanced story on some happenings. Trust me. I'm giving you the best I've got in my storehouse of memories, all the main highpoints from ninety exciting years.

I haven't slowed down a whole lot. People won't let me. I don't mind that. I still like to help people, if I can. My phone has never been unlisted. I keep it right beside me and I usually answer every time it rings. And that happens many times a day. Some sports writer is calling from New York, or San Francisco, or New Orleans. A little girl wants to set up an appointment to interview me for a school essay. A politician wants some advice. The mayor or some judge downstate wants me to come make a talk. The kids over at the University of Kentucky want me to sing "My Old Kentucky Home" in Rupp Arena, and make the "Y" with the cheer leaders. If I can, I do all these things.

Somebody calls or comes to get my help in making a bank merger. Or there's a fellow who's in a jam and trying to keep out of the penitentiary. I'm still a lawyer, and in the last year or so I've handled a couple of matters for fees.

I told somebody I never advised anybody to run for public office. They asked why. I said, Well, I learned quite early that if they ran and won, it was because they were irresistible and smart as hell and nobody could touch 'em. But if they lost, I beat 'em. So I had no way to win that sort of thing, and just didn't tell anybody to run.

Every now and then I get a little flood of fan mail. I always write and thank 'em. Got a call the other morning. Woman wants an autographed picture and wants me to send one to her friend in Boston. So I do that two or three times a week. She just said she loved me, and I said that's mighty nice. When I go into a restaurant or on a trip, ladies will come up to me and say, "Governor, my, aren't you looking well." I get a chuckle out of that. There's three stages of life—youth, maturity, and my-aren't-you-looking-well.

It's kind of shameful how they keep bestowing honors on me. I guess that comes with the territory. They even put me in the Confederate Hall of Fame, on account of Grandpa Dan riding with General Morgan's Cavalry. They made a television documentary not long ago. I'm something in the Boy Scouts, the Newsboy of the Year, recipient of a gold medallion from the Daughters of the American Revolution, a few hundred citations like that. One I'm extra proud of is being designated "Kentuckian of the Century" by the Kentucky television and radio broadcasters. I sure hope they know what they are talking about!

What I read these days in the newspapers doesn't go down too well sometimes. Some of those cartoonists are vicious. They hadn't ought to treat President Reagan as mean as they do.

And those TV correspondents...that Sam Donaldson and Chris Wallace, why they ought to be run out of the country. I do have to thank television for one thing—soap operas. For twenty years I have been watching "Days of Our Lives." That's exciting. It comes on at one in the afternoon; I hate to get interrupted while I'm watching.

Every Thursday I go over to Lexington to have lunch with some of my favorite cronies. It's a mixed crowd. They don't all show up every week; it depends on what business appointments they might have. I show up practically every Thursday.

In this fine group—most of whom I say I've known since they were little boys, and that's about right on some—are Hoover and Frank Dawahare, Dr. Charles Sachatello, Joe Weddington, Russell Lutes, Dr. E. C. Seely, Walt Robertson, Bill Keightley, Otis Singletary, Cliff Hagan, Eddie Sutton, J.T. "Red" Denton, Bucky Blankenship, Lloyd Alexander, Dr. Floyd Poore, Bill Henry, Roger Wilhoit, and always Foxy DeMoisey. Since his older brother Frenchy died in 1963, Foxy has been my main man. That's not easy because he's one of the top-flight pharmaceutical sales reps in the country and does a lot of traveling on his own. But he serves as my appointments and business secretary and is on hand, coming down from his home in Fort Thomas, to drive me to a lot of functions in addition to the Thursday lunch.

In the Spring of 1987 Foxy took me on a nostalgic visit to Washington. John Sherman Cooper thought it would be a good idea for us to go back to the floor of the United States Senate and sit for old times' sake in our seats again. That was quite a day—for it was the first time I had been back in the chamber since I left to become baseball commissioner. Once is enough; I don't think I'll go back any more.

Not consciously do I live on memories—but I can assure you it is nice that people do not forget you. I've got friends all over and especially in the commonwealth. They keep trying to turn me into some sort of folk hero. As an example, in December 1976 I was invited to come to Frankfort and speak to the legislators. I guess I made a pretty big hit.

At least that was the reaction of my editor friend Vance Trimble at the *Kentucky Post* in Covington. He published this editorial:

One of a Kind

Albert B. (Happy) Chandler visited the state Senate chamber this week and gave a 30-minute speech that kept 'em on the edge of their seats when they weren't clapping.

It was more than a speech, actually.

It was an oratory. An oratory the likes of which few of us can ever have the chance to hear any more.

It was a side-heaving, no-punch-barred, pepper-red talk from the twice-former Governor, U.S. Senator, state senator and baseball commissioner that would have put grins on the faces of the Websters and Lincolns and Barkleys of the speech world.

It was Happy, all right. No doubt about it. And he is as spirited, as funny, as opinionated and as oxen-strong in physique and handshake as ever.

The Senate paused just long enough during this busy and hard-worked legislative session to hear Chandler take his listeners back to another time in Kentucky politics and history.

He reminisced. He joked. He tore after those who are against the death penalty, and said of taxes:

Folks get taxed "from the cradle to the grave and from the womb to the tomb."

He's said it before. But it sounds so original, so true, so Happy Chandlerish, it's always funny.

Happy Chandler came back to the Capitol and found a home. It suddenly was like he'd always been there.

Well, one thing's for sure: He'll always be there in the minds of the people in state government, the legislators, those in high office, and the plain folks of Kentucky.

There's never been another Happy Chandler. No sir, never.

And it's good to know he's still spinning those yarns.

When the All-Star game comes around, sports interviewers are always asking me to name my all-time All-Star team. For years I gave them the selections right off—in the outfield, Babe Ruth, Ty Cobb and Ted Williams. The infield was Lou Gehrig at first, Eddie Collins at second, Honus Wagner at shortstop, and Pie Traynor at third. My catcher was Roger Bresnahan and the pitchers were Walter Johnson, Christy Mathewson and Lefty Grove.

In recent years several new men have come to the fore, changing my lineup.

There have been a lot of good catchers—Bill Dickey, Mickey Cochrane, Gabby Hartnett. But Bresnahan was the greatest defensive catcher of them all. He was a real stylist. Until Johnny Bench of the Cincinnati Reds. He's my man now. He developed beautifully.

Gehrig was the Iron Man. He played in more consecutive games than anybody else and he hit the ball harder than anybody else. But at first base now I put Stan Musial. He bloomed later. He really blossomed.

Eddie Collins was one of the first college graduates to play in the major leagues and later became general manager of the Boston Red Sox. But now at second I put Joe Morgan. In 1975–76 Joe Morgan was just the best ball player in the country.

Wagner was a throwback. Pete Rose is the nearest thing to him. Wagner was bowlegged and had hands like hams. But at shortstop now I put Joe Cronin.

I kept Traynor at third. Brooks Robinson is good, but he'll have to go behind Traynor at third. In the outfield I have taken Babe Ruth out and kept Cobb and Williams. My new nominee is Joe DiMaggio. DiMag was a better outfielder and hit .325 for twelve years. Ruth struck out more times than he knocked home runs, generally.

Williams was one of the greatest hitters of them all. If he hadn't lost those four or five years in the military service, there's no telling what he would have done.

But I'd have to say the greatest hitter was Shoeless Joe Jackson. He didn't play too long, but he was the purest hitter I saw. Of course he was banned by Judge Landis for his role in the Black Sox Scandal, when several members of the Chicago White Sox were accused of throwing the 1919 World Series with Cincinnati.

Shoeless Joe was a natural hitter and they mistreated him. He wasn't guilty of anything. That's my view about it. He was not educated. The Carolina legislature and the courts down there acquitted him. And still the old judge put him out. That was a tragedy, I thought.

Shoeless Joe was such a natural hitter if you woke him up at midnight and he had a bat in his hand, he'd hit you. Good eyes. Ted Williams used to say Jackson could see the stitches on the ball and could tell you what it was doing.

"Big Train" Johnson might have been the best pitcher of all time. He could throw faster; I don't know if any of these fellows today are faster. Mathewson threw three shutouts in one World Series—you can't beat that. Grove was the best lefthander. I'd put Sandy Koufax up close, but Grove was the best.

You want some managers, too? I'll take Connie Mack, John McGraw and Joe McCarthy. There's one extra thing about Connie Mack—he was a splendid gentleman of the old school.

Most of my all-star roster is made up of old-timers. You could name good players all day. Bob Feller would have been close up there. I never was too much on Willie Mays. He was a good outfielder, but I always thought he was over-exaggerated. I guess I'm an old-timer myself, but the way I see it: records live, opinions die. I'm just going by the book.

Greed is too prevalent in sports today. Churchill Downs in Louisville is determined to make money. Box seats for the Kentucky Derby used to be $200. I've had one all my life, of course. Then they went up to $300. This fellow came along and now it's $1,070. They collect the money six months in advance and put it in the bank and draw interest. You pay for your tickets in November and get them in April. Not much excuse for that.

The Racing Commission is responsible for permitting that. That's an outrage. I told them so. If I were governor, they couldn't do it, because I wouldn't let them.

Baseball ticket prices are too high. When I was commissioner I wouldn't let them charge more than a dollar for a bleacher seat at the World Series. You're a half mile from the ball game. And you have to stay up all night in line to get a ticket. They cost thirty dollars apiece!

People are being very much imposed on by people who can impose on you. Everything is inflated. I don't know—this country is going broke.

I am often asked how I rate the commissioners who succeeded me. It's an insult to even mention Ford Frick's name. He was an absolute zero. Bowie Kuhn was one of the nicest men I ever encountered. And I'd say the same thing about him that Frenchy DeMoisey said about me: If Kuhn could find out what was right, he'd do it. And I helped him. I helped him every way I could.

That Eckert was an accident looking for a place to happen.

They named an Air Force general who didn't know a baseball from a bale of hay. How he got the job, I don't know. Some bunch of smart alecs got together and put his name in. Dan Topping may have had something to do with that. Eckert lasted only two years. He never knew where he was.

But Bowie Kuhn was a first-rate fellow. And I think this new fellow, Peter Ueberroth, is all right. I exchanged notes with him. He's asked for my views on some things, and I've tried to help him. A good baseball man? Well, he didn't start with the knowledge or experience. But he will be a good man.

If we don't make another penny, Mama and I can get through the winter all right. My Scotch blood has made me a pretty careful person in finances. They asked my friend Joe Leary if Chandler has any stock. He said, "If he ever had any, he's got it. He didn't sell it." And Joe is right about that. I made some money and I made some wise investments.

I bought thirty shares of stock in the bank over at Lexington for thirty dollars a share forty-five years ago. I didn't sell any of it, and it has split and split and split and grown to be one hundred thousand shares. It's mine. I don't owe anything on it. That's a billion-dollar bank down there now, and I helped create their merger. I got approval from the Comptroller of the Currency. I can make my voice heard down there. I've also got some stock in the Woodford Bank and Trust Company here in Versailles.

Through banking I've developed two of my most long-standing friendships—with L.D. Sweazy, chairman of Woodford Bank and Trust, and in Lexington with W.T. "Billy" Young, who's a businessman and on the board of First Security bank.

I'm not a stupid, wide-eyed speculator. As far as I'm concerned, they're all dead. I'm conservative. I bought stock that was good and paid for it. I never bought anything I didn't pay for. Lots of people live by their wits and bet on stocks. I don't do that. I own this place at 191 Elm Street and also that little farm across the road. I guess modestly speaking Mama and I are worth maybe two million dollars and no debts.

I don't have any Visas or charge accounts. I wouldn't pay a nickel for an American Express card. They want to charge you. Why should I pay them for a card? I can buy anything I want to. I don't need them to tell somebody I'm all right.... All this talk about advertising and handling, I'm not going to pay handling charges. I've been in *Who's Who in America* since 1932 and every year they raise the price on me. Last time they sent me a book, $125 for the book, three dollars for postage. I sent 'em the $125 and said I been getting this thing since 1932 and I'm not going to pay you to send it to me. You either pay the $3 or keep it. I didn't hear from them any more. I think that's an outrage. They hold you up, if you let them. I'm queer about that.

Another thing I don't do. Lots of fellows, if you have a bill goes over thirty days they want to charge you. I don't pay those. I say don't give me a carrying charge, because I'm not going to pay you.

Somebody asked if I was serious about Mama's overdrafts. I sure am. It's not a joke. She doesn't give a darn. I'll bet she is overdrawn right now. Financially, she's a disaster. I've put up with it. I don't spend any money except for her. I need five dollars to get my hair cut. That's all I need. So I give her all the rest of the money. She takes it all. I don't have anybody else I'm paying anything for, so she does not give a darn, and she's financially reckless. Lord have mercy!

Do I consider myself a banker as well as a lawyer? Well, I'm sort of a banker. I was on the board of a bank once and I resigned. I didn't want to be a member of a board where you're responsible for too many things that you don't know about. I got out. I helped sell a bank. I can do that pretty well.

22

Wearing the World
Like a Loose Jacket

As I have often said, I've never looked back on my actions with regret or tried to second guess the hands fate dealt me. Some of the cards I drew in ninety years of living were not all that wonderful. I've suffered blows and dirty tricks, just like most everyone else in public life—maybe more than my share. Yet I've never played crybaby, and I'm not going to start complaining now.

The plain truth is that I was sober and I meant to do everything I did.

That is not to say there haven't been disagreeable results, and in fact a couple of right disagreeable incidents came along not many weeks before my ninetieth birthday—July 14, 1988.

One episode was what some newspapers called the "Zimbabwe ruckus" or the "nigger flap." The other was the couple of little mini-strokes I suffered. I'm mentioning them in this last chapter because both events got considerable publicity, and folks wonder what effect they had on me.

The "nigger" incident was the only blemish on my long service on the board of trustees of the University of Kentucky. I have been on that board a long time—fifty-three years. During my two terms as governor, I served as board chairman. Three other Kentucky governors appointed me to serve as a trustee. Two did not; they were John Y. Brown Jr. and Martha Layne

Collins, both of whom took away my right to cast a vote in trustee decisions, but left me to serve as an honorary member of the board, stripped of any authority.

That situation changed when our present governor, Wallace Wilkinson, took office. He thought highly of the modest contributions I have made over half a century to the university, especially its sports programs, so he appointed me in early 1988 to serve again as a full-fledged member of the board of trustees, with all rights and privileges. He thought I could once more make a real contribution to action of the trustees.

On April 5, 1988, I attended a meeting of the trustees investment committee in one of the little offices at the university. Four or five other board members were there and we took up the university's decision to dispose of its investments in South Africa.

The committee chairman was discussing in a general way how to get rid of our investments over there, and I said, just apropos of nothing: "The question of Zimbabwe [formerly Rhodesia] has arisen, and you know what's happened there. It's now all nigger. There are no white folks there anymore. The streets of Salisbury are boarded up. Grass is growing in the streets. And it's just changed."

There was a girl sitting in the back of the room I didn't know. She was a reporter for the *Lexington Herald-Leader;* she picked up on that remark, called it a racial slur and went to her supervisor at the newspaper and he said, "Print it!" Then they embarked on a campaign to make it stand up and make it a national issue.

My statement was not said in anger. It was not said in jest. It was just said. And not said to be offensive toward anybody living or dead. And as I told them later, I was born in a town of 800—400 white and 400 black—and we all called 'em niggers, and they didn't seem to mind, you understand. They answered me by saying that the blacks were afraid to remonstrate. I said I didn't believe that.

The Lexington paper was just nasty and low and mean. I've always insisted that criticism of public officials ought to be just and tempered and decent—but it ought to be just and tempered, it ought to be decent, and if it is not any of those things it ought not to be.

When the Lexington paper broke the story and quoted a

group of U.K. students, and some others, as saying I should be punished by being forced to resign from the university board, Governor Wilkinson called me on the phone. He said he did not intend to ask me to resign, but suggested that I should make an apology.

"Governor," I said, "I do apologize for having said anything they construed to be offensive because I hadn't intended to be offensive." And I did make such a public apology—to anyone who might have been offended by my remark.

But that wasn't enough to satisfy the rabble-rousers. A militant campus group, virtually all black, and numbering about forty, according to the newspapers, said the word "nigger" was a terrible insult and demanded that I be forced off the university board.

These protestors waited on the president of U.K., David Roselle. He was weak at the start; the newspapers quoted him as saying that "the university completely and totally repudiates what it is Governor Chandler says. Completely. We do not support his statement." He never showed me the courtesy of asking me about what I had said, or meant, and most assuredly never suggested personally to me that I should resign as a trustee. One student leader and a Lexington city councilman, both of whom are black, began fanning the flames and got the football players, who are also mainly black, stirred up so much they staged a one-day walkout of spring practice and threatened to boycott the annual Blue-White intrasquad game on April 23 or wear black arm bands as a symbol of defiance. Only my resignation, they asserted, would appease them. That was something I had no intention of doing.

To be honest, I was flabbergasted by this football squad walkout. Since the 1920s I have always maintained a healthy and close relationship with football players and coaches in Kentucky, especially at the university. Paul "Bear" Bryant and I were close; he called me "Skipper." I was frequently asked for counsel by coaches Blanton Collier and Fran Curci. Dr. Otis Singletary, during his time as UK president, insisted I serve on the athletic council. Of course, in later years I haven't shown up at Wildcat practice sessions like I used to, so my sports record probably is not so well known now to late-comers over there on the Lexington campus.

That present set of young men probably haven't the slightest concept of the Old South I grew up in when the word "nigger" was commonly used and was not necessarily a term of disrespect. I am proud of the strong political and personal friendships I have developed over the years with Negroes. Earlier in this book, I have recounted many instances of going to bat for colored people because I believe they are entitled to equality under the law. And I have never deviated from that position in the slightest, and the record clearly shows that.

I am aware that the word "nigger" went out of style and became an offensive buzz word years ago. But even so, there was a period when the Negroes themselves could not settle on the terminology we were supposed to use. My son Ben reminded me that in a speech at the Woodford County Courthouse during the 1959 gubernatorial contest I remarked that I appreciated the help of the "black boys" in the current campaign. A black man, who still resides in our area, stood up and interrupted my speech by saying his people were "Negroes" and that they resented being called "black." Well, that was all right with me, but for quite a period of years there was a lot of confusion and indecision over whether they wanted to be known as "colored," "black," or "Negro." Now the preference seems to be "black."

Maybe I have lost touch with young black men like those trying to create a ruckus on the University of Kentucky football squad. I have to admit they dismayed me, seeing some with earrings and so forth in their noses and ears; I don't know what kind of people they are.

Naturally this was the kind of a furor that was picked up by news wires and was broadcast all over the country. And phone calls started flooding in on me at Versailles. My guess is that of the first 1,000, only three were negative. Baseball Commissioner Peter Ueberroth offered to fly down to Lexington and meet with football coach Jerry Claiborne and his players.

"Thank you, commissioner," I told Ueberroth, "but I believe Coach Claiborne will handle it all right." Actually I was not certain of it at the time; Claiborne seemed then to be just pussyfooting and not coming to grips with the situation.

Joe Morgan, one of the greatest black baseball players who ever lived, called wanting to help. We've been good friends since the days when he was the stellar second baseman for the Cincinnati Reds. Joe called the situation an "outrage" and said he would do what he could to stop it. I thanked him and told him not to worry, everything would settle down.

In retrospect, my *faux pas* was not a big deal, and certainly didn't deserve all the attention it received. It was one word, a racial slur, if you want to call it that, and spoken not in a public forum but in a small committee meeting and without any animosity or bad feeling. It was plain and simple my reversion to the language of my youth. Except for a reporter being present and deciding to turn it into a *cause célèbre,* the episode would never have created a ripple.

But the strike by the football squad stunned Coach Claiborne and infuriated most, if not all, of his assistants. Jake Hallum, who's a line coach, and Jerry Eisaman, offensive coordinator, flew into pretty near a rage. So did the rest of the coaches, and they took these black boys on, you understand. Jake told them: "Go ahead, walkout—we won't play! Lose your scholarships; all of you leave, go play some place else. Leave!"

They were forthright and rough on the players. Then Claiborne came around. He called me, and I told him I had told Ueberroth I thought he could handle it and would handle it. He did. He moved in then, and told his squad to go ahead and leave if they were going to boycott the Blue-White game. The reaction of a whole lot of people to that threat was they wouldn't go see 'em anyway. Said they'd better learn to play football if they wanted to have the support. I got more support than they did from the football fans.

The Lexington paper kept saying that three or four thousand people were going to march on the state capitol in Frankfort and demand that Governor Wilkinson fire me from the university board. I had already apologized to anyone who felt offended, and I knew the governor was not going to request my resignation.

A bunch of protestors, not any three or four thousand but maybe a couple of hundred civil rights activists, gathered at the capitol on April 13, and Governor Wilkinson went out to hear what they had to say and tell them flatly he had no intention of asking me to give up my trusteeship.

It was an angry, unruly mob. They booed the governor and several times one protestor shouted "That's bullshit!" when Wilkinson made a statement. That was a worse offense, in my opinion, than my quiet, non-violent use of "nigger" in a more or less private meeting. But the same newspapers that made a hullabaloo over my so called racial slur did not even mention that the cry of "bullshit!" was thrown in anger several times in the face of the governor of Kentucky. What kind of evenhanded, fair journalism is that?

Somebody who knows my heart about as well as I do, Mama, came to my defense in her typically noble and beautiful style of prose in our family weekly, the *Woodford Sun,* on April 14, 1988, in her regular "Opinions and Personals" column, which said:

> The fact that Governor Chandler used an unfortunate word in a private conversation which was overheard by a reporter was not worth reporting. The fact that it was used by a man known as the best friend our black brothers have in America was enough to make a good reporter discount it. She must have felt she could use it in a way to gain a little publicity for herself. The net result has been that the *Lexington Herald-Leader* has done the greatest disservice to the state. The effort to discredit Governor Chandler has not only infuriated the majority of Kentuckians but has brought a flood of expressions of support from all over the United States. The *Herald-Leader* has tried to repair the damage by reminding its readers that Governor Chandler's record proves he is no racist but has actually been the most effectual friend our black citizens have had in their long fight for their rights. The *Herald-Leader* editor was out of town when his paper made this mistake. To their dismay they found that trying to do Governor Chandler in had as little chance in Kentucky as getting Santa Claus indicted for breaking and entering.
>
> Governor Chandler's remark was not meant as a slur and his urgent hope now is that the ensuing furor will not hurt the cordial friendliness that has existed between the blacks and the whites. The many calls he has had from black friends, both in Kentucky and from all over the nation, have been a great support. It is heartening to know that his contributions to the cause of equal rights are so widely known. His efforts have come from a genuine belief that God created us equal. The rest we have to do ourselves.
>
> The suggestion that he is too old to be on the UK Board of Trustees is a thoughtless remark. His mind is as acute as it ever was. His experience on that board is priceless. Governor Wilkinson would never have appointed him

if he hadn't found out from experience that he definitely had all his marbles, as he likes to say.

Any person, especially any politician, picks up enemies along the way. And Happy has collected a few. I hope they will be willing to cease and desist in the interest of cooling this unpleasantness before it does irreparable damage.

Fortunately, since the whole incident was such a minor event, it did evaporate like the proverbial tempest in a teapot. Wise heads prevailed. The rabble-rousers saw they were not getting anywhere. They quietly faded—just before they were about to get inundated by a general backlash.

And frankly, I have written more here than I really wanted to about such a transient episode in my long life; I have done it just so that anyone who cares can have a clear understanding of the dimensions of the ruckus.

Even so I think I should tack on a couple of postscripts that do much to illuminate how decent folks reacted to the unfairness of the criticism of me.

Right on the heels of the "nigger" flap, I went over to the UK Chandler Medical Center to present, as I have done for twenty-five years, a silver cup to the top man in the graduating class. We turned out ninety-two new doctors this year, and the Singletary Center was crowded for the ceremony.

As president of the university, David Roselle spoke, and got a fair reception—just fair. And almost unfair for the president of the university. He didn't speak very long.

When I got up to give that cup, the audience cheered and darn near knocked the place down. So I said to Roselle after it was over, "Mr. President, I don't believe these people want me to leave here." He didn't know what to say. He just stammered. I didn't expect him to say anything because it was apparent the folks were not mad with me. I think Roselle would have been a whole lot better off if he had kept his mouth shut in the first place when he popped off about repudiating anything I said. He's new on his job; perhaps he'll learn with experience.

The other postscript involves former heavyweight champion Muhammad Ali, who grew up in Louisville as Cassius Clay and reigned fifteen years as king of his boxing division. Just as the furor was ending, Ali telephoned me at Versailles and said he needed my help. He had in mind setting up a Boxing Hall of Fame in Louisville and wanted me to set up a meeting with Governor Wilkinson and go with him to talk to the governor. I made the arrangements and met him in Frankfort.

The Lexington reporters got wind of it and descended on Muhammad Ali at the state capitol.

The old champ doesn't walk well any more, on account of all those shots to the head he took in the ring, and he looked sort of feeble. But he hugged me, and some of those reporters tried to make it appear he didn't even know me. Good Lord, I've known him since he was a little boy, but some of those newspapermen tried to make it appear I had sent for him to come down to Frankfort and make a public testimonial for me. They just didn't have their facts right.

But Muhammad Ali set them straight in a hurry. When the first one stood to question him, Muhammed Ali leaned forward and poked his finger in the reporter's chest, and said, "Did you ever say nigger? And if you say you didn't I'm going to say you're a liar! Everybody says nigger. I say nigger. Everybody says nigger. What Governor Chandler said was not offensive to me!"

That just chilled the press, for Muhammad Ali to say that!

Enough on that controversy; now about those two T.I.A.s that hit me about six weeks before my birthday. The medical term, I think, is transitory ischemic attack, which partially interrupts the flow of blood through the carotid arteries to the brain. Most folks call them mini-strokes. Fortunately, mine turned out to be very minor, and caused no damage.

My health has been good, except for some sort of a pinched nerve in my lower spine which has caused a lot of pain in my legs for nearly five years. It's something the surgeons don't want to operate on, I suppose on account of my age, and because I tell them to just let it be. I can handle the pain—most of the time—and I don't take pain pills either. I have started using a walker, but that's no big deal. If I want to go some place, I just stand up and tell my old legs, "Get movin', fellows."

I wasn't aware of suffering either T.I.A. The first came toward the end of a long day—too long, I suppose. A writer for the *Courier-Journal* magazine came to my home in Versailles to interview me for a piece he said would pretty well review my entire career. That meant he had a lot of questions for me to answer. We sat down in my front study about nine or ten in the morning and talked steadily all day, just taking time out for lunch in my dining room.

Looking back, I can see that I put a little too much stress on myself with such a long interview. Usually after lunch I relax watching my favorite soap opera and then stretch out for a nap. During the many months of recounting my experiences for this book, my co-author would come two or three times a week with his tape recorder and we would talk two or three hours, then eat lunch together and sign off until another visit, so I could get my rest. That was no strain.

I don't remember the tail end of my interview with that *Courier-Journal* writer. They say that late in the afternoon I suddenly just stared off into space and didn't respond to any of his questions. I recall Mama coming in and saying she was going to put something under my tongue—that was a nitroglycerine pill. They got me into my bedroom and all of a sudden I woke up in bed and my physician, Dr. Benjamin Franklin Roach of Midway, was there. He said he was going to take me over to the Chandler Medical Center at Lexington, and he drove me there in his car.

They gave me a lot of tests—brain scans, ultra sound, everything you can think of. I didn't feel bad, and they gave me some blood thinner and sent me back home the very next day. I thought I was okay, and I guess they did, too.

Foxy DeMoisey drove me back to Versailles. Mama had run short on money and asked me to get her some, and I took out some bills and was standing there in my bedroom holding the money in my hand. My son Ben was there. Somebody asked me about Foxy DeMoisey, and I said I hadn't seen him in a week—but he'd just driven me home from the hospital! Then they say I looked down and saw the money in my hand, and asked, "Where did this come from?"

So they said, "Oh! Oh!" And rushed me back to the hospital.

This time the doctors turned me every way but loose. I have never been through so many thingamabobs in my life. Every time I turned around a nurse was sticking me with a needle. I have no enthusiasm for hospitals. But I stayed there three or four days and got better quick, and they let me come home.

Dr. Roach seems pleased with my progress. When he checked my blood pressure the first of June it was 122 over 75—

and that seemed to be just fine. From those two mini-strokes I never did have any ache or pain. I just blacked out for a little while. Now I feel fine again, and my legs are no weaker, except when I'm sitting real easy and careful they cramp something awful, and if I turn around in my chair they give me real fits.

With so much happening in my "bad news department" it was truly gratifying to get a call from Commissioner Ueberroth that showed organized baseball hasn't yet forgotten me. He invited me to come to the 1988 All-Star game in Cincinnati. That was just like the old days. I enjoyed visiting with a lot of my long-time friends in baseball. They seemed very glad to see me, and Joe Morgan came up and hugged me. Commissioner Ueberroth asked me to bring a friend to the game, so I took our governor, Wallace Wilkinson, who seems to be doing a good job in bringing Kentucky government out of difficult times.

Then came my ninetieth birthday party. I could go on quite a bit about that day. It is truly humbling to find that after such a long life of public service you have kept such a host of real loyal friends. Some of my closest pals got together with Bucky Blankenship and held a reception at his Bright Leaf Golf Club over at Harrodsburg. I don't know how many people were invited, maybe a thousand, but it seemed like I was around there four or five hours shaking hands, kissing folks, and giving bearhugs. I love all that, partner; if you know me, you know that.

The people over at the state capitol tried to make my ninetieth memorable. The Legislative Research Commission adopted a resolution declaring July 14 "A.B. 'Happy' Chandler Day." Governor Wilkinson came over to my party at Bright Leaf and was one of the last to leave. Good wishes came from all over the country by telephone, telegram and mail. Ronald Reagan sent a letter from the White House:

> Dear Happy:
>   Nancy and I want to add our congratulations to all those you are receiving as you celebrate your 90th birthday. We wish you all the returns of the day as you reflect on a full life and many years of service to the people of Kentucky and our entire nation. Your countrymen know you as the concerned and enthusiastic public servant from your

terms as a governor and United States senator from the Bluegrass State and as commissioner of Baseball.

We join your fellow Americans in the hope that your special day is one of good cheer. Again congratulations and happy birthday and God bless you.

Sincerely,

RONALD REAGAN

It turned out to be not only a day of good cheer for me—but also for Mama. My friends had planned a little surprise. When we drove up to Bright Leaf there it was—a special gift parked out on the clubhouse lawn, a beautiful 1988 Cadillac ElDorado! By golly, Mama's eyes just about jumped out of their sockets. She knew who would be driving *our* new car (since I haven't been driving in about fifty years!) Besides Mama has been bugging me for a long time to get her a new car; her old Cadillac was about twelve or so years old and she kept lamenting that it was falling apart. Now I hope she's satisfied.

Partner, that was quite a birthday party!

Not far from Versailles at a village named Pisgah is an old-fashioned country cemetery. It's a quiet and beautiful place—and very old. The Presbyterian church there was built of native stone in the 1780s. In the cemetery are graves of Revolutionary soldiers. George Washington, Aaron Burr and Thomas Jefferson made contributions to help erect that old church.

It's near the old Whitney Dunlap place; he was the father of my daughter-in-law Tossie, and he and Mrs. Dunlap are buried there. That's the place Mama and I have chosen for our final resting place, and I suppose some of our children will also wind up there.

As far as my feeling about the hereafter, I'm not sure. Mama thinks she is going there, and Mama, of course, is the only hope I've got. If there is anything to this hereafter business, I just don't know. She'll make it. They'll tear the thing down and start all over if she don't make it.

She's good enough. All she's done her whole life is do justice and practice mercy and walk humbly with her God. Ain't no better girl than Mama. She is confident about the hereafter. Thing is, when you don't know . . . . And who does know? I've told 'em I've been here a long time, and I have yet to see some fellow that's traveling a route come back and say, This is the way.

People who know I'm a very religious person ask if I pray a lot. No, not for something frivolous like a sunny day, a safe journey . . . . My cousin Claude Terrell said the best thing. He'd been a fisherman all his life, and said he hoped when he made his final cast and was safely in the Master's net he hoped and prayed that he'd be worthy of being kept.

I never did pray to win. I said, If it's in Your name and it's in Your plan and You consider me worthy of this trust, why let me have it. I never asked for anything I didn't think I deserved. And whether prayers help or not, I've got to agree that the prayers of the righteous availeth much. That's the reason I always said I get Mama to pray for me. Because I guarantee if there is anything to the efficacy of prayer, hers will get there. She's a religious girl, if there ever was one on earth.

People have asked me if I visualize God—someone with a long white beard. That's very difficult to contemplate and difficult to understand, and very few people understand it. I'm not sure I do. In the beginning it was God and He created heaven and earth and He shall come to judge the quick and the dead, whose kingdom shall have no end.

That's a matter of faith. That's a matter of believing in an omnipotent and final power. Now all this thing just didn't come about. Man didn't make this. Somebody made this heaven and earth and somebody declared the glory. Somebody did this . . . and if you don't figure it out that way, I don't know how else you can.

How do I see God? Is it a him? Has to be a him, I guess. Just standing on the ramparts of Valhalla and looking at the scene and can't improve it. By golly, bound to be . . . . He said, My spirit will not always strive with man. So that means He calls on you to do certain things, and if you do them you got a better chance, I think. And if you don't, you take the consequences, you understand.

Is there a contest between God and Satan? Yes, sometimes I've tried to reconcile that. I don't know how to do that. I don't know whether He consigns you to purgatory or oblivion or some other place because of failure to keep His commandments. But all things—and of this I am sure—work together for the good of them that love the Lord and keep His commandments.

Once somebody asked me if I felt any resentment when my little brother died, if I prayed, if I blamed God or the Devil. I just watched over him, and watched him die. I thought it was tragic that he didn't have a better chance. I didn't blame anybody, oh, no, you can't do that. Vengeance is Mine...that is what the Lord said. You can't get vengeance from the Lord. Anybody who tries that is in a bad state. My father didn't blame God. He never got over that, though.

Do I visualize Heaven as a place? Will I see my loved ones in the hereafter? I don't know. I wish I did. It's difficult. There are plenty of people who believe that's true and there are plenty who are skeptical. Plenty of people think this is all. And this is a mixed up situation.

I'm sorry to say occasionally all of us have doubts. We have hopes, we have fears, all the things that anybody else has, and then at the end we're hopeful that it will come out all right.

I have vigorously read and studied the Bible and I have explored religious theory. I have sought the Lord and He delivered me from all my fears. I have not been fearful. I have not been unmindful of the fact that in this life you have to take the consequences, and I have been willing to take the consequences. I'm responsible for my own actions, and if I make a move, I don't blame somebody else if it fails.

When anyone asks me about the future, I always give the same answer: I wear the world like a loose jacket. I live each day like it's gonna be my last, and sleep each night like I'm gonna live forever.

Index

C